... this story. The author is in the diplomatic service of South Africa.

Zack is 12 now.

Love,

Dad.

HOSTAGE

IN

TAIPEI

McGill Alexander

HOSTAGE

IN

TAIPEI

McGill
Alexander

CLADACH
PUBLISHING

HOSTAGE IN TAIPEI
Copyright © 2000 McGill Alexander

Published by CLADACH PUBLISHING
Santa Rosa, CA
Mailing address:
P.O. Box 355
Fulton, CA 95439 USA
Website:
http://www.cladach.com

Editor: Catherine Lawton
Cover design: Chris Wagner
Front cover photo of the hostage crisis:
Fan Lee

ISBN: 0-9670386-2-6
Library of Congress Card Number: 00-108581

Printed in the United States of America

To my family
with love
and
to all other
innocent victims
of terror
around the world

Our hope in the Lord when we were held hostage
and our comfort when we had been delivered,
these verses accurately reflect our feelings at the time:

In you, O Lord, I have taken refuge;
let me never be put to shame.
Rescue me and deliver me in your righteousness;
turn your ear to me and save me.
Be my rock of refuge,
to which I can always go;
give the command to save me,
for you are my rock and my fortress.
Deliver me, O my God, from the hand of the wicked,
from the grasp of evil and cruel men.
For you have been my hope, O Sovereign Lord,
my confidence since my youth.
From birth I have relied on you;
you brought me forth from my mother's womb.
I will ever praise you.
I have become like a portent to many,
but you are my strong refuge.
My mouth is filled with your praise,
declaring your splendor all day long.

(Psalm 71:1-8)

~ The Alexanders

Table of Contents

PREFACE 7
1. "WHY IS THIS HAPPENING TO US?" 11
2. HOSTAGE! 23
3. STREETS OF TAIPEI 35
4. TERROR IN TAIWAN 45
5. HORRORS OF HELPLESSNESS 61
6. SHADOW OF DEATH 73
7. POLICE ASSAULT 81
8. CHIEF HOU YOU-YI 95
9. WILD DOGS 101
10. A MOTHER'S GUMPTION 115
11. A LONG, LONELY NIGHT 129
12. CHRISTINE'S DRAWING 139
13. NO TEARS TO SHED 147
14. HOSPITAL VIGIL 156
15. A HEAVYWEIGHT ARRIVES ON THE SCENE 162
16. ARMED ONLY WITH LOVE 177
17. AFTER SHOCKS 189
18. CELEBRATIONS 205
19. CONFUSIONS 211
20. VISIT TO THE PRISONER 221
21. THE GOOD-BYE WHIRLWIND 235
22. BACK TO SOUTH AFRICA 245
23. THE MIRACLE BULLET 251
24. THE MIRACLE CONVERSION 257
25. A MIND-BOGGLING REQUEST 271
26. EXECUTION 277
27. DEAD TO SIN; BUT ALIVE TO GOD 287
EPILOGUE 297
NOTES 299
ACKNOWLEDGMENTS and SOURCES 307

Preface

SHORTLY AFTER OUR HOSTAGE ORDEAL I was asked whether I intended to write a book on the experience of our family. I said I had no intention of doing so.

However, people continue to display curiosity as to just what happened and we are still asked to share our experience at churches, groups, and organizations. Many have declared that they have been encouraged, blessed and even awed by what took place. We as a family know that God has used what happened to us to touch the lives of hundreds of people, especially in Taiwan. Inevitably, there have been misconceptions regarding what took place. Evidences of this are the questions which we are repeatedly asked by various people whose curiosity overcomes their reluctance to pry.

Witnessing all this, I reviewed my initial reservations about recording the events. Encouraged by my very special friend Anne, that remarkable woman who consented to marry me, I decided to commit pen to paper. It has not been easy. Time, as always, has been in short supply. Much of the manuscript was written under canvas while I was commanding a military peace-keeping force in the strife-torn Richmond area of the KwaZulu-Natal Province of South Africa.

It is our prayer that those who read this story, if they are Christians, will be blessed and uplifted by the confirmation of God's love for each individual and His faithfulness towards His children. If they are not Christians, then we pray that the reality of God's love would become apparent to them from these events.

This is our story, as we experienced it. There is much that we cannot explain and the skeptic will no doubt be very critical. We have no arguments to counter criticism; we only know what happened — and I have tried to set that out in these pages.

We do not regard ourselves as special people because of what happened to us. A great many people (far too many!) have gone through greater terror and have suffered far more than we have. Many innocent victims have died in similar or worse incidents. Our hearts go out to such people and their families, and we feel humbled that we should have survived when people are suffering and dying every day in this broken world. If our story bears telling, it is only because God used what happened to us to touch the lives of so many people.

We know that many people's lives were changed because of what happened in Taiwan on 18 and 19 November 1997. We know that a brutal killer eventually found peace for his tormented soul, and that we were delivered from a terrifying and life-threatening situation. For these things we give glory to God and praise to Jesus Christ.

McGill Alexander
Port Elizabeth, January 2000.

HOSTAGE

IN

TAIPEI

1

‣Why Is This Happening To Us?‹

DARKNESS HAD FALLEN as I drove up Cherry Hill and stopped at our official attaché residence. I glanced at my watch as the garage door opened. It was exactly 7:00 P.M..

The thought didn't enter my mind that someone could be standing in the shadows of our Taipei neighborhood, watching me.

"I've made it on time," was all I was thinking. "Anne's going to be pleased." I drove into the garage, and the door closed behind me. At the same time, I mentally closed the door on the challenges of another day at the embassy. I was ready to relax for the evening.

The house was built over the garage, and as I mounted the stairs I heard my twelve-year-old daughter Christine practicing piano in the lounge above. I greeted her with a kiss before ascending the next flight of stairs to the large landing which we used as a TV lounge. Anne was busy on the computer. Twenty-two-year-old Melanie was watching TV. On her lap she held the Chinese baby boy we were fostering, seven-month-old Zachary. The only family member missing was nineteen-year-old Shona, who was halfway around the world from us, serving in the South African Air Force.

I kissed them all, then methodically placed my briefcase in

my adjoining study and hung my jacket over the bannister before reaching for Zachary and settling with him into an easy chair. We treasured evenings together as a family.

The author, Mac, relaxing with Zachary the night before the hostage taking. (Photo: Melanie Letts)

Though five stories high, our house had only two or three rooms on each floor.

The island of Taiwan is only slightly larger than South Africa's Kruger National Park. With a population of more than twenty-one million people in an area of less than 36,000 square kilometres—and with much of the island too mountainous for human settlement—living space is limited. Even our house, which was large enough for the entertaining we had to do as diplomats, was squeezed between other houses on a very small piece of land.

Our neighborhood in Taipei—called Cherry Hill because at one time, before the suburb of Peitou encroached into the hills, it had been a cherry farm—seemed quiet and safe.

The people of Taiwan may worry about rising crime rates; but it is by no means a country besieged by violent criminals. There is no comparison with the lamentable situation in our own country of South Africa. There, people who can afford it live in fortresses in an effort to secure their safety; cars are hijacked at gunpoint by murderers who casually shoot the drivers; cash-in-transit vehicles are ambushed on busy highways by military-style gangs spraying automatic gunfire from assault rifles; farmers in isolated areas have been attacked and murdered for trifles; and no one in their right mind would walk around alone at night in the streets of cities such as Johannesburg, Durban, and Cape Town.

In the city of Taipei the pavements crowd in the evenings with shoppers and fun-seekers, while young girls walk along the streets at night without much concern. A murder or a rape becomes a major news item, and the worst crime that most people are likely to encounter is pick-pocketing or bag snatching. Burglars are interested in money or jewelry and generally ignore electronic items, cameras, appliances, and clothing. Houses seldom have burglar bars fitted to the windows.

As we relaxed in the evening, we watched TV news reports of the violent crimes that had been taking place in Taiwan throughout the last year—1997. This unusually high outbreak of crimes elicited a vehement response from the population. This response itself indicated how accustomed people were to a safe society in Taiwan. True, the incidence of white collar crime is probably far higher than is generally realized, and kidnapping is far more frequent than in most Western countries. Yet the average person could feel safer on the Taipei streets than in many Western capitals.

Before going to bed, we'd lock our house, but we seldom bothered to do so during the day. We had a security gate on the street, with an intercom to the house. The gate was always locked, and could be opened electronically from inside the house. An athletic person could climb it, but the busyness of the street made that likelihood small, especially in the early evening. Surely an intruder would be seen.

These things didn't enter my mind while I chatted with Anne and Melanie, bouncing Zachary on my knee. Vaguely I was aware that the piano playing had stopped and Christine was coming up the stairs to my left. I turned toward her.

Then I froze. A stranger was with her, a Chinese man with shaggy hair; stocky and stony-faced. He had one arm around our girl's neck, and he was pointing a grey pistol to her head. The barrel was thrust through Christine's long black hair.

Stunned, my family and I could do nothing but watch as the thug marched Christine into the middle of the room.

I grasped desperately at the forlorn thought that this must be some sort of a macabre joke.

Christine cast a terrified glance toward me as the intruder pulled her past me.

"Dad, he's one of *them!*" she whispered.

"What do you want?" I asked him in English, as my heart raced.

He ignored my question. With growing horror, I saw this was no joke.

For a moment the intruder faced me and his steely eyes took in the scene. With his pistol he motioned Anne across the room, closer to Melanie and me. The blood pounded in my temples.

"Do exactly as he says," I cautioned my family. "Don't anyone make any sudden moves."

Anne crossed the room. The stranger reached into one of his pockets. He wore what appeared to be a shooting jacket or photographer's waistcoat under his nylon windbreaker. Still holding the pistol against Christine's head, he pulled out a pair of open, steel handcuffs. He motioned me to approach. I handed baby Zachary to Melanie and stood up.

My military training told me that now was the moment to act. But the presence of my family told me that I dared not. The intruder indicated that I should turn around. I obeyed him. Then very slowly and carefully he leaned across and clipped the cuffs onto my wrists with one hand. He never let the gun leave Christine's head. With my hands secure behind my back, he led me to my chair and made me sit down. He then made Anne, Melanie, and Christine sit on the sofa.

Again he dug into his ample pockets and pulled out some rolled sections of black electrical cord. Kneeling in front of me, he tied my ankles together. Then he spoke for the first time.

"I'm sorry," he muttered in a heavy Taiwanese accent.

Removing his windbreaker, he began to tie up the rest of the family.

Barely ten minutes had elapsed since I had arrived home. How could this be happening?

Christine had immediately recognized this man, and we all knew who he was. We had seen his "wanted" posters. This was the man who was wanted for kidnapping, murder, rape, assault, arson, robbery, and a string of other crimes. We had been taken hostage by Chen Chin-hsing, Taiwan's most violent and wanted criminal fugitive.

He tied Melanie's hands behind her back with a piece of electrical cord. He then made her sit down and tied her ankles together. Next he did the same to Christine. She turned toward me.

"Daddy, why is this happening to us?" she asked.

Why indeed? What could I answer my youngest daughter? Of the millions of people in the teeming city, why us? Surely the odds were stacked in our favor, and yet here we were, being taken hostage. Melanie was terrified, Christine frightened and confused. What could I say to them? My own mouth felt dry.

"I don't know why it is happening to us," I replied. "But we have to trust the Lord Jesus. All things are in His control and He has a plan."

Anne and I had brought up all our children to trust in the Lord. But now my own faith was being sorely tested.

"Are we going to die?" Christine wanted to know. I had no answer. I watched the hostage-taker turn to Anne, with a

15

piece of cord in his hand. She held up baby Zachary, whom she had taken from Melanie.

"No!" Anne said very firmly.

The notorious Chen Chin-hsing seemed momentarily taken aback by Anne's unfazed attitude. He squinted at her for a moment, then shrugged.

"Okay," he replied.

Kneeling, he tied her ankles together, leaving her hands free to hold Zachary. Again he muttered "Sorry" as he tied her up.

The buzzer on the intercom at the front gate sounded. Anne and I looked at each other. We thought it must be the Pakistani carpet salesman who had made an appointment to see us that evening. Chen just ignored the buzzer.

Fortunately, the salesman persisted. From outside, he and his nephew (who was with him) could see lights on inside. Soon they saw several lights being turned off, and they thought they saw movement inside.

. They were right. With his captives tied up, Chen took a cursory look inside my study, then propped an armchair against its door. Pointing upstairs he asked us whether there was anyone up there. When we replied "No," he took the chair from in front of the computer and jammed it upside down on the stairs leading up to the bedrooms, together with a glass-topped telephone table. This formed an effective barricade on the narrow stairway.

He then switched off the TV lounge lights, leaving the TV set on. He ran down the stairs, made sure that the house was locked, switched off all the lights, and collected a two-litre plastic bottle of water from the fridge in the kitchen.

The two men at our front gate, seeing lights extinguished one after the other, couldn't understand why we refused to answer our intercom. Pulling out his cell phone, the salesman tried phoning us. By then Chen was back in the TV lounge with us. He picked up the ringing phone and handed it to Anne.

"Hello," Anne answered.

"Hello, this is Saif Sindhu with the carpets. We are ringing your buzzer at the front gate, but you are not answering us."

"We can't let you in now," Anne replied in a low, deliberate voice, striving to keep control of her emotions. "We have been taken hostage."

A few seconds of disbelieving silence followed as Sindhu absorbed the full meaning of this statement.

"Oh my goodness!" he exclaimed and rang off.

Immediately he phoned one of his customers who was a colleague of mine from the embassy, Wouter Badenhorst. This quiet and amicable family man who had been stationed in Taiwan for almost four years, was a solid and dependable friend.

Agitatedly, Sindhu told Wouter something strange was happening at the Alexander home and suggested that he phone us. Mrs. Alexander claimed that the family was being held hostage!

Wouter immediately tried to call us, but in the meantime Chen was using the phone, so all he got was a busy signal. Wouter kept trying.

Chen had phoned what seemed to be the police. Anne and I have a very basic understanding of Mandarin Chinese, so we were able to communicate in a rudimentary fashion with the intruder, who spoke no more than a dozen words of English. But now on the telephone he used Taiwanese, a dialect we couldn't understand at all.

He became very angry as he spoke during that first telephone call. We gathered that the people he was speaking to (we later deduced that it had been the police) would not believe what he was telling them. He gruffly terminated the conversation and immediately called another number. We got the impression that this time he was speaking to a newspaper or television station. Abruptly, his manner became calm and friendly. Again, the party on the other end seemed not to believe him. This time he made a visible effort to convince them, never losing his temper. He gestured toward us on several occasions as he spoke.

As the conversation ended, he seemed well satisfied. He switched off the TV and pulled out a second pistol, a 9mm Beretta—identical to my own service pistol in South Africa—and several spare magazines. The many pockets of his camera jacket bulged with loose ammunition. He produced two long 32-round 9mm magazines and began to check the first few rounds. Noticing me watching him intently in the half-light cast by the lamp in my adjoining study (the only light left on in the house), he walked over to me, removed the first round from one of the long magazines and held it close for me to see.

I went cold. The point of the bullet was hollow and had been tampered with. He smiled sardonically at the expression on my face.

As a soldier, I knew what one of those dumdum bullets would do to a human body on impact.

At this point Wouter's call got through to us. The phone rang. Thrusting one pistol into his waistband, Chen picked up the receiver and answered.

When Wouter heard the strange voice, he immediately realized that Mr. Sindhu had heard correctly. His face paling with horror, he nodded to his wife, Mericia, who understood at once. Her eyes widened in shock.

Wouter asked to speak to me, but as Chen could not understand him, he handed the receiver to Anne. She confirmed his worst fears, and then held the receiver to my ear. I hurriedly explained to Wouter what had happened, described to him our exact location inside the house, told him the apparent state of mind of the gunman, what weapons he had, and asked Wouter to notify the police. However, I cautioned him to stress to the police that they should do nothing rash and warned him that the man was loading his pistols with dumdum bullets.

Wouter promised to take immediate action, and rang off. Wouter had served for several years in the South African military and had a particular interest in handgun shooting as a sport. I knew that he understood, and reliable person that he was, I knew that he would do all he could to help us.

Chen took our carved, round Spanish coffee table with a copper top and barricaded the stairs coming up from the lower lounge. Then, he called our attention to the telephone. "TV, TV!" he repeated in English. "Not Taiwan! World-wide!" He then reverted to Mandarin and several times uttered, "CNN." Clearly, he wanted us to contact the international media for him.

Of course we didn't know the telephone number of CNN or any other TV station. Melanie, however, had been seeing a young American journalist, Michael Letts, who was in practical training as a reporter at the *China Post*, a Taipei English-language daily newspaper.

"Phone Michael," Anne told Melanie.

We all tried to use body language to indicate to Chen that he should give the phone to Melanie. He held the phone near to her and with great difficulty she twisted her bound hands far enough from behind her back to be able to dial. Michael was working in the newsroom of the *China Post* at the time, but the number was busy.

Nearly hysterical, Melanie was white and shaking. Never had I seen my slender daughter, with her "wanderlust" and love of rock climbing, so frightened as she was now.

Anne suggested phoning Michael Letts's aunt and uncle, an expatriate American businessman with whom Michael lived while working in Taiwan. Desperately Melanie tried their number. Martie Olson, Michael's aunt answered. While Chen Chin-hsing held the phone to her ear, Melanie tried to tell Martie what had happened. Her emotions got the better of her and she became hysterical, crying over the phone for Martie to contact Michael and the media, and to help us.

In a state of near-panic, Martie managed to phone Michael at the *China Post* and relay the message to him. Michael says he felt his head begin to spin. Earlier that day, the newsroom

had received a report that Chen Chin-hsing had been apprehended. Although this was obviously fake, Michael did not
know it at the time, so he assumed the gunman holding us
hostage to be a "copycat killer."

He wanted to call the police, but he spoke no Chinese, so
he asked deputy editor Mr. Jason Blatt to call.

Blatt didn't believe his story. Michael became frantic. He
asked him three or four more times and got the same dis-
interested response. Michael blew his top. Screaming at the
editor in language interspersed with expletives, he finally got
the reaction he required. By now, the whole office reached a
state of uproar and Blatt had little choice but to call the police.

In all the confusion, an *Agence France-Presse* reporter, who
happened to be in the *China Post* newsroom as the story was
breaking, hastily scribbled down our home phone number.

As soon as Chen hung up, the phone rang again. Hearing
that the caller spoke English, he again held the receiver to my
ear. It was Brian McLeod, deacon at the Calvary International
Baptist Church where we as a family worshipped. We had a
church meeting planned for the following evening, and he
was phoning to postpone it. I used the opportunity to tell him
what was happening to us, to ask him to contact the police
and to pray for our safe deliverance from this frightening
situation.

Brian was flabbergasted. He knew me well enough to
know that I was not pulling his leg. He immediately contacted the police, and then phoned our pastor, Bill Martin. They
started a prayer chain that would encircle the globe within a
few hours. As Christians heard about it, they phoned others.
Many were expatriates who had been sent to work in Taiwan
for a few years by their companies, and they phoned their
families and friends in their home countries. Christians began
praying in the USA, the UK, Australia, and South Africa.

Later, as television crews arrived on the scene and the
story was beamed right across the world, more and more
Christians added their prayers like links in the chain: there

would be those who knew us, friends and family in South Africa, the UK, New Zealand, USA, Spain, Italy, the Czech Republic and the Netherlands; there would be our fellow military attachés in countries all across the globe; and there would be the thousands, perhaps millions of Christians and others who didn't know us and whom we had never seen who would be earnestly praying for our safe deliverance. But all this was still to come in the uncertain hours that lay ahead.

What was happening to us was being experienced in unusual ways by our friends in Taipei. Marcus and Myra Stinson, American friends from church, were normally members of the Church of the Nazarene. They, like we (who are members of the Assembly of God), had arrived in Taipei for a period of time while Marcus worked on a communications project and, finding no English-language church of their own denomination nearby, joined Calvary International Baptist Church.

That evening, Myra was driving home with their children, Sarah and Trevor. They stopped at McDonald's in Tien Mu to buy hamburgers as a treat. As they drove through to pick up their hamburgers, they heard sirens blaring and saw streams of police cars and motorcycles scream by.

"Look," exclaimed Myra. "They're heading toward Cherry Hill, where the Alexanders live. I wonder if they've caught the last of those bad guys?"

The Stinsons thought no more about it, but at home Myra found an urgent message to phone Joye Martin, the pastor's wife. She did.

"Myra!" exclaimed Joye in an anguished voice. "He's taken the Alexanders hostage!"

Back in our TV lounge, the phone rang again. It was the *China Post*. The sub-editor Jason Blatt, who knew Mandarin, was on the line to speak to Chen. After his initial dismissal of Michael Letts's pleas, he began to take the situation seriously. It dawned on Blatt that this was a story worth getting in on. Chen eagerly obliged.

2

▸Hostage!◂

INSIDE THE DARKENED HOUSE on Cherry Hill, tension mounted. Chen sat on the sofa, the telephone in one hand and a pistol in the other. As he spoke on the phone to Jason Blatt of the *China Post*, he stretched out to make himself more comfortable — at the expense of Melanie and Christine, who perched on the edge of the sofa. Chen placed his legs behind them, lying on his back, but propped up on the armrest. Because Anne was sitting deep in the sofa against the other armrest, he unceremoniously plopped his feet on her lap. She still held little Zachary. His eyes widened in puzzlement.

Blessed with a bubbling sense of humor, my wife invariably sees the funny side of any situation. She found a vicious criminal's relaxed repose with his feet crossed on her lap to be funny. She brought my attention to it with a laugh. I didn't find it at all funny under the circumstances and neither did Melanie and Christine.

Though Chen spoke on the phone in a relaxed manner, his eyes displayed a ruthless and steely resolve. There could be no doubt that he knew what he wanted and intended to get it at all costs. He was a man with a mission. He was using my

23

family. I looked at Melanie, who showed signs of extreme agitation and Christine, who was pale with fright. Only Anne remained calm. Her blue eyes sparkled as always, and she tossed back her strawberry-blond hair almost defiantly.

But I was gripped by sheer terror. I envisioned a scene of carnage unfolding, with my family being shot to death in front of me, or of them witnessing my own bloody execution. My dry tongue cleaved to my palate and my head throbbed. I was reminded of the sensation I had once experienced prior to doing a free-fall parachute jump after not having parachuted for several years. The essential difference, though, was that this time I had no choice in the matter.

There was nothing I could do.

Nothing, that is, except pray. I began to pray out loud, so that my family would hear me. I prayed that God would send a miracle so that we would be delivered from that impossible situation. I also prayed that God would touch this man, Chen Chin-hsing, and replace the aura of evil which surrounded him with an aura of love.

As I prayed I felt a calmness descend upon me. The image of impending slaughter which plagued my thoughts disappeared and I found myself able to focus on what was happening around me.

I became aware that Anne and the girls were praying out loud also.

Chen ended his conversation with Blatt and gazed at my praying family with mild curiosity. Blatt said later that Chen told him he was holding us hostage and he emphasized the presence of the baby. Chen demanded that Blatt come over to the house immediately, as he wanted international media coverage.

Chen told Blatt his grievances. He claimed that his imprisoned wife and relatives were innocent. He accused law enforcement agencies of having wronged his wife and family. A note of desperation crept into his voice as he stated that he no longer cared about anything.

Blatt phoned the police, told them about his conversation, and then set off in a taxi for Cherry Hill through Taipei's swarming evening traffic.

Chen appeared content with the phone calls. He settled down to wait. He showed no aggression toward us and allowed us to talk freely. Grabbing the remote control, he switched on the TV again, and flipped through the channels. He watched one of the Chinese-language stations for a while.

Then he noticed that we were all very uncomfortable, so of his own accord he untied our ankles. Again he muttered "I'm sorry" in English. Our passive response to his actions and our relative calm seemed to make him a little complacent about us.

Yet the ruthless resolve never left his eyes.

I tried to engage him in conversation. He obviously had difficulty understanding me though, since my Mandarin is poor and my deep, resonant voice is not exactly suited to the high-pitched, tonal Chinese dialects. He did begin to talk, and from what Anne and I could understand he was saying that he wanted to talk to his wife and that he was concerned about his children. When he spoke of his children, he would smile at baby Zachary.

Discovering this weak chink in the man's armor, Anne tried to exploit it. Pointing to Christine, Anne asked Chen whether she could phone a friend. He readily consented and held the phone for Anne. Anne dialed the number of Paula Perkins, whose daughter Lindsay was Christine's best friend. Anne held the receiver to Christine's ear, telling her to explain the situation and ask them to call the police. No one was home, so Christine left a message for Lindsay.

Zachary was hungry and began to cry, so Anne showed Chen the empty baby bottle and told him that she needed to replenish it. He gave her permission to go downstairs to collect milk formula and baby food. Then she fed Zachary, and he quieted down.

Chen asked me in Mandarin if we were Americans.

"We are not," I replied in Mandarin. "We are South Africans." He looked at me blankly.

"But you are from the embassy?" he queried.

"Correct," I answered.

He smiled slightly and nodded, looking satisfied.

▶▶▶▶▶▶▶◄◄◄◄◄◄◄

I am not a career diplomat. I was merely serving another term of duty in the constantly changing, challenging, and exciting life of an army officer, this time as a military attaché. My wife Anne and I had longed for a posting abroad as an attaché couple.

Travel was something we enjoyed. Anne had worked in London before I met her. Pathfinder training with the Israeli paratroopers, then commando training with the Chilean special forces and airborne exercises with the British Parachute Regiment in the Netherlands had taken me around the world. When our two eldest daughters were very young, we lived for two years in Madrid, where I was sent to study at the Spanish Army Staff College, and we used the opportunity to tour through most of Europe.

During military demonstrations in South American countries, I had accompanied marketing teams from South Africa's armaments industry on several occasions as an interpreter and commentator. In addition, I had travelled to various African countries on active service and to conduct military training programs. Both Anne and I had travelled extensively on holidays to countries in Southern Africa.

Eager to experience more of the world, in late 1994 when we saw the list of upcoming postings abroad, we applied, hoping to be sent to Belgium. But when we appeared before the selection board, they told us that the Belgian post was reserved for an officer from a staff division of Defence Headquarters. An infantryman and paratrooper, I was excluded.

"Is there any country in which you would prefer not to serve?" a board member asked.

"Yes," I replied, "we would rather not go to Taiwan."

"Why not?" asked the brigadier who was chairman of the board, narrowing his eyes.

"Because, Sir, all the indications are that we will be breaking off diplomatic relations with them within a year or two, and we would not like to have our tour cut short."

"You have no grounds to make that assumption," admonished the brigadier, looking annoyed.

With that, our interview was terminated. I was indignant; Anne was amused. It seemed I had once again been too outspoken, upsetting the pompous brigadier. It felt as though my grey beard bristled with annoyance.

"Don't worry about it," Anne reassured me with her disarming smile, "If the Lord wants us to be sent abroad, we'll go and we'll end up where He wants us."

In time I was notified that I would be posted abroad in January 1996 as the Armed Forces Attaché to Taiwan! The ways of the military are devious indeed. I should have known better than to make my preferences known.

Because of the political uncertainty surrounding South Africa's diplomatic relations with Taiwan, Anne and I had very real reservations about being sent there. Our enthusiasm knew no bounds, however, at the prospect of our living in an oriental country. Neither of us had ever seen the Far East. In order to prepare ourselves, we began reading avidly about Chinese culture, history, and customs.

Early in 1995, I handed over to my successor the duties of chief instructor of the Senior Command and the Staff Duties Course at the South African Army College in Pretoria. Anne and I reported at the South African Military Intelligence College to attend the Military Attaché Course. For the next six weeks we were versed in the protocol, predicaments, and pitfalls of the diplomatic world. Our instructors honed us in the social graces. They fed us copious amounts of background information about the ongoing dynamics of change in South Africa. Together with other couples bound for countries on five continents, we were systematically equipped to represent our country abroad. After sitting for the diplomatic examinations of the Department of Foreign Affairs, at last we were ready. We all anticipated exciting challenges ahead.

South Africa's first fully-democratic election took place only a year earlier. For the first time in half a century we had a government which was recognized and accepted by the general international community. Still fresh in our minds was the euphoria accompanying the elections which, against all expectations, had taken place with a minimum of violence. The interest of the international media and the world-wide respect for, and status of, our new president Nelson Mandela had brought South Africa into the world's focus.

South Africa had become respectable, consigning *apartheid* to the trash heap of history. Our future looked bright. The countries who had previously shunned South Africa now scrambled to open embassies in Pretoria, and many expressed eagerness to exchange military attachés with the newly-constituted South African National Defence Force.

New worlds quickly opened for South African diplomats. Anne and I could sense the excitement among our fellow students in the course. I recall experiencing a pang of regret that Anne and I were the only ones being sent to one of the old "pariah states."

During the bad old days of *apartheid,* only a handful of countries accepted military attachés from South Africa—those who also, for one reason or another, were rejected by a large section of the international community. Sanctions against *apartheid* South Africa had systematically whittled away diplomatic representation, and with it military contact.

Only countries where right-wing military dictatorships flourished—such as Argentina, Paraguay, Uruguay, and Chile—maintained significant military links with the white oligarchy of Africa. In the early 1970's, military cooperation grew between South Africa and the Republic of China on Taiwan. South Africa sent a select group of paratroop officers to a special forces course in Taiwan, and shortly afterward diplomatic relations upgraded from consulate to full embassy level. In 1978, the two countries exchanged military attachés.

Taiwanese officers attended South African military courses. The two countries exchanged high-level visits and instituted conferences on military intelligence and technology.

Then came the demise of *apartheid* and the election of a democratic government in South Africa. The Republic of China (ROC) on Taiwan saw the handwriting on the wall. They hustled to provide substantial financial support for Nelson Mandela's African National Congress during South Africa's election campaign. But, alas, it was too late to switch sides. Taiwan's Communist arch rivals on the mainland of China, the People's Republic of China (PRC), had supported South Africa's liberation movements during all the years of their armed struggle. During those years, Taiwan (ROC) had openly supported South Africa's oppressor government in Pretoria. Now it was payback time, and the payment demanded by the government of mainland China was diplomatic recognition. By implication, this would require South Africa to terminate diplomatic recognition of Taiwan's ROC.

But while the politicians tried to make up their minds about the two Chinese states — the PRC on the mainland, and the ROC on Taiwan — the South African National Defence Force prepared a military attaché replacement — me.

From July to November 1995, I attended the Joint Staff Course required for colonels from all the arms of service who want to be considered for promotion to brigadier general.[1]

Melanie had a year to go before she would graduate as a social worker from the University of Stellenbosch, so she'd remain behind in South Africa. Shona had just finished high school and planned to take a secretarial course at the Pretoria Technikon; so she, too, would remain behind.

Christine, our freckle-faced and fun-loving ten-year-old would go with us to Taiwan.

In January 1996, Anne, Christine and I flew to the busy,

vibrant capital city of Taipei, on the beautiful, mountainous island of Taiwan. We moved into a house in Peitou, a quiet though crowded suburb in the hills on the outskirts of Taipei. A few cherry trees still remained in the tiny gardens of some homes, a reminder of the area's rural past.

During the halcyon days of the *apartheid* government, the military mission at the South African embassy in Taiwan had included an attaché each for the army, air force, and navy, as well as an assistant attaché and a non-commissioned officer for administration. Now there was only myself.

Fortunately Anne, who had a security clearance, assisted me with much of the classified typing and computer work.

I did have an excellent Chinese secretary, the demure, attractive and dedicated Carol Lee. She did my unclassified typing, made contact with senior Taiwanese officers, arranged dinners, receptions, and other programs, undertook some translation work and did all my non-classified administration. Carol soon became my right hand. She had served five consecutive military attachés before me and she knew every senior officer in the Taiwanese military.

The fourth member of our little team, Jimmy Chuang, was my driver and messenger. He knew all of Taipei and most of Taiwan backwards; he had phenomenal driving skills in Taipei's energetic traffic and valuable knowledge of Mandarin, Taiwanese, and English. And after twelve years of service at the embassy, the strange customs of the people from *Nan Fei* (South Africa) no longer surprised him.

Taiwan and South Africa enjoyed excellent military relations. My predecessors had worked hard to bring about this state of affairs and I walked into a situation where I had ready access to the ROC armed forces at all levels. The Chinese people are by nature friendly and helpful, and it did not take me long to find my feet.

The Chinese Lunar New Year celebrations, shortly after our arrival, introduced us to the hospitality and generosity of the people of Taiwan. We were inundated with invitations and gifts. The social activity continued throughout our stay on the island, particularly during the Dragon Boat Festival and the Mid-autumn Festival. Anne and Christine loved the excitement and vibrancy of life in Taiwan. We enjoyed sightseeing with Melanie and Shona when they came for vacations.

My intensely stimulating work kept me busy and happy. The Republic of China has the thirteenth-largest armed forces in the world, with almost half-a-million persons under arms. It is equipped with modern, high-tech defense systems. I lost no time in making contact with the Taiwanese airborne forces and soon qualified as an ROC Army paratrooper.

My job as the Armed Forces Attaché primarily encompassed four fields: 1) liaison with the ROC armed forces on behalf of the Chief of the South African National Defence Force; 2) overt collection and exchange of intelligence; 3) handling of official visits by senior South African military officers and officials from the South African Department of Defence; and 4) promotion of South African armaments sales abroad.

Least enjoyable for Anne and I were the social commitments. We don't find appealing large receptions with vast numbers of distant acquaintances mouthing obligatory and inane pleasantries. We prefer intimate groups of friends sharing an informal dinner in someone's home. This we could do with the military attaché corps in Taiwan, since it was an embarrassingly small group. Besides South Africa, only El Salvador, Guatemala, and Paraguay sent attachés in uniform to Taiwan. Only thirty countries of the world gave recognition to the ROC, and most of those were such tiny states that they were unable to provide military attachés.

Several significant countries which recognized the rival Peoples Republic of China did however have representative offices in Taipei, doing the work of an embassy, though giving it a different name. These countries had interests in Taiwan which warranted this, and some of them even employed retired military officers in the role of unofficial military attachés. So it was that the "attaché corps" found itself in the rather unique situation of having a second group, not wearing uniform and not officially accredited. These highly professional former officers included men from the USA, France, Israel, South Korea, and Singapore. With such a tiny attaché corps, Anne and I were able to quickly build up a close friendship with most of the couples involved. The nature of the social functions we attended with them therefore tended to be close, informal, and friendly.

Unfortunately, the officially-accredited attachés all spoke Spanish, but no English; while the rest spoke English, but no Spanish. Few of us spoke Mandarin well enough to conduct a relaxed conversation or hold a meaningful discussion.

Anne and I took the lead to overcome this quandary, because we both had learned Spanish in Madrid. We arranged dinners one night for official attachés, at which we only spoke Spanish; and a different evening for the unofficial attachés who spoke English. It worked well. Our life abroad proved to be animating and enjoyable.

Street scenes in Taipei. Above: Taipei, city of architectural asymmetry. One of the ancient city gates, restored to its original glory, is flanked by modern office buildings and surrounded by incessant traffic. Below: One cyclist, among Taipei's thousands (millions?) of motor scooters, shows off her well-behaved dog.
(Photos: Mac Alexander)

ABOVE: Cuts of meat for sale at a Taipei street market.
BELOW: The scene at every traffic light in the city—the leggy ladies of Taipei. (Photos: Mac Alexander)

34

3

▸Streets Of Taipei◂

DURING LUNCH TIME on that fateful November day, I left my
office to take a break from uninspiring administrative tasks
and walked the city streets of Taipei, enjoying the vibrant life
and friendly people.

To an Occidental like myself, the street scenes held exotic
appeal: narrow residential alleys draped with clean laundry;
ingenious home-made motor tricycles; smiling street vendors;
pretty girls on motor scooters; pavement restaurants where
animated customers consumed bowls of noodles.

On that particular day, I set off down the pleasant and
wide, tree-lined boulevard known as Tun-hwa North Road.
With so much on my mind, I was glad to get out of the office
for a while.

By this time, the diplomatic isolation of the Republic of
China had intensified. South Africa, following the rest of the
world, had finally made their decision and would switch
recognition to the People's Republic of China in a few short
weeks from now. The uncertainty that had surrounded this
decision had hung like a sword of Damocles above our heads,
threatening to end our tour abroad. Now the sword had
fallen. I had been instructed to close down my office and

return to South Africa. Soon the bustling streets of Taipei would be history to me.

While closure had merely been a threat, however, it had served as an incentive. I worked extremely hard to promote military relations between South Africa and the ROC in the hopes that this would in some way contribute towards the postponement of the decision which we knew was inevitable. And even if we switched diplomatic recognition to Beijing, I reasoned, if I could show what benefits were to be gained from continued contact with Taipei, we could maintain an "unofficial" military attaché there, like other countries. My South African colleagues in the Departments of Foreign Affairs and Trade and Industry worked equally hard towards the same end.

Though these work conditions caused tension, it was incredibly stimulating as well. Fighting for survival, one invariably taps otherwise-untouched resources, and I fired off regular reports containing what I considered to be ingenious suggestions and recommendations. It took me six months to realize that no one in South Africa bothered to read them!

Obviously those in Pretoria responsible for handling whatever I submitted had already written off Taiwan. For whatever reason, they had decided that no matter the potential in Taiwan, no matter what arms deals might benefit South Africa, no matter what investment might materialize, the South African military would dump Taiwan once diplomatic recognition had been terminated.

Shortly after we arrived in Taiwan, the ROC held its first fully-democratic presidential election. Determined to thwart this blatant display of democracy, the People's Republic of China on the Chinese mainland made concerted efforts to disrupt Taiwan's election and intimidate the voters into either staying away from the polls or not voting for President Lee Teng-hui.

The PRC's People's Liberation Army along the Chinese mainland shore opposite Taiwan conducted massive military maneuvers. The sabre rattling reached a climax with the firing of inert surface-to-surface missiles which straddled the island, landing in the sea just kilometres from the coast.

I found myself carrying out a formal military appraisal of the situation and drawing up a contingency plan for the evacuation of embassy personnel, their families and other South African residents in Taiwan. Fear that the war between the Chinese Communists and Nationalists would resume gripped many of the expatriates living in Taiwan. The world held its breath as the USA sent two potent Naval carrier battle groups to the area, and the ROC placed all its forces on alert. Enormous military power was concentrated in and around Taiwan.

Most Taiwanese, however, remained unfazed and refused to be intimidated. The election proceeded. President Lee and his running mate Lien Chan were re-elected. The PRC backed down. Then, in our official capacity, Anne and I were invited guests at the lavish and colorful inauguration of President Lee.

After this spectacular highlight to our first few months in Taiwan, more excitement followed when typhoon HERB struck the island. During the worst storm in more than thirty years, we locked ourselves securely in our home for two days. The windows rattled and rain fell in solid sheets. We listened terrified to the onslaught of gale-force winds that hurled branches and debris across the streets. Shards of glass flew from buildings, and Taipei's incessant traffic ground to a halt. No one dared venture outside.

In mountains and valleys, mud slides and floods cut off whole communities for weeks. We had no electricity or piped water in our home. More than twenty people were confirmed killed, and some forty others disappeared without trace in raging rivers or under tons of sliding earth.

After the balmy weather of South Africa, we were awed by the unstoppable power manifested in the elements.

Political issues remain the prime source of excitement for a diplomat though, and we had no shortage of these, either. When our fears were finally realized and President Mandela announced in November 1996 that South Africa would sever diplomatic ties with the ROC at the end of 1997 in favor of the PRC, my job changed markedly.

Overnight, the flow of VIP military visitors from South Africa virtually stopped. My friendships with senior Taiwanese military officers became strained. Ambassador Viljoen retired in February 1997 after more than forty years in the foreign service and for almost six months the South African embassy functioned without an ambassador. This sent out very negative signals to the ROC government.

Although I still visited ROC military units, I no longer experienced the open, free interaction I had before Mandela's announcement. In June I received word that I was to close the military mission in Taipei at the end of 1997 and return to South Africa to be placed at the disposal of the South African Army.

Anne and I felt deeply disappointed that we couldn't complete three years as an attaché couple. It was policy in the South African National Defence Force that members of the South African armed services would be afforded only one opportunity to serve as a military attaché. This signaled the end of our foreign travels.

Professionally, I felt bitter. Everything I had worked towards in Taiwan disappeared like the proverbial puff of smoke.

I was the only South African military attaché between Kuala Lumpur and Washington, D.C.. Now I was to be withdrawn, my mission closed, and no replacement sent to any country in the Western Pacific. This area is surrounded by countries which are friendly towards South Africa, with fast-growing economies and their military establishments are burgeoning, while elsewhere in the world they are shrinking. I felt it very unwise to have no military finger on the pulse of that region which includes the world's most populous and third most populous countries and the largest armed forces in the world. But as my opinion apparently counted for nothing, these facts merely served to frustrate me.

I was bluntly told that there was no money to replace me or to open another mission elsewhere in the Western Pacific. Looking at the dubious potential of some missions which we were maintaining in other parts of the world, I had strong reservations about this argument. However, as a soldier I could only commit my viewpoints to paper and then accept the decisions made by my superiors.

I set about the closure of the military mission and booked our flight back to South Africa for 31 December 1997, the last day on which our embassy would function in Taipei under that name. I planned farewell functions and purchased farewell gifts for the senior officers of the ROC armed forces. With only five months left in Taiwan, a busy time lay ahead.

In the meantime, South Africa sent a new ambassador to Taiwan, just five months before the embassy was due to close. It had been decided that an unofficial representative office would be maintained in Taipei after the embassy ceased to exist, and that the embassy would convert into a liaison office. The new ambassador Mr. Nikki Scholtz would simply change his title and then head up the new office.

During the last few months of 1997, these changes created a climate of uncertainty within the embassy. In negotiations with Pretoria, the ROC tried hard to gain certain advantages under the new relationship. But the South African government remained intransigent on these issues.

Ambassador Nikki Scholtz saw a great need for continued military relationship with Taiwan, but his appeals also fell on deaf ears. He and I spent long hours discussing the political and military situation in the Far East, and he regularly requested my advice for his reports back to South Africa.

I was informed that the South African Army would, on my return, post me to Pietersburg, capital of the country's Northern Province, where I would serve as the Senior Staff

Officer Operations at Headquarters, Far North Command. My assignment would be to coordinate border protection in an area where starving illegal immigrants were streaming into our own land from neighbor countries searching for better opportunities.

I would not be leaving Taiwan on a high note. I would not be able to look back on satisfying professional accomplishments. I felt cheated, almost betrayed. But, as the premature and anticlimactic end of our tour abroad loomed, the last thing that entered my mind was being caught up with my family in an international hostage drama!

▶▶▶▶▶▶▶◀◀◀◀◀◀◀

I had not walked far on my lunch time stroll through downtown Taipei when I heard sirens and saw police cars and fire engines tearing up the street in the general direction of the embassy.

Often fire drills occurred in downtown buildings, and sometimes actual fires. A screaming cavalcade of fire engines weaving through the city's traffic was not unusual. I thought no more about it. I knew if it affected the embassy, my secretary Carol would call the cell phone I carried.

Back at the embassy an hour later, I found the Chinese staff in a state of great excitement.

"The criminal Chen Chin-hsing has been spotted in a building very near to the embassy," they told me. "The police have surrounded the building and they hope to capture him."

Over the past few months, the news media had given extensive coverage to this high-profile criminal. Everyone spoke of the reign of terror he and his two cronies had caused, and of the inability of the police to apprehend them. Police plastered wanted posters with photographs of the infamous trio all over Taiwan. We had seen one at the local convenience store just a block away from our house. When one of the criminals, Lin Chun-sheng took his life during a shoot-out with the police in August, someone had drawn a diagonal cross through his picture on the poster. When I saw it, I thought, "One down, two to go!"

False alarms and fruitless police cordons became common, as a jittery public reported sightings. In fact, I assumed what I had witnessed that day was another false alarm.

I smiled at the excitement, shrugged, and got back to my work. If Chen was there, the police would get him. That was their job. I needed to get on with mine. I had lots to do in the next six weeks, and Chen Chin-hsing had nothing to do with me.

Carol kept me informed during the course of the afternoon anyway, as she monitored developments on her radio. A woman had appeared at a sixth-floor window in a building in Mingsheng East Road, opposite the Sherwood Hotel, a block away from the embassy.

The woman yelled down to passers-by in the street below, "Chen Chin-hsing is inside my home." Within minutes police arrived on the scene and cordoned off the area. Protected by bullet-proof vests, face masks, and helmets, the heavily-armed police covered the apartment while their colleagues broke in. The media arrived in force. The police found two hysterical women inside who claimed that Chen Chin-hsing had held them hostage.

But two hours of searching the building revealed no sign of Chen—not a trace.

Skeptical, I thought perhaps Chen had been there, perhaps not. Little did I know that only a few hours later, I would be his hostage in my own home in a different part of the city.

In any case, I thought no more of it except to mention it when I phoned home later in the afternoon. Anne reminded me that we had made an appointment with a carpet salesman to come to our house between seven and seven-thirty that evening.

Like most people, I had more important and urgent things on my mind than the antics of a local criminal. The death of Chen's accomplice was probably making people overreact, I thought.

▶▶▶▶▶▶▶◀◀◀◀◀◀◀

Chen Chin-hsing was born in 1959 in Sanchung city, Taipei county, the illegitimate son of a poor woman. Newspaper reports and comments made by police officers who had long been on his trail revealed a picture of a classic social misfit. No one seems to know who his biological father was — certainly Chen never knew him. It is said that his mother didn't even know the man's name. Later, when Chen was still very small, she married another man and evidently there was no place for the little boy in the new union.

Brought up in poverty by his maternal grandmother, Chen showed early signs of antisocial behavior. He soon became the typical, euphemistically-labelled "problem child," a constant headache to his teachers. Yet he was devoted to his grandmother, who seems to have been the only one to show him affection. Despite his otherwise-violent nature and the harshness of the world around him, he apparently received from his grandmother a soft side — an ability to respond to love.

He seems to have had a poor school career. In Taiwan the first nine years of schooling are compulsory. Chen, however, never completed even this minimum requirement. Yet his Chinese calligraphy was surprisingly artistic, he displayed a bent for turning a fine phrase, and he had a penchant for writing letters.

His first brush with the law came at the age of twelve when he was arrested for larceny and theft and placed in protective custody. The following year, 1972, he was sentenced to a three-year reformatory term for assault. Then Chen suffered a devastating blow to his pride in junior high school. Faced with the highly competitive Taiwanese educational system, he found that his lack of English skills made it impossible to keep up with the other kids academically. So he dropped out.

In 1976 he was sentenced to a lengthy prison term for robbery and intimidation committed in Taipei. Chen did not complete the sentence, but managed to escape. Though Chen may not have even completed his high school education, there can be little doubt that he was a man of considerable intelligence.

After his escape it seems that Chen went on a crime spree, alleged to have included theft, robbery, and even murder. Eventually, however, it came to an end when he was recaptured by the police, tried by Taiwan's rushed judicial system, and sent back to prison. When he emerged again in 1991, he had spent seventeen years behind bars.

In view of the nature of his alleged crimes and his escape from custody, it is surprising that Chen did not remain in prison longer. More surprising, he seemed to go "straight" for a while, becoming involved in the underground loan system, which, although considered shady, was a far cry from his former violent and angry life of crime.

Possibly this was due in part to the influence of the gentle Chang Su-chen, a girl he met the year he was released and six months later married. Except for his maternal grandmother, Chang seems to have been the first person to have shown Chen affection. As he had with his grandmother, Chen responded with an almost ironic tenderness.

He seems to have held a deep love for his wife, and they had two sons. Home video footage screened on television showed Chen Chin-hsing at home, playing with his young sons while his smiling wife looked on. The whole reason for his precipitating the hostage drama at our home in Taipei was to secure what he would consider a fair deal for Chang Su-chen.

So what went wrong? Why did he go back to his violent ways when things seemed to be looking up for him and his family?

Not being privy to his personal situation and commitments, his financial resources, his social pressures as a jailbird, and the influence of his questionable friends, it would be presumptuous of me to venture answers to such a question.

It does seem that Chen Chin-hsing attempted a series of business ventures. One of these was the opening of an illegal video arcade. However, the government began a large scale crackdown on the island's video arcades, and, like his other efforts, this one also folded. This failure seems to have precipitated Chen's teaming up with Lin Chun-sheng and Kao Tien-min, a partnership which led directly to a string of crimes, mostly against young and helpless women.

Whatever the reason, 1997 saw a return to crime by Chen Chin-hsing in a spectacular and horrifying way.

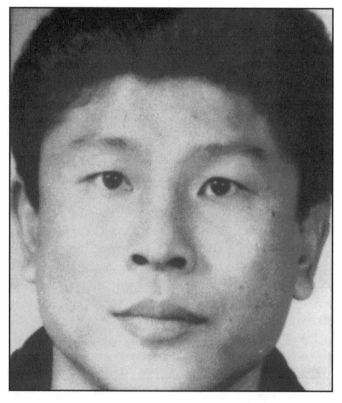

Fugitive Chen Chin-hsing, kidnap/murder suspect, Taiwan's most-wanted criminal. (AP Photo, PictureNet Africa)

4

▶Terror In Taiwan◀

On 14 April 1997, three thugs kidnapped a seventeen-year-old girl named Pai Hsiao-yen, daughter of the attractive Taiwanese television celebrity Pai Ping-ping and Japanese comic-book artist Ikki Kajiwara. The kidnapping took place in Linkou, a town just outside Taipei, while Hsiao-yen was on her way to school. The three thugs were Lin Chun-sheng, Kao Tien-min, and Chen Chin-hsing.[1]

They took pretty Pai Hsiao-yen to an apartment in Wuku, Taipei County. That night at 8:00 P.M. the trio of hoodlums contacted her mother and demanded five-million US dollars in ransom money. Over the next three days the kidnappers made several phone calls to Pai Ping-ping, giving her details of drop-off locations, which they constantly changed.

On 17 April Pai's car approached the latest location, but the kidnappers spotted what they thought were members of the local media following her; so they did not appear. The next day the kidnappers instructed Pai to pay the ransom at a location in Linkou, but again failed to appear to collect the money.

Convinced that Pai had notified the police, the enraged

kidnappers apparently beat her daughter so badly she went into shock and died from internal bleeding and liver damage. Her body was dumped in a drainage ditch in Taipei County's Taishan Township. While she was held captive, it was later claimed, she had been guarded by Chang Chih-hui, the brother of kidnapper Chen's wife, Chang Su-chen.

The kidnappers continued to demand the ransom money from the dead girl's mother. Before she had died, the most brutal of the thugs, Chen Chin-hsing, had cut off one of the girl's fingers, and on 23 April they sent the finger to Pai Ping-ping together with a note warning her against contacting the police. Until the 24th, they continued to arrange rendezvous after rendezvous, but never showed for fear of being ambushed by the police.

The police, it seems, were indeed involved, though they kept the whole matter from the media. On 25 April the police converged on Chen's home in Sanchung, Taipei, to arrest him. But he managed to escape when his wife saw them and warned him. Police arrested his wife, Chang Su-chen, together with two of his friends.

On 26 April, after failing to capture Chen in a shoot-out, the police finally made a public statement revealing that Pai Hsiao-yen had been kidnapped, and that Lin and Chen were suspects but had so far avoided police efforts to capture them. The police launched a massive manhunt in the mountains of Wuku and Pali, west of Taipei. The three kidnappers, however, were apparently hiding out in the suburb of Shulin, in an apartment leased by a woman named Hsu Chia-hui.

At 5:15 P.M. on 28 April, Pai Hsiao-yen's decomposing body was found. The same day, police investigations revealed that Kao Tien-min was the third member of the trio. The next day, they released photos and criminal records of the three. It was a major news item. Newspapers carried the photos, and "wanted" posters began to appear around the island.

Clearly, things were getting hot for the three fugitives. Splitting, they went separate ways. Rumours crackled through

Taiwan as conflicting reports came in that they had escaped to mainland China, had committed suicide, had kidnapped other people, were hidden by wayward police elements, or were enjoying the protection of one of the powerful and mysterious criminal Chinese triads.

Crime had shown a steady increase in Taiwan during the nineties, and among the population of the ordered and peaceful island concern grew. Prior to 1988, martial law prevailed in Taiwan. After his 1949 defeat at the hands of Mao Zedong's Communists, President Chiang Kai-shek had fled the mainland with his Nationalist government.

Taiwan and a few small islands were the only remaining territories over which the Republic of China had been able to exercise sovereignty after their withdrawal. Chiang Kai-shek had ruled this land with a fist of iron. Crime was virtually unknown.

But after Chiang's death in 1975, the ROC slowly transformed from a dictatorship to a democracy. In March 1996 the first truly democratic election in 5,000 years of Chinese history took place when President Lee Teng-hui was elected for a second term of office, this time by universal adult suffrage. However, the new democracy was showing cracks in its social fabric. For such a previously safe society, crime had reached alarming levels. During 1996 some 13,000 violent crimes such as murder, robbery and rape were reported to the police — double the number of a decade earlier.

The kidnapping and brutal murder of young Pai Hsiao-yen was a symptom of Taiwan's new and spreading malaise. The teenager's murder sparked widespread public outrage. The government's popularity plummeted.

President Lee Teng-hui held a top-level security meeting on Friday 2 May 1997 to discuss the growing crisis in social order.

Two days later, tens of thousands of people took to the streets to protest over the increasing breakdown of public law and order. The people of Taiwan exercised their new democratic rights to let the authorities know that they were deeply dissatisfied with the government's inability to prevent criminals from carrying out their deeds with impunity. Protesters demanded that the president apologize to the public at large and that Prime Minister Lien Chan step down.

The crisis in government continued, with opposition parties using the opportunity to pile on the pressure. The government could not ignore the criticism. On 8 May 1997 Interior Minister Lin Feng-cheng resigned. The same day police closed in on Hsu Chia-hui, the woman in whose apartment the three fugitives had hidden. She confessed to concealing the kidnappers and confirmed to the police that the three men were heavily armed.

None of this appeased the general public, and social activists and civic action groups mobilized a second large-scale protest on 18 May. The public felt that too many crimes remained unresolved, and the inability of the police to arrest Pai Hsiao-yen's murderers was a high-profile example. Within a week, on the 24th, a third protest march convened on the streets of Taipei.

On 2 May the police pulled in Lin's girlfriend and a video game parlor operator for questioning. On 24 May the police questioned and detained the younger brother of kidnapper Chen's wife. The next day they received a tip-off that Chen was spotted on a motorcycle in Wuku. However, a massive police search failed to turn up any trace of the wily fugitive.

The media castigated the authorities for their apparent inertia. It seemed that everyone in Taiwan knew about the Pai Hsiao-yen case, and the anger of the common people was intense. Citizens felt insecure, and every robbery, rape, and assault committed in Taiwan seemed to further vindicate their feelings. The three kidnappers, their fingers dripping with the blood of their victim, were acquiring an aura of invincibility and their continued evasion of the police seemed to make every unlawful act committed by any petty crook another example of criminals thumbing their noses at the enforcers of law and order.

On 28 May the trio of fugitives wrote a letter to the two Panchiao District prosecutors responsible for investigating the Pai case. They admitted responsibility for the kidnapping and murder of Pai Hsiao-yen, but denied that any of the relatives and friends who had been arrested as suspects had had anything to do with it.

Every criminal on the island with a known record was nervous about being implicated. Just having been acquainted with one of the fugitives could turn a person into a suspect. The police seemed desperate for results.

Some of those who were arrested began to crack under police interrogation. On 29 May, Chen's brother-in-law Chang told prosecutors that he had helped guard Pai Hsiao-yen in an apartment in Wuku. He also told them that he had watched Chen cut the little finger off Pai's hand.

For the next two months, the three fugitives maintained a low profile. The police manhunt reached a stalemate. Citizens hoped the trio had left the country.

During July, protestations of the anti-crime lobby became so vehement that the Minister of Justice hinted that corporal punishment such as whipping and caning might be introduced in an attempt to check the worsening crime wave.

By 22 July police investigators, made confident by the confessions they had obtained from suspected accomplices, turned seventeen of them over to the prosecutors. The public had been howling for results and the authorities were anxious to relieve the pressure by showing some signs of progress.

These confessions eventually led to the hostage-taking. Controversy surrounded the manner in which the police had extracted the confessions, particularly that of Chang Su-chen, the wife of Chen Chin-hsing.

Suddenly, on 8 August the fugitive trio re-emerged to kidnap a businessman in Taipei's Peitou suburb. They extorted four-million New Taiwan dollars (about US$150,000) from him and again disappeared. Public outcry ensued as fear gripped the island afresh.

Wealthy Taiwanese began taking extended overseas holidays. In the areas of Taipei where the three hoodlums had been seen, property prices crashed to rock-bottom. Parents resorted to taking their kids to school and picking them up again in the afternoon. Many people stopped going out at night.

A few days after the latest kidnapping, fugitive Chen Chin-hsing poured scorn on the authorities by robbing a household in Taipei, temporarily abducting the three women in the house, and wounding a police officer who tried to intervene. It was apparent that, despite the efforts of the police and the public, the three were still moving about within the capital city almost at will. The police and the government came under heavy fire from a critical and skeptical public media.

Under extreme pressure from the beleaguered government, the police stepped up their efforts.

Then came a breakthrough. A tip-off on 19 August led police to a building on Wuchang Street in central Taipei. They trapped two of the fugitives, Lin Chun-sheng and Kao Tien-min.

Two-hundred police reinforcements speedily cordoned off the area. During a furious shoot-out one policeman was killed and another seriously wounded. They cornered Lin in a dead-end alley, and rather than surrender, he shot himself in the head, dying instantly. During the final shoot-out with Lin, Kao slipped through the police cordon, and escaped.

Although the police tried hard to portray Lin's death as a success, the public were unimpressed. The whole affair was generally seen as a botched operation and the police came in for fresh, sharp criticism from the media.

Two days later, on 21 August, the investigations into the cases of twelve suspected accomplices in the Pai kidnapping were closed. Prosecutors recommended the death penalty for Chen's brother-in-law, Chang Chih-hui; life imprisonment for

Hsu Chia-hui and for Chen's wife, Chang Su-chen; and twelve years for Lin Chi-neng. They awaited trial.

A few weeks of quiet followed, then on 15 September the police released the contents of a letter written by fugitive Chen Chin-hsing. In the letter, Chen claimed that the only people involved in the kidnapping and murder of Pai Hsiao-yen were himself, Lin, and Kao. He protested that his wife, relatives, and friends were innocent and he threatened retaliation if any of them received a heavy sentence. He offered to surrender if his wife was released.

Then, on 18 September, apparently unable to control his sexual appetite, Chen raped a female student from a vocational high school in Taipei County. A worker unintentionally photographed him leaving the crime scene. (Chen was ultimately accused of eighteen rapes, although he admitted to as many as twenty.)

Four days later, Chen was seen in Yungho City. A tip-off alerted police to his presence. Two traffic police encountered him in a narrow alley. Evidently intimidated by the notorious criminal, they allowed him to escape on a motor scooter.

In September the police launched a nation-wide crime crackdown and arrested seventy-one gangsters, including a former city councillor alleged to have used violence to win commercial contracts. But no trace was found of the two remaining fugitives.

For a month no more was heard of either Chen or Kao, though rumors circulated. Then, on 23 October, at a clinic for plastic surgery on downtown Taipei's busy Roosevelt Road, the bodies of a plastic surgeon, his wife, and a nurse were discovered. They had been brutally murdered. The doctor's wife had been tied up, and all three victims had been stabbed several times before being shot at close range with a 9mm handgun. The murdered nurse was believed to have been raped before she was killed. The victims had their eyes taped closed, and there was evidence someone had undergone plastic surgery in the clinic.

Speculation was rife that the perpetrators had been Chen and Kao who, it was thought, must have had their appearances changed. (Chen later confessed that Kao indeed had minor surgery to his eyelids and that they had killed the three people to silence them. DNA tests of blood found at the clinic matched the blood of Kao Tien-min.)

The local media, transfixed by the appalling antics of these arrogant assassins, fanned the fears of the populace with almost daily stories. Police bore the brunt of unrelenting criticism from the outraged public.

All police received orders to shoot to kill if they encountered Chen or Kao. This instruction later had a direct bearing on what took place in our home.

Police stations in all those districts of Taipei known to have been frequented by the killers were reportedly reinforced by members of a specially-trained police task force.

A man resembling Chen allegedly grabbed a woman and held her at gunpoint in front of her fifth-floor apartment off Fuhsing North Road in central Taipei. Though he didn't identify himself, he told her that he was "someone worth twenty-million New Taiwan dollars." This was the amount of the reward money offered by authorities for information leading to the arrest of the two wanted men.

The man asked her if she worked for an airline. She produced her identity card to prove otherwise, and the man released her unharmed and fled. Police investigations did reveal a woman living in the same apartment block who was a flight attendant.

This prompted fears that Chen and Kao might have plans to hijack a plane and flee abroad or go to mainland China. Taipei's Sungshan Domestic Airport stepped up its security measures.

Then, in the late evening of 3 November, Kao was spotted in the suburb of Shihlin. He initiated an exchange of gunfire with police in an alley off Tehsing East Road before abandoning the motor scooter he had been riding and fleeing up

Yang Ming Mountain in the darkness.

Thousands of civilian and military police cast a dragnet over the steep and densely-forested mountain overlooking Taipei. Vehicle check points were set up on the busy Yangteh Avenue in the vicinity of the National Security Bureau Headquarters in a suburb dotted with the mansions of the rich and famous of Taiwan. The search continued all night. The next day helicopters arrived to assist searchers. They found nothing; and public confidence in the police dropped to an all-time low.

A damning editorial in the English-language *China Post* on 6 November stated: "In the minds of many, the failure of the police to capture Kao and fugitive Chen Chin-hsing has resulted in a complete loss of confidence in the police's ability to maintain safety. It is an indication of depressing incompetence on the part of the government."

It was thought that both Chen and Kao had at one time worked as grave diggers, so speculation grew that they were using their knowledge of the vast, elaborate graveyards with their huge, ornate Chinese tombs covering large sections of the mountains, as a labyrinth in which to avoid the police. But searches revealed nothing.

Chen and Kao were not hiding in the mountains. They were in the city.

▶▶▶▶▶▶▶◀◀◀◀◀◀◀

While police combed the forests and the graveyards, Chen hid in the suburb of Peitou. He had already decided what he had to do in order to get a retrial for his wife and relatives — he would take hostages and try to force the hands of the authorities. But, convinced that no policeman would hesitate to shoot Chinese hostages in order to get at him, he determined that his hostages would have to be foreigners.

In Taiwan, policemen who shoot wanted criminals are rewarded with promotion and a substantial cash bonus. This practice tended to make any fugitive from the law wary of encounters with ambitious police officers.

The National Police Administration in Taiwan reportedly drew up a special reward system for the Pai kidnap-murder case. Any police officer who would catch or kill any one of the three suspects in the case would get a two-rank promotion. On 14 November, over fifty Taipei police officers were promoted for their contribution in the death of suspect Lin Chunsheng. The police rivalry created by this bounty system hampered progress.

Chen believed by holding foreigners (and to most Taiwanese, "foreigner" was synonymous with "American") during a confrontation, he would deter the police who would not be anxious to create an international incident by risking injury to such hostages.

The houses in our section of Peitou off Hsing Yi Road were almost identical, and these houses were eminently suitable for holding out against a police siege. All Chen needed was to find one in which foreigners lived. He identified a young American couple, living in a corner house in Lane 154, number 20. Now he would just wait for what he considered the right time.

At the same time Chen was looking for foreigners to abduct, Anne and I had travelled to South Africa to attend her father's funeral. Melanie, Christine, and Zachary remained at home.

Melanie had been living with us for several months, having graduated from the University and now undertaking a research project among AIDS sufferers in Taipei, for which she would receive credit towards a masters degree. It was Melanie who had brought home little Zachary as a foster child. When the tender-hearted and outgoing Melanie had visited an orphanage for abandoned children, she had spotted one tiny baby boy lying on the floor and yelling for all he was worth. She had picked him up and exclaimed jokingly, "Oh, I'll take this one home with me!"

Her jest had been lost on the Chinese nurse, who replied,

"Of course. If you come back tomorrow, we'll have the paper-work ready. You can keep him until his adoption has been finalized. We will provide you with diapers and formula, and you must bring him back every Wednesday morning to be weighed and for his inoculations."

And that is how Zachary came into our lives. And how it was that our two daughters and baby Zachary were home when Chen Chin-hsing was casing our neighborhood. But Chen evidently did not spot them.

When he chose the house next to ours, he didn't realize that number 22, where we lived, was also occupied by for-eigners.

On Tuesday 4 November, the *United Daily News,* a local Chinese-language newspaper received an open letter from Chen, and the following day so did TVBS, a local cable tele-vision news channel. When these letters were made public on Friday the 7th, they caused seething anger among police and government senior officials. In them, Chen strongly criticized and ridiculed the police for their inability to catch him for more than six months.

Chen accused the police of destroying their one means of finding the fugitive trio by having arrested all the people who knew them well. In a display of metaphorical prose with peculiarly Asian imagery, he likened their actions to cutting the string of a flying kite. He added ominously that he and Kao would not be arrested unless it was their destiny as mapped out by the "King of Hell."

Referring to his wife, her brother, and his friend, whom police were holding, he threatened to commit more violent crimes unless they received justice. He accused the police of framing them, and he claimed again they were not involved in the kidnap and murder of Pai Hsiao-yen. Their confessions, he insisted, were forced from them through police torture.

Arrogantly offering to surrender if the senior policemen (whom he named) in charge of the investigation subjected themselves to lie detector tests in front of the media, he reiterated his intention to continue harming innocent people if his demands were not met. Referring to himself as a demon bent on a fiendish imposition of justice, Chen asked the public to forgive him as he had no other means of accomplishing his aim.

Police and government leaders rejected his demands out of hand.

Pai Ping-ping, mother of the murdered girl, denounced him contemptuously for being concerned about his family after having shown no mercy to her daughter.

On 8 November Chen's mother-in-law published an open letter in the press, appealing to her son-in-law to give himself up. This, she said, was the only way he could help those detained under suspicion of being his accomplices. On the same day, a well-known opposition politician and human rights lawyer, Frank Hsieh, announced that he was willing to provide legal assistance to Chen's wife, on condition that Chen surrender to the police.

Chen said later that when he learned of Hsieh's offer, he immediately wrote a letter to Hsieh. In it he requested Hsieh to hold a press conference and make public his promise to be his wife's defense attorney.

Sadly, this letter was not read by Hsieh until after Chen took his hostages. Whether it was delayed in the post or whether it languished in Hsieh's office is unclear. Whatever the case, since he got no response, Chen began to desperately consider other measures. He was running out of time.

Acting on reports of sightings of Chen and Kao in Yungho City, the police dispatched a large force to comb the small and densely-populated urban centre on 10 November. Again, their efforts proved fruitless.

The next day, Chen again wrote a letter to the *United Daily News* promising that he would not kill innocent people, but he also warned that he would never surrender to the police. Again displaying his flair for metaphorical writing, Chen claimed that if he and Kao Tien-min turned themselves in, the police would make meals of them, placing them on a table to be "cut, fried and cooked" in whatever way the police chose.

The police then resorted to psychological tactics, trying to appeal to Chen Chin-hsing's emotions. They released a tape recording in which Chen's wife, Chang Su-chen, urged him to turn himself in. She told him in the recording that his "eye-for-an-eye" and "blood-for-blood" desire for revenge would never come to an end and that by turning himself in he would save his family and friends who had been arrested.

Crying while she spoke, the emotional Chang, addressing her husband as "Ah-Chin," pleaded with him to end his run from the police and castigated him for causing trouble for his family and their children. She told him that she would have to shoulder his guilt until he surrendered.

The recording was generally seen as a desperate attempt by the police to counter Chen's letters to the media. It did not persuade him to surrender.

▸▸▸▸▸▸▸▸◀◀◀◀◀◀◀

At this time, a group of Chinese Christian women, mothers from a Ladies' Fellowship in Hsinchu, felt deeply burdened for the spiritual state of Kao and Chen. They prayed fervently that the two men would repent of their terrible sins and ask Jesus Christ to forgive them and to save their souls from eternal damnation. In a desire to convey this message to the two fugitives, they collected enough money to place a half-page advertisement in a national newspaper.

Anxious to place their ad on a Sunday when the newspaper's circulation was greatest, the ladies approached the *United Daily News*, Taiwan's largest-circulation Chinese newspaper, and requested that it be published on Sunday 16 November. The newspaper was sympathetic, but Sunday's space had been booked for several weeks. The best they could do was to offer a space on Monday the 17th. Though disappointed, the ladies accepted the offer.

The ad ran on a red background (which for the Chinese is a very auspicious color that would attract attention), and it displayed the famous "Hands Joined in Prayer" by Albrecht Dürer. In their ad, the Christian ladies addressed Kao Tien-min and Chen Chin-hsing by name and explained the way of salvation through Jesus Christ. They listed scripture verses. The newspaper placed this ad on the front page.

The same day the ad appeared, the police received a tip-off and cornered Kao in an illegal brothel in the crowded and busy Taipei suburb of Shihpai. In the ensuing, spectacular gunfight, prostitutes leaped from windows to escape, and two civilians and a police officer were wounded. Kao realized the game was up, so he turned his gun on himself and committed suicide. Again, hopes of one police officer gaining a substantial reward were thwarted. But government and police were clearly relieved that they could at least show the public that they had accounted for a second suspect.

Kao had two semi-automatic handguns on his person, and police reportedly discovered a hand grenade concealed in his scooter outside the brothel.

With the news of Kao's death, Chen became acutely aware of the dragnet drawing in around him. Concerned whether the police had any inkling of his whereabouts, he scrutinized the newspapers.

Then the red ad placed by the Christian ladies caught Chen's attention. He later admitted that what he read deeply moved him. This newspaper ad was providential, and it was to be the first of a series of spiritual events to touch Chen in the next few days.

Right now though, Chen had made a decision on his next move. The time had come to take his hostages.

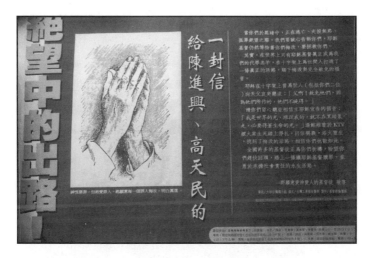

The ad, placed by Christian ladies in the United Daily News, appeared later in several papers, here on the front page of the China Times, Nov. 17. The Chinese words appealed to Chen Chin-hsing and Kao Tien-min to accept Jesus Christ as saviour. Kao died that same day. (Photo: Mac Alexander)

Chen Chin-hsing's wanted poster on wall of police station in Taipei. (Photo: Fan Lee, *The Journalist*)

The Alexander's official attaché residence
on Cherry Hill, a suburb of Taipei.
Anne stands in foreground.
(Photo: Mac Alexander)

5

▸Horrors Of Helplessness◂

CHEN CHIN-HSING BROKE into the house of the young American couple just after dark on Tuesday 18 November. To his consternation, he found no one at home. It happened that the husband was on a business trip to South Korea, while his wife was on holiday in the United States.

Chen waited, then when no one came home, he again emerged in the dark street. It was winter, and although the semi-tropical climate of Taiwan seldom produces really cold weather in Taipei, it grew dark quite early. Night fell before six o'clock in the evening in November.

In the street, Chen wondered what to do. Then he saw a dark green Honda Accord drive by, slow down, and stop in front of the garage of the house next door. As the electronic garage door opened, he noticed the registration number on the car's plate. It was a diplomatic number plate.

Chen must have felt a surge of triumph when he realized that he had found another foreign family. He watched me drive inside and close the garage door. Then he re-entered the home of the absent American couple. From there, it was an easy matter to jump over the wall into our garden.

He skirted our small swimming pool, found a partially-open window in the laundry, and climbed in. That window we normally left ajar by day, so our cats could come and go as they pleased. Quickly he moved through the dining room to the lounge, where Christine sat at the piano.

Christine heard the sound of him jumping through the window and stopped playing. She turned to see a short, stocky Chinese man with unkempt hair, thin moustache and wisp-like goatee peering around the corner and pointing a gun at her. She started up in alarm, but the man motioned at her with his finger across his lips to be quiet. He moved to the foot of the stairs and beckoned to her to approach him. Grabbing her and clamping his arm around her neck, he then marched her up the stairs, while he held the gun to her head.

▶▶▶▶▶▶▶◀◀◀◀◀◀◀

The intruder who had taken us hostage no longer lay back on the sofa where my family sat, bound. Chen began to display signs of nervousness. It seemed that he was expecting the arrival at any moment of those he had notified. He kept looking down from the parapet at the lounge windows below. Every so often, he switched on the TV and surfed through the Chinese stations to see if there was any news on his hostage-taking. He held a pistol in each hand: the Italian model 92 Beretta with a 15-round magazine; and an Austrian Glock 17 with an extended 32-round magazine.

His glance fell on the baby, and he indicated to Anne by pointing a pistol over the parapet that there was going to be shooting. Gesturing towards Zachary, he then covered his own ears with his hands, still holding the pistols. He spoke to Anne in an exhorting tone.

"When the shooting starts, cover the baby's ears," we understood him to be saying.

Zachary, this baby boy who had come to occupy a special place in our household and in our hearts, now fixed his intelligent gaze upon this strange man. Those bright, alert eyes, that showed curiosity and wonder at everything around him, now concentrated on Chen's hardened and determined face.

Even in the darkness, the light from my study adjoining the TV lounge was sufficient for us to see fairly well. At the same time it was so dim that nobody looking into the house from outside would be able to distinguish anything clearly.

I now realized that Chen expected a gun battle with the police.

"Immediately lie flat on the floor if any shooting starts," I cautioned my family. "And don't move at all."

Christine complained that her wrists hurt, so Anne and I brought Chen's attention to this. When he became aware of her discomfort, he immediately untied her, but indicated that she should remain seated on the sofa.

The phone rang again and Chen answered. After a brief conversation he handed the receiver to Christine. It was our young cousin Matthew Simmonds, who was living in Taipei while studying Mandarin. He and Melanie were good friends and earlier that afternoon she had phoned him to suggest that they go out to a movie together in the evening. Since he had been out, she had left a message for him and he was now returning her call to accept her offer.

Christine quickly told him what was happening. The incredulous Matthew found her account difficult to comprehend. But he soon realized that she was deadly serious, so he asked to speak to Chen again. He exchanged a few words with him in Mandarin. Matthew obtained assurances that Chen did not intend to hurt us. Then he rang off and rushed out of his lodgings to find the police. The whole business seemed unreal and he felt sick in the pit of his stomach. It just couldn't be happening!

Matthew hurried outside to a small tea shop where the students often gathered to absorb the local gossip. The old Chinese lady who ran the little establishment listened to his garbled account as he explained to her why he needed to get to a police station. Then, with an inscrutable expression she pointed to the TV in the corner. Matthew went cold. There was our house, with an animated announcer giving the latest update. The screen showed crowds of people, police cars, and flashing lights everywhere. Here was the confirmation he had hoped would not come.

The old woman directed him to the nearby police station. Shocked and disbelieving, Matthew raced to the station. They already knew about the hostage-taking. Matthew wanted to help. No one could think of a way that he would be able to help. So while the police discussed the matter and asked him occasional questions, he fretted and watched the drama unfold on their television set.

Shortly after Matthew had first phoned and spoken to Christine, we had heard the buzzer from the front gate's intercom sounding in the TV room. We all jerked in alarm. It was about 8:15 P.M., just over an hour since Chen had walked in. Chen picked up the receiver and spoke into it. The police had arrived.

▶▶▶▶▶▶▶▶◀◀◀◀◀◀◀

The intruder gesticulated wildly. Waving the pistol in his hand, he exchanged angry words with the police over our intercom. In horror, we watched this man holding our destiny in his murderous hands. His dark eyes flashed as he jabbed the gun in our direction. If my wrists had not been tightly clamped behind my back, I could have reached across and touched him.

Chen shouted something at the police in Taiwanese. It seemed his anger had to do with their refusing to believe who he was. Alternatively, he could have been telling them that he did not wish to speak to them and was only prepared to talk to the media or to their superiors.

With what sounded like a Taiwanese curse, Chen ended the conversation and slammed the intercom handset into its receptacle. Immediately the buzzer sounded again. He picked it up and spoke very curtly to the person at the gate, this time in Mandarin, which I could understand a little. He seemed to be making his demands known. Then he listened a moment.

"*Duì!* (Correct)," Chen said. Then he deliberately pointed the gun at each one of us in turn and counted in English.

"One, two, three, four, *gēn* (and) baby!"

He seemed dissatisfied with the police response to what he was saying. He again shouted very angrily into the handset. Then he slammed it down again.

The people at the gate buzzed again. This time Chen flew into a rage, grabbed the intercom receptacle, ripped it out of the wall and with tremendous force hurled it to the floor.

We had two other intercom points in the house: downstairs in the lounge, and upstairs in the main bedroom. The police kept pressing the buttons at the gate and we heard the buzzing at the other points, but Chen ignored them. His display of unbridled fury frightened us indeed. We felt at the mercy of this unpredictable and angry man.

Chen's rage seemed to abate somewhat, but he muttered darkly to himself as he fingered and checked his two pistols. My family all stared in wide-eyed fear. Melanie prayed softly that the Lord would not let him kill us.

Getting no response from Chen, the police stopped their buzzing and began shouting in abusive-sounding language, as if they were threatening and insulting him. Chen became extremely agitated and kept up an angry tirade back at them.

It was then that I realized that the arrival of the police signalled danger rather than deliverance. They clearly were provoking him.

From where I sat I could not see the windows downstairs in the lounge, but judging from the direction of the voices outside, the police had entered our garden and were moving into positions around the front of the house. Chen swore back at the police and waved his guns about threateningly. He knelt on the sofa between Melanie and Christine, leaning over the parapet toward the high lounge windows opposite him. I gathered that he was yelling at them not to come near the house or he would shoot.

I started to tell my family to lie down. Then Chen saw something or someone through the window. He whipped a pistol across and fired a shot in the direction of the window.

The report from the gun amplified thunderously in the vault-like lounge. Melanie screamed.

"Get down on the floor!" I yelled at the family. I tried to slide down onto the floor from my chair.

Then, to my horror, I heard the police return fire. I heard distinctly at least two shots fired from outside.

"Stop shooting! You'll kill us all!" I shouted in English at the police.

Chen grabbed Melanie, holding our helpless daughter in front of him as he fired a volley of shots at the window. The noise was ear-shattering, the muzzles flashed in the dark like lightening on a stormy night. The smell of cordite filled the room. Zachary wailed. Anne held him tightly where she lay on the floor. Christine lay flat on the floor beside Anne and Zachary. Chen tightly clasped his human shield.

"Don't shoot! Don't shoot!" Melanie pleaded, screaming at the police.

As soon as the police returned fire, Chen backed off from the edge of the parapet, dragging Melanie with him and firing as he did so.

The shooting stopped as suddenly as it had started. I was overwhelmed with anger at the police for acting so irresponsibly. The house was in virtual darkness. They had no means of seeing or knowing where we were positioned. Such indiscriminate shooting could as easily have resulted in injury or death to the hostages as to the hostage-taker.

"Are you people crazy?" I shouted out furiously. "Don't shoot out there! You will kill us or this man will kill us! Whatever you do, don't shoot!"

There was no reply, but the police were making a lot of noise. Outside, they shouted. And inside, Chen shouted back at them.

Reporters had gathered in the street outside. They later reported that Chen had shouted at the police not to make any reckless or sudden moves and to stay away from the house. There was still no response by the police to my yelled pleas; but probably no one out there understood English.

My voice does not lack timbre. The people outside must have heard me. That thought consoled me. If the police and onlookers had any doubts before, now they must know that Chen was holding foreigners inside the house.

Melanie's face reflected sheer terror. Chen had one arm clamped around her slender neck, and he pressed the Beretta pistol against her cheek. The other gun, the Glock with the long 32-round magazine in it, he held ready to fire at the police.

As soon as the shooting stopped, and while he was still shouting at the police and holding onto Melanie, he released the magazines of the guns he was holding, one at a time, and immediately replaced them with fully charged magazines. He then commenced refilling the partly-used ones. Like a well-trained soldier, he kept both his pistols fully loaded at all times.[1]

Sticking one pistol into his waistband, Chen picked up the two-litre plastic bottle and took a swig of water. The tension had dehydrated all of us, and I again became aware of my dry tongue cleaving to the roof of my mouth. Catching Melanie's eyes as he drank, he held the bottle up with a questioning gesture. Melanie nodded vigorously. Her thick brown hair fell untidily across her tearstained face. Holding the bottle to her lips, he allowed her to take a few mouthfuls. She showed clear relief and appreciation.

The man then offered each of us water. I shook my head. I was reluctant to give him the acknowledgement that he had total power over me. I could not relinquish to him all of my self respect. It was as if this was the last vestige of independence left to me, and I was not prepared to give him the satisfaction of holding this bit of power over me, despite my raging thirst. As my anger mounted, I found it increasingly difficult to control my feelings and maintain my composure.

Chen moved cautiously back to the sofa and peered over the parapet behind it. All the while he held onto Melanie, the cold steel of his Beretta held against her face.

"Please don't hurt me," she pleaded with him. "Please don't shoot me." He held her right against him. His finger was constantly on the trigger. He took no notice of Melanie's pleadings. Certainly he did not understand her words, yet he could surely understand the desperation in her voice. It didn't move him, though. His attention remained fully focused on the direction from which the police had fired.

"Is he going to shoot us?" Melanie asked me. "Daddy, what does it feel like to be shot?" Then her voice took on an even more urgent note.

"Mommy! My chest is closing up!"

Like Anne, Melanie occasionally suffered from asthma. They both carried a small ventilator when they went any-where, but now both their ventilators were upstairs in the bedrooms. Anne understood the dangers of asthma in this situation.

"Just calm down, my girl," Anne encouraged her in a steady tone. "Take it easy, stay calm and don't get yourself into a state."

Anne's soothing, reassuring voice had a settling affect on all of us. We all knew that Anne's calmness was not feigned; she was no good at hiding her feelings. In her heart, Anne was praying that the asthma attack would pass, and her faith is such that she had complete confidence that it would pass. It did, and Melanie showed no further symptoms of the asthma that night.

Volleyed shouts again erupted between Chen and the police. I guessed he was telling them that he had one hostage as a shield, that she would be hit if they tried shooting, and that he would not hesitate to kill all the hostages if the police did not do exactly as he said. Although very highly-strung and tense, he still appeared very much in control of himself.

My confidence in the police now thoroughly shaken, I feared greatly for Melanie's life. I pleaded with Chen in my limited Mandarin to release her and to take me as his shield. He understood me, but shook his head emphatically and kept his hold on her. She was close to hysteria.

Irrepressible frustration welled up from within me. With brutal indifference this man was sacrificing my daughter's life for his own ends. It was happening in front of my own eyes and I could do nothing about it.

As commander of a parachute brigade I once had several thousand people under me. When I issued an instruction it was carried out with alacrity. I was accustomed to being in control. In a crisis I had resources at my disposal to draw upon. I am a physically fit, strong man who had got out of tight spots often in the past. I had fought in wars, had been under fire, had led paratroopers in battle. I was not a complete stranger to fear; but I had always had recourse to some action in times of danger. Until now.

Here I was trussed up like a chicken for slaughter, my daughter was likely to be shot right next to me any moment, and I could do absolutely nothing about it.

Never had I felt more helpless in my entire life.

Chen moved away from the sofa and the parapet with Melanie, to a position in the room from where he could watch both the stairs coming up from below and those going up to the bedrooms. He held one gun always ready to fire at whichever stairs might yield an assault by the police. He seemed to think they were already in the house.

Melanie cried out as Chen walked cautiously back and forth, always holding her close in front of him, pointing the gun at her head, and keeping an eye on the stairs. Chen and Melanie were merely a few metres in front of me in the dark room. I told Melanie to try to keep quiet and not to annoy him. And I prayed very hard.

The contrast between this short, burly, ugly hoodlum and my slender, beautiful daughter was agonizingly sharp. He reeked of stale tobacco and perspiration; his teeth were stained brown and rotted from betel nut juice; his wrinkled clothes were soiled and his nails were long and dirty. Melanie had just had a bath, she was wearing a brand-new track suit, and her brown hair had been washed and dried. She smelled fragrant and looked lovely.

Again I pleaded with him to let her go and to take me as his shield. Again he refused. Melanie is a slim, petite girl. She was light and easy to move around in front of him. I was much bigger than Chen and my heavy frame, with my hands tied behind my back, would have been difficult to move around. Chen needed to maintain mobility, and he seemed wary of his only male hostage. He kept his distance from me and showed clear distrust.

The phone rang again.

It was Michael Letts, calling from the office of the *China Post*. Chen again held the phone to Melanie's ear. Crying uncontrollably, Melanie told Michael what was happening, and she told him about Chen's demands for international media coverage.

"Michael, he's got a gun to my head, with his finger on the trigger," Melanie sobbed. "He's going to kill me!" She begged him to tell the police not to shoot at the house, as this man was ruthless and would kill the whole family.

Stunned at what he was hearing, Michael assured her he would do something, but after he rang off, he was badly shaken. Twice he misdialed his aunt's number and found it difficult to decide what to do. He collected himself sufficiently to make sure that someone had informed the South African embassy and that the police had been called again. But what now? What else could he do in these unreal circumstances? He felt quite helpless.

Once again our phone rang. Chen now handed it to Christine.

"Hello!" she said curtly. (I had often scolded her for her abrupt telephone manner.)

"Christine!" said the distressed voice on the other end. "This is Habiba."

Mohammed (Mo) and Habiba Elhamdaoui were our other next-door neighbors. Originally from Morocco, this Arab family had lived almost all their lives in the Netherlands, then had moved to Taiwan to work at a Dutch factory. Christine had practiced speaking with them in Afrikaans, because it is so similar to the Dutch which they spoke.

That evening, Mo and Habiba had returned from visiting friends, only to find crowds in the neighborhood and a squad of police ensconced in their house. It took half an hour to convince the police to let them in, and then only on the condition that they wore bullet-proof vests. They couldn't communicate effectively with the police; and with horror they found their furniture had been unceremoniously dragged away from windows to allow armed police to take up firing positions.

They gathered that there was a gunman in the area and that it was probably Chen Chin-hsing. Police were using their house, which had an identical layout to ours, to rehearse an entry. But Mo and Habiba had no idea that the fugitive was in our house.

Concerned about us, Habiba immediately phoned. When she heard Christine answer, she thought that Anne and I may be out.

"You must make quite sure that your house is properly locked up," she admonished Christine. "That man the police are looking for is in the neighborhood. Or are there also police all over your house?"

"No," replied Christine. "The police are all outside. The only one in our house is the guy with the gun, and the police are trying to shoot him!"

Habiba felt her heart jump into her mouth.

Then shooting broke out in front of the house. Christine

screamed and rang off.

I went rigid. Had the police gone completely mad? They were trying to shoot their way into the gigantic, aluminum double door which formed the entrance to our home. I was appalled.

The gunman dived across to the sofa, roughly dragging our screaming Melanie with him. She hollered at the police to "stop shooting!" I joined her.

"You idiots!" I yelled. "What do you think you're doing? Stop shooting!"

Leaning across the back of the sofa and over the parapet, Chen fired a burst on automatic at the front door with the long magazined Glock. He then swung his gun across to fire briefly at the tall lounge window. Empty shells ejected by the pistol struck Melanie in the face. Between the shots we could hear the sound of shattering windows, while shards of glass and chips of plaster fell to the floor.

He fired several more single shots with both pistols, then quit when he realized that the police had stopped.

Had the police decided to sacrifice our lives in their insane desire to kill this man at all costs?

The pale face of my eldest daughter broke my heart. With desperation I pleaded for the third time with Chen to let her go. This time, incredibly, he released her and she immediately fell to the floor on her face and crawled awkwardly between the sofa and the armchair. Her hands were still bound behind her back. I struggled to my feet and moved with dread towards the psychopath who had invaded our privacy and terrorized my daughter at gunpoint.

6

‣Shadow Of Death◂

As I APPROACHED the man with deadly eyes and a pistol in each hand, he motioned toward the sofa. I sat down. He crouched on the sofa next to me. He pressed one gun into my ribs, and he leveled the other gun over the parapet, aiming at the downstairs lounge window.

Anne had crawled across the floor of the room to the far corner, where she lay behind an armchair, shielding baby Zachary and trying to calm him. The shooting noise was quite terrifying, and made him cry. However, with Anne holding him tightly and comforting him, he quickly quieted down each time the shooting stopped. Then he would coo and cluck, and struggle to get away from Anne and crawl around. Anne worked hard to keep his attention.

We had no doubt that what was taking place around us was a spiritual battle. That much we had shared with one another and we acknowledged it to God in our prayers at the time. What we didn't know was just how much the forces of the Lord were being boosted by the prayers of His people. We weren't aware of the prayer chains that had been set off all over the world.

Yet at this crucial time Anne was filled with peace. As she lay there on the floor in the dark, holding onto the wriggling and restless Zachary, she recalled a story from the insurgency war in Zimbabwe, then known as Rhodesia.

A Christian family was besieged in their isolated farmhouse by a band of insurgents who were in a position to wipe them out. But the attack never came and the attackers backed off. Later, authorities apprehended the insurgents and asked them why they had not attacked. The rebels replied that they could not, because they saw an army of men dressed in white surrounding the homestead. The Christians believed that the attackers had seen the heavenly angels that God had sent to protect His children.

Now, besieged in our home, Anne had an impression of God's angels surrounding us and she *knew* that we would be all right. Her calmness and steady composure inspired the rest of us, confronted by this violent man with a gun in each hand.

Waving one gun in the direction of the stairs leading up to our bedrooms, Chen told Christine to sit at the bottom of the stairs and warn him if anyone tried to come down from there. Apparently he expected the police to penetrate the house at any moment. And he thought they might enter from the roof.

Not understanding him, Christine looked at me in consternation. I told her to go to the foot of the stairs and warn him if the police came down. She gaped incredulously.

"What must I do if the police come?" she asked, obviously convinced that she'd heard me incorrectly.

"Warn him immediately!" I demanded. "If you don't, we'll all get shot."

Christine dubiously crossed the floor to the stairs. This wasn't the time to reason with her; she must do as she was told. But her questioning child's mind was unconvinced. Surely the police are the good guys and this character is the bad guy? It follows that we should not be helping him and that the police would not do anything to endanger our lives in their efforts to get him.

Reluctantly, she lay at the foot of the stairs; but she ignored them, riveting her attention on Chen Chin-hsing, instead.

He placed one pistol momentarily on the sofa, repeating his instructions to Christine in Mandarin. He pointed his second and middle finger at his eyes, then indicated the top of the stairs. Cupping his hand to his mouth, he mimicked a shout, making quite sure that Christine understood how she was to warn him.

"I'm going to die," she whimpered to her sister.

Just then the phone rang once again and Chen answered. After a brief conversation, he held the cordless receiver to my ear. It was Nate Showalter, pastor of the Taipei International Church. (We had become acquainted with him and his wife at a Marriage Encounter weekend shortly after we had arrived in Taiwan.)

Nate was conducting a Bible study at the home of David Ni, a Taiwanese member of his church. Someone phoned to tell them what was happening to the Alexanders. The prayer chain set in motion by Brian McLeod was running like wildfire, as Christians all over Taiwan were notified. Now, David and Nate were asked to pray for our safe deliverance.

The Bible study came to an abrupt halt as everyone joined in a period of intense prayer.

Then they decided to switch on the TV and see what was happening. The situation was confused; but they could tell we were still inside the house. Then someone suggested that they try to phone us at home, in case there was anything that they could do.

Because David Ni spoke Taiwanese, the little group of Christians agreed that he would talk if Chen answered the phone. Twice they phoned; and twice Chen answered. David spoke to him at length, and tried to keep him calm and to assure him that a peaceful resolution was possible. While he spoke on the phone with Chen, the Christians gathered around him to intercede for David, for Chen, and for us.

Ni kept Chen talking as long as possible, while his wife

called the police on the other line, keeping them abreast of Chen's comments.

Chen informed Ni that he had three pistols, lots of ammunition, and several hand grenades in his possession. During the second call, Ni told Chen they had contacted the police.

Seeing that the police were still not in proper communication with Chen, the group of Christians decided, after further prayer, to dial again. This time, David asked the gunman if he could speak to me. Chen agreed and held the handset to my ear. Nate came on the phone. He asked me how things were going. I felt encouraged to hear his voice.

I told him just what our position was and that Chen was holding the phone to my ear because I was tied up. With his other hand, I explained, he was jabbing a gun into my ribs. Nate assured me that people all over the city were praying for us. He asked if we could pray together right there over the phone. Of course I'd been praying almost constantly since this crisis began, but I was immensely grateful to be able to pray with someone from outside.

Nate prayed, and it felt like a spiritual injection to hear him calling on the Lord to keep His hand upon us and upon Chen. Nate then asked me if I would like them to speak to Chen again.

"Yes," I replied. "Please do."

I turned to Chen and told him that someone wanted to speak to him. He lifted the receiver to his ear and began speaking. I was unable to follow the Taiwanese, but Nate and David later told me the gist of their conversations with Chen.

David asked Chen why he was holding us. Chen replied that he was trying to get a fair deal for his wife and family, who, he claimed, were innocent.

"I know I'm going to die," Chen told him. "But I want my wife to go free."

David asked him not to hurt our family. Chen reassured him that he had no intention of doing so, provided the police did not do anything rash. It was fortunate that I could not understand that, as I would certainly not have felt reassured, given the police actions until then!

Chen asked David who these people were, and why they were praying aloud all the time.

David explained to him that his hostages were Christians and they were praying to Jesus to keep them from harm and to get them out of there safely. Then he added, "And they're also praying for you and your situation."

Another spiritual encounter for Chen!

Chen put down the phone and crouched on the sofa next to me again. He seemed a lot calmer after speaking to David Ni, but he still kept one pistol barrel pressed into my ribs. And he kept an eye out for any movement at the downstairs door or window.

Chen became aware of me watching him intently. He held my gaze for a few moments. Then he slowly raised the pistol in his right hand and placed the point of the barrel under his chin. He indicated that he intended to shoot himself.

I was appalled by the thought of him doing such a thing in front of my wife and children. Besides, I knew that he would be more valuable to the police alive than dead. And even the thought of suicide repulsed me. I knew that though he might escape any earthly trial by taking his own life, he still would have to face God's judgement if he failed to set his life right with Him before death.

I pleaded with him not to shoot himself. He lowered his pistol and stared hard at me. Then he returned his attention to the door and window downstairs. Later, he repeated the suicide threat, and I again dissuaded him. It became obvious that he was not intending to shoot himself then and there. But he was warning me this was to be his ultimate act once he achieved what he wanted—or if the police forced his hand.

Then the police started shouting again at Chen from outside. He shouted back. His demeanor changed immediately and drastically. The pensive look vanished from his face and he became angry and aggressive. I found his unpredictability frightening.

I began to pray desperately out loud that he would calm down and that the police would not do anything rash.

An impending sense of extreme danger pressed about us.

I prayed to the point of exhaustion. I didn't know what more I could say, but I knew that I had to pray. As I prayed in the Spirit, I felt my spirit rise. Crumpled on the floor near my feet, Melanie also prayed.

Chen looked at us, heard the strange sounds, but never attempted to stop us. All the time I felt the gun pressed into my side. He wasn't letting his guard drop. But he appeared puzzled by what he saw and heard.

Without warning, our captor suddenly swung around on the sofa. He pointed his gun towards the door and window downstairs. Seriously disturbed by whatever was happening down there, he opened fire in that direction with one gun, while the other remained pressed into my ribs.

I crouched lower on the sofa. Again I shouted to the police, "Don't fire!"

The gunman also shouted at the police as he kept firing shots in their direction. It was a scene of confusion. I was not sure whether the police outside were also firing. It sounded like it—but Chen was firing his gun right next to my head and the house acoustics resulted in a deafening din. Between the shooting and the shouting, as well as Zachary's screaming and my family's praying, I wasn't able to distinguish with certainty whether shots were being fired from outside.

After the initial volley, the shooting became sporadic. Highly agitated, Chen switched his guns from one hand to the other, replacing a magazine as soon as there was a lull in shooting; and yelling abuse at the police all the time. They shouted back from different positions outside the house. I got the distinct impression that the noose was being tightened— and I think, so did Chen.

My adrenaline pumped hard and fast. Dread rose within me. The whole crisis was reaching a head. I had no more

words to pray; no more words to encourage my family. I only
had the Word of God. Loudly, I began to recite the scripture
that came flooding to my mind:

The Lord is my shepherd; I shall not want.
He maketh me to lie down in green pastures:
he leadeth me beside the still waters.
He restoreth my soul:
He leadeth me in the paths of righteousness
for His name's sake.
Yea, though I walk through the valley
of the shadow of death,
I will fear no evil:
for thou art with me;
thy rod and thy staff they comfort me.
Thou preparest a table before me
in the presence of mine enemies:
thou anointest my head with oil;
my cup runneth over.
Surely goodness and mercy shall
follow me all the days of my life:
and I will dwell in the house
of the Lord for ever.
(Psalm 23, KJV)

As I uttered the words "though I walk through the valley
of the shadow of death," uncontrollable emotion rose from
within me. In the dark, tears sprung to my eyes. I struggled to
keep my voice even. I didn't want my family to know how
frightened I was. They needed encouragement.

But truly that valley of shadow was closing in about us.
An almost tangible sense of imminent death hovered.

As I finished the psalm, the firing stopped. Then came an
eerie silence. Outside, the police stopped shouting. We waited
in the darkened room, hardly breathing.

Chen tensed, clenching his jaws, poised like a cat ready to
spring. He displayed signs of great nervousness and seemed
to be anticipating an assault by the police.

Warily he watched the stairs leading up to the bedroom. I

envisioned our roof, which was a large, flat balcony with a door leading in to the top of the stairs. The houses stood so close together that it would have been an easy matter for the police to lay a makeshift bridge across from the roof of the house next door to our own.

Every so often, pinpoints of red light played across the walls of the room, as if the police were seeking a target by aiming laser beams through the windows. But with those methods police were not going to spot him, since he was hiding behind the sofa and the curtained railings of the parapet.

The flashing lights from police vehicles outside weirdly illumined our darkened house.

"I know I'm going to die," Christine repeated to her sister, who lay hiding beneath the table.

An expectant hush followed, in which we could hear crowds on the street, murmuring—no shooting or shouting. The decisive moment had come!

7

▸Police Assault◂

INSIDE THE HOUSE we had no way of knowing what was happening outside. We later learned that, after speaking to me on the phone, Wouter Badenhorst called the Foreign Affairs Police to report that we had been taken hostage. He found one officer who called himself "Scott" and who spoke English well. But Scott had difficulty believing Wouter. He thought Wouter was saying that Chen was in *his* house. Then he had difficulty understanding the address which Wouter gave him for our house. There is another Hsing Yi Road in Taipei, spelled the same in Roman letters but having different characters and sounds in Chinese.

In desperation Wouter told Scott he could wait no longer to try to explain things to him. He was leaving now to go to our house and would meet Scott there. He rang off, and then contacted our friend Jacolene Spangenberg, the embassy's Head of Administration. She knew every room of every house rented by the embassy, and was aware of every item of furniture in each room. She could describe to police the inside of the house.

She and Wouter agreed on the telephone to get to Cherry

Hill as quickly as possible, so they could liaise with the police. Then, Jacolene had to have her car filled with petrol, something she'd intended to do earlier that evening, but had not yet got around to doing. This delayed her considerably.

Wouter and Mericia, leaving their two small daughters in the care of their *amah*, or maid, hurriedly pulled on warm clothes, and jumped into their car.

The normally-heavy evening traffic of Taipei was worse than usual. By the time they drew near to our house, some police were already there, and the public were beginning to arrive in small groups. The news had leaked out; our address was flashed on television screens across the island.

Wouter and Mericia parked a short distance from our house and ran towards the nearest police. One officer approached them, asked who they were, and then introduced himself as "Scott." Concerned about the police all waving guns around, Wouter told Scott that there must be no shooting. Scott nodded good-naturedly.

But, the next moment, Wouter saw a motley bunch of very young-looking policemen come bolting down the road past them, heading towards our house and bristling with guns, shields, and body armor. No one seemed to be in charge of them; and several of the men managed to drop bits of the equipment that bounced around on them as they ran.

Wouter could see a disaster in the making. He tried to push forward through the crowd. Police restrained him.

"This has nothing to do with you," they told him.

Wouter exploded. "It has everything to do with me! Those are my people in there!"

Then, rushing across to a nearby guardhouse outside a block of flats, he grabbed the surprised guard's telephone and phoned Ambassador Nikki Scholtz. When Nikki heard what was happening, he wanted to come down to our house right then; but Wouter suggested that he remain at his residence, as there would soon be many people making contact with him. He asked him to request the authorities to exercise restraint.

Then, constrained by the police, Wouter rejoined Mericia and the two of them waited for Jacolene to arrive.

The police made no effort to control the traffic and the growing crowds, other than to cordon off our road to vehicles, so Jacolene was unable to drive down the crowded street to our house. She doubled around and approached from the other direction.

Leaving her car, Jacolene ran to the corner nearest our house. As she did so, a shot rang out. Her blood froze. Then she heard a volley of shots. She had arrived just as the first exchange of gunfire took place.

Mortified, she accosted the first police officer she saw. They all had their eyes on the house, their guns drawn and ready to fire. No one would speak to her. She ran from one to the other, trying to find someone in authority with whom she could speak, but it was a vain exercise. There didn't appear to be anyone in charge and no one was interested in speaking to her.

Jacolene is a woman of action. An accomplished SCUBA diver with a great love of adventure and the outdoors, she was also the epitome of professionalism in her work. This chaotic situation was more than she could tolerate.

Systematically, she began working her way through the police officers, trying to find one who could speak English. Then Wouter arrived and joined her in the street in front of our house.

Scott and another policeman tried to get them both away from the scene, but they wouldn't go. Wouter just kept shouting at Scott, "Tell the police to stop firing."

"I do not have the authority to order them to stop," Scott replied.

"Authority! I'll give you authority!" Wouter roared back at him, towering over the diminutive Chinese man. In almost a blind fury, he yelled, "I authorize you in the name of President Nelson Mandela to tell those policemen to stop shooting or they will have the blood of that family of South Africans on their hands."

Wouter gestured threateningly toward the house and the police officers, and the frightened Scott scuttled off to join his young colleagues as fast as his legs would carry him.

More shots!

Diving for cover, police and members of the public all shouted at once. Jacolene and Wouter heard Melanie and me shouting from inside the house. At least they knew someone was still alive inside there! Police officers then began moving spectators out of the way, and again tried to chivvy away Jacolene and Wouter as well. But they weren't budging.

An elderly watchman, who controlled access to the parking garage of another block of flats opposite our home, found it all too much to handle. Sitting in his tiny guardroom while the police rushed around outside shouting and shooting, and shots from the gunman in our house ricocheted off nearby walls, he fainted. He was carried off on a stretcher, to be evacuated to hospital with a suspected heart attack.

Wouter in the meantime had run back to the guardhouse with the telephone in it and he again phoned the ambassador to tell him about the shooting. He told him that it was urgent and essential that Nikki speak to the highest possible authority, even the president if necessary, to get the police to stop all further shooting. Then Wouter phoned our house to try to find out whether anyone had been injured.

Christine answered the phone, frightened and crying.

"Uncle Wouter," she sobbed. "Tell them to stop shooting. They're going to kill us."

He tried to reassure her and asked her to give the phone to Chen. Several police stood around him, including Scott, but when he tried to get them to talk to Chen they all declined and moved away.

Wouter lost his temper. Grabbing Scott by his bullet-proof vest he lifted him up and deposited him unceremoniously down in the guardroom.

"Now you talk to him!" growled the normally-docile

Wouter at the terrified policeman, and shoved the phone
receiver into his hand. Nervously, he held a brief conversation
with the criminal. To the people outside, our house seemed
ominously quiet.

Media representatives converged on the scene en masse.
Newspaper and radio reporters, TV camera crews, photographers; everyone wanted to muscle in on the action and get a
scoop. Taiwan's notoriously-competitive media have a cut-
throat approach to getting the news first. With sixty-five radio
stations, four TV stations, 371 newspapers and 151 cable TV
stations on the island, the late ones didn't survive.

This was such big news ("The Final Act" was how one
banner headline described it) that television stations cancelled
all scheduled programming to broadcast the drama live. TV
crews swarmed into the surrounding houses and blocks of
flats; soon veritable batteries of cameras with high-powered
lenses were mounted on roofs all around.

In fact, by then the police had set up a command post of
sorts in a house about a block away, on the opposite side of
the street from our house. Jacolene and Wouter eventually
gained access to this "command post," but wondered why no
senior police had arrived. It was probably no more than an
hour since the police had been notified of the situation, and
evidently at this stage, only local precinct police had come. [1]

Jacolene boiled with anger that the police would not talk
to her, particularly when shooting erupted at the house for the
third time. Scott had apparently been cowed by Wouter's
aggression and was trying to avoid the South Africans. So the
one policeman on the scene who could speak English was
nowhere to be found.[2]

Their helplessness under these circumstances frustrated
Jacolene and Wouter beyond measure. With her cell phone,
Jacolene kept constant contact with the ambassador. As soon
as he had been informed of the hostage-taking, Ambassador
Scholtz contacted the Africa Section of the ROC's Ministry of
Foreign Affairs, who assured our South African ambassador

that everything possible would be done to ensure the safety of his people. However, things were happening too fast for these good intentions to take immediate effect.

Then Wouter observed that someone who clearly had authority had arrived on the scene. When this man spoke, the police scurried around frantically. Wearing a helmet and a bullet-proof vest, but carrying no weapons, he hurried down the street toward our house. Wouter later learned that he was Police Chief Hou You-yi. Whether the decision was Hou's, or that of some subordinate in command of the police who were surrounding the house, the order to carry out an assault had already been given. Those on the ground at the scene of the crisis had not yet received any instructions from the government, and they were springing into immediate action.

Jacolene, in the meantime, kept in regular contact with Secretary Jaap le Roux at the embassy. Jaap immediately went to the embassy, where he later manned the telephones and other communications systems back to Pretoria right through the night. As Jacolene obtained information on what was happening at the house, she continued to notify Jaap and Nikki Scholtz, and Jaap updated his colleagues at the South African Department of Foreign Affairs back in Pretoria and answered the South African media's questions. Wouter managed to keep Jacolene supplied with recharged batteries for her cell phone. She had to replace her battery at least six times during the entire crisis.

▶▶▶▶▶▶▶◀◀◀◀◀◀◀

In the house, we were not-too-blissfully unaware of all this going on outside. Chen began shouting at the police again, and they shouted back at him. We could see flashes from cameras outside, and the street noise grew louder. A lot of people were out there, apparently.

Trying to crouch as low as possible on the sofa, I heard something between all the other noises that made my hair stand on end. Someone was opening the electronic garage door.

It was 9:00 P.M.. Our cuckoo clock struck the hour. Convinced the police were penetrating our house, I felt myself begin to shake. If there was an exchange of gunfire inside the house, my family were certain to be caught in the crossfire. Helplessness engulfed me.

Now I realized the police had been distracting Chen by keeping a shouting match going with him. He didn't hear the garage door. I was grateful for that. No telling what he'd do if he knew the police had entered the house. Silently and desperately I cried out to the Lord to preserve us at this crucial point. A calmness came to me immediately.

Christine kept creeping across the floor, away from the steps leading upstairs, moving towards Melanie and me. This placed her between Chen and the steps from downstairs — right in the line of fire if the police assaulted up the stairs! I kept telling her, almost angrily, to go back to her position at the foot of the upward stairs and to watch for any sign of the police. She couldn't understand why I did not want her near me. She needed comfort and reassurance. But I simply had to keep her away from where I knew bullets would soon start flying.

Anticipating them, I heard the police moving around downstairs, underneath the balcony on which we were being held. The gunman still had not heard them, and continued with his shouted exchange with the police outside. I found it incredible that the police were intent on killing this man at all costs, even if it meant that we all had to die in the process. Why else would they attempt an assault at this dangerous stage?

I warned my family again to lie flat on the floor and not move. Then I shouted out loudly in English, "Whoever you are down there, do not try to come up the stairs and do not shoot! You will place our lives in danger, and if you do not kill us, this man will!"

I knew that Chen would not understand me, and that he

would think that I was joining in his shouting to the police outside. I just hoped that there was a police officer downstairs who understood English.

It was to no avail. In my heart I knew that the assault would take place no matter what I did.

The gun barrel pressed against my head as Chen half stood on the sofa, moving his gaze alternately from the two sets of stairs to what he could see of the lounge below. All I could do now was try to distract his attention from the stairs up which I knew the assault would take place, so that he might be caught unawares. Perhaps this would enable the police to identify him and get off a clean shot, and the whole thing would quickly be over.

I raised myself upon the sofa as best I could and craned my neck so that I was peering over the parapet towards the large lounge window downstairs as if I had heard something down there. If I could get him to turn towards the window, he would be forced to turn away from the stairs.

But Chen ignored my efforts. Though he steadily moved his gun with my head as I moved, he fixed his attention on the stairs leading up from below. Perhaps he had heard the police in the lower lounge.

The sound of footsteps pounded up the stairs. I steeled myself for the attack.

Deftly, Chen jumped up from his kneeling position on the sofa — always keeping the gun in his left hand against my head. He aimed the gun in his right hand at the top of the stairs. There was a shattering crash as he fired a volley of shots down the stairs.

The whole room erupted. Gunfire exploded right in front of my face, deafening and blinding me.

Just as he began to fire, I glimpsed several dark figures bunched together on the stairs — two or three, it may have been more. Through the darkness, I thought I saw black uniforms and helmets; flak-jackets and face-guards; and large items like guns and shields in their hands.

As these figures rounded the bend of the stairs, they ran into Chen's barricade formed by our round, copper-topped, Spanish coffee table. At exactly this moment they came into Chen's sight. From where the barricade stopped them, they would have looked directly across the TV balcony toward the dimly-lighted study. Chen held me on the sofa, to one side, providing no silhouette and ensuring that they could not see him in the contrasting light—evidence of either his extreme criminal cunning or simply the sound application of basic military tactics.

With his Glock pistol, he discharged a veritable fusillade of shots at the attacking police. The nightmarish flash and noise of gunfire right next to my head confused me. I was convinced that the police were firing back. It was so intense. To their everlasting credit, though, they had not fired at all. Had they done so, both Chen and I would almost certainly have been hit, and probably also other members of my family. As it was, I crouched low on the sofa, trying to avoid the line of fire.

The police faltered. In the dark I glimpsed them falling over one another on the narrow stairs. Pressing his advantage, Chen whipped the Beretta in his left hand away from my head and added its firepower to that of the Glock. He was determined to generate a sufficient volume of fire to turn the wavering of the police to a full flight.

As he pulled the gun away from my head, he discharged its first shot prematurely. The muzzle-flash right in front of my face synchronised with the explosion of my left knee.

The impact took my breath away, and I cried out in pain and shock. When I tried to shout, all I could manage were short, screaming gasps. I tried to move my leg, but a sharp, numbing pain stopped me. I'd been shot.

Chen continued with his two-gun broadside and the attacking police fled in disarray. On the narrow stairway they trampled over one another to get away. No casualties were reported, but I am convinced—at that point-blank range and with such an intensity of fire — that Chen must have hit them. Certainly not many of his shots left marks in the wall behind them. Doubtless their body armor, shields and the bullet-proof face masks sometimes worn by Taiwan's police saved them.

The shooting stopped. I became conscious that both my daughters were screaming.

During the shooting, Christine saw the gunman swing one pistol in her direction and fire several shots at the flight of stairs directly above her. No doubt he was anticipating a dual assault. (He was thinking way ahead of the police, however, because in actuality they had not carried out a pincer assault.)

Christine had thought Chen was trying to shoot her. She hugged the floor. One bullet slammed into the wall just above her head. As the muzzle-flash occurred, she stared into the barrel of the gun.

Another shot ricocheted up and hit the wall just below the ceiling — right above where Anne lay covering the baby's ears and protecting him with her body. The spent, flattened bullet dropped down and hit Anne on the head. It caused no harm.

Once the shooting stopped, Chen again yelled angry threats at the police.

With difficulty I cried out that I had been shot in the knee. Then I shouted to Melanie, who was still screaming.

"Are you all right?" I asked her. She stopped screaming and began to cry.

"I've been shot," she whimpered.

"Where were you hit?"

"In my wrist and in my back."

The bullet that hit me must have passed through my leg and hit Melanie. She was lying just behind and below my leg, face down on the floor with her hands bound behind her.

My first thought and greatest fear at that instant was that her spine may have been damaged.

"Don't move at all, Melanie."

She said it felt like "everything inside has blown up three

times."

Chen saw that we had been wounded, and that he had wounded us. After a quick, cursory look, he shouted to the police that he had accidentally injured two of the hostages.

"Send up a doctor to see to them," he yelled in Chinese.

We tried to assess the extent of our injuries. Anne, Christine, and Zachary were unhurt. Melanie appeared to have suffered serious damage. I was wearing black trousers, and in the dark I couldn't see what sort of injury I'd sustained. With my hands handcuffed behind me I could not use them to ascertain the damage. But I was beginning to feel faint. I tried to move the wounded leg, and to my relief I found that I could straighten it. However, it kept sliding across the floor and bumping against the edge of the carpet. And I could not lift my feet. Then I realized what made the floor slippery — it was my blood!

I had seen people die from loss of blood. I knew it could happen quickly, even if the wound appeared superficial. I recalled a young officer under my command who had died soon after receiving a gunshot wound in combat, even though he was quite coherent and calm. As my imagination worked overtime, I ascribed my faintness and light-headedness to loss of blood. I had no way of knowing how much I was bleeding, and I felt that I might soon pass out, or even die.

My family needed to be warned, so it wouldn't come as too great a shock to them, but I didn't want to cause them to panic. I tried to spell it out softly, so Anne could understand, but so Christine wouldn't grasp the implications.

"I'm losing a lot of blood," I called out. "I think I might be going. Whatever happens, just do what this man says — and trust in Jesus," I urged them.

But I had not succeeded in being sufficiently ambiguous.

"Daddy, don't die!" Christine cried out, scurrying across the room on all fours right past the man who had shot us and very nearly shot her too. She grabbed my leg (fortunately the uninjured right leg) and hugged it.

Leaving Zachary behind the chair where she had been protecting him, Anne crawled across the room past Chen to where Melanie and I were groaning in pain. In the dark, she tried to establish the extent of our injuries.

"You've got to try and stop the bleeding, Sweetheart," I told her. Despairingly, I pulled against the handcuffs that held my hands uselessly behind my back.

Christine grabbed a T-shirt, which had been lying on the floor, and handed it to Anne. Anne tried to staunch Melanie's wounds with it, but there was not much bleeding and the wounds hurt so much that Melanie screamed every time she tried to apply pressure.

She left the T-shirt covering Melanie's back and looked around for something to use on my leg. By this time everything was swimming in front of me, and it was a battle to retain my consciousness.

"Your tie!" Anne exclaimed, and immediately undid my necktie. She tied it around the upper part of my leg as a tourniquet.

"Tighter!" I gasped, feeling that she was being too gentle with me. She redid it, knotting it tightly and firmly above the knee. It seemed to stop the bleeding, and I certainly began to feel better. I am convinced that Anne's quick thinking and unhesitating action saved my life.

Someone shouted up the stairs. This person did not wait to reason or argue with the gunman. He ran straight up the stairs with his hands held above his head. As best I could make out he was shouting, "I am unarmed and I am coming up."

The man jumped over the barricade and stopped right in front of Chen, who stood next to me, and who still held a pistol in each hand. I believe that was the bravest act by any man I have ever witnessed.

Chen frisked the man, and stopped when he got to his belt. He apparently felt something suspicious.

"What is this?" demanded Chen.

92

"Don't be ridiculous," the man reprimanded him. "It's my electronic bleeper." Chen continued his body search.

Satisfied, Chen motioned him toward us. First, the man briefly embraced Chen, apparently in a gesture of gratitude, and then knelt down beside us.

I had thought until then that he must be a doctor. But his dark clothing, helmet and bullet-proof vest, as well as his demeanor soon made me realize that he was a police officer. He spoke no English, so we couldn't describe our condition to him.

We later discovered that this gallant man was Hou You-yi, Chief of the Criminal Investigation Division of the Taipei City Police. Hou had long been on the trail of Chen and his deceased accomplices, and had arrived on the scene outside our house just before the police commenced their assault. His first action after the shooting was to enter the house to confront Chen about his wounded hostages. Subsequently, he seemed to take charge of the police operation, bringing order to the chaos.

Anne showed him Melanie's wounds. Then he examined my leg. Deceived by the amount of blood on my leg, he assumed my injury to be the worst, and without further ado he grabbed hold of me and tried to lift me onto his shoulders.

The Chinese are generally not large people and I am not a small man. He was unable to hoist my eighty-five kilograms, but then without any hesitation, he simply dragged me over the barricade and down the stairs.

Feeling foolish and helpless with my hands bound behind my back, I tried to walk, but my leg collapsed. As we brushed past a couch in the lounge, my glasses were knocked off. I recall feeling a silly twinge of annoyance, knowing I could not read without them.

As Chief Hou dragged me toward the front door, the gunman shouted instructions from upstairs. Hou immediately changed direction and pulled me toward the main window instead. Bullet holes riddled the panes and curtains of the windows that were edged with jagged pieces of broken glass. Obviously, Chen did not want the front door opened, as that would enable the police to rush in.

Hou yelled something out the window. Glass shattered as officers began breaking shards of glass from the frame with their pistol butts. Hou lifted me. Several policemen outside reached through the window and grabbed me. They pulled me out the window.

Hou immediately rushed back upstairs to get Melanie. Chen restrained him, saying that Melanie was not badly injured, so she must stay behind with the others. Impatiently and indignantly, Hou dismissed Chen's protest and easily lifted Melanie's slight frame over the barricade and carried her down the stairs. He passed her out the same window, with Chen threatening him from above. He climbed out after her.

Anne, Christine, and Zachary were left alone with the gunman.

There is no doubt in my mind that Chief Hou You-yi's valor saved the life of my daughter and quite possibly my life as well.

8

▸Chief Hou You-yi◂

WHO WAS THIS MAN who risked his life for ours? When our opinion of the police and their actions hit rock-bottom, how did it happen that it was a policeman who had come to our rescue? His arrival brought a marked change in the handling of the situation. What made his presence so influential?

Much later I would learn more about the man Hou You-yi—that he was approximately the same age as Chen Chin-hsing, but that his life had followed a very different path.

Coming from a stable background in the Pu-tse township of Chiangi County, Hou became a hard-working and high-achieving student. Hou always had an ambition to become a policeman. He specialized in criminal investigation at Central Police College and graduated third in his class.

Posted to the Criminal Investigation Corps of the Taipei City Police, he served on the front lines of the Violence Prevention Unit, dealing with the worst criminals. Hou made a study of violent criminal behavior and the triggers that activated such behavior.

Hou's arrest of three gang leaders of the "Chutangkou"

branch of the notorious organized-crime syndicate known as the Bamboo Union made headlines. And it gained for him both the enmity and the respect of the underworld of Taiwan. Here was a policeman who stood out as dedicated, not open to corruption and above all, a professional.

In 1983 Hou was responsible for the arrest of Liang Kuo-kai, a known gangster and Taiwan's most-wanted criminal at the time. For this, Hou was awarded an early promotion. Thus started a phenomenal rise through the ranks by the devoted and ambitious police officer. As head of Criminal Investigation at the Chungshan Police Precinct, Hou solved a number of sensational cases, including a triple murder. Next, he became second-in-command of the Taipei Criminal Investigation Corps. In this position, he distinguished himself by rescuing a kidnap victim and arresting the perpetrators.

His philosophy of leadership was the simple military principle that had been proven through many centuries: lead from the front, lead by example, and don't ask your subordinates to do anything they know you're not prepared to do yourself.

In an interview ("A New Breed of Cop") conducted by Jane Rickards and published in the *China News* on 1 December 1997, Hou spoke of his belief that a commanding officer must set an example by showing his willingness to take on the most dangerous assignments.

"I have been in the police business for many years," Hou was reported as saying in an expression of humility. "Now that I'm the chief, I don't think that I'm better than anyone else. I treat everyone equally."

He added that he does not place much value on outward things like the mandatory salute his subordinates have to give him. Rather, he likes his officers to feel they are part of a family.

"I treat them like sisters and brothers," Hou is reported to have said. "That way when I want them to crack cases and make arrests, they must do it well. If they don't, they feel like they've let down a friend. It's not just a job obligation."

Hou's outlook is indicative of both his grasp of human nature and the application of his own Asian culture. To the Chinese, honor towards the family is a matter of the highest importance.

Even more, Hou epitomized the ideal commander as described in the Chinese military classic written over 2,300 years ago by the great general and strategist, Sun Tzu, and still studied by military men today. Sun Tzu described the qualities of leadership as wisdom, confidence, compassion, courage, and firmness. Hou You-yi demonstrated all five qualities in an undeniable manner in his handling of the hostage crisis.

Promoted to Chief of the Criminal Investigation Corps of the Taipei City Police, Hou was the logical choice to lead the investigation into the high-profile kidnap case involving teen-aged Pai Hsiao-yen. While the public decried the ineffectiveness of the police, Hou and his team were involved in painstaking and time-consuming detailed police research.

Known as Special Task Force 0414, they conducted a detailed analysis of the three suspects based on available evidence and information about their personality types, their behavior patterns, and their likes and dislikes; their addiction to the infamous, cancer-causing betel nut, a mild stimulant chewed by millions of people in the Far East and a mainstay of the agricultural economy of Taiwan; their preferences in clothing, their most-liked make of motor scooters (the favoured form of transport among the Taiwanese); what items they usually bought at roadside stalls; their favourite foods; the methods they used in committing crimes; the parts of the city they frequented.

The Special Task Force interviewed people acquainted with the criminals, or who had come in contact with them. Landlords, shop owners, shady employers with underworld links, fellow petty thieves, relatives, neighbours, video arcade managers, massage parlor girls, and Taiwan's disreputable mini-skirted betel nut vendors. Hou even had handwriting experts carefully analyze Chen's calligraphy.

In building this picture, Hou You-yi harnessed his vast firsthand experience with the world of gangsters and other criminals. Clinically and objectively he examined the background and childhood of each of the three fugitives. The hard work of Hou and his special task force did not enable them to capture the trio. But it did give them a very good understanding of the devious workings of their minds. Undoubtedly, this knowledge enabled Hou to handle the hostage situation with such professional competence.

Evidently, Hou You-yi arrived on the scene at our home at the moment the assaulting police were retreating in the face of Chen's final fusillade of firing. He must have had to fight his way through the hordes of reporters, photographers, and inquisitive public milling in the street outside our house. He claims he could hear the screaming and shouting coming from our family inside the house.

As an experienced policeman, he later stated, he knew a bullet wound could result in death very quickly. Realizing people had been wounded in all the shooting, he felt it vital to get them out and to medical attention as soon as possible. Mounting the steps from the street into our garden at a run, Hou approached a window of our house and heard Chen calling out from inside that there were people wounded.

"How were they injured?" he yelled through the window at Chen.

"I don't know," Chen replied. "But send up a nurse or a doctor."

"No one would dare enter this house with all the shooting that has been taking place," Hou retorted. "I will come in and take a look at them."

"Okay," called out Chen. "But no guns."

"No problem," returned Hou and immediately climbed in through the broken window.

Asked afterwards whether he had been afraid on entering

the house, Hou answered with words typical of a man who always puts duty first.

"I never even thought about the danger. Actually, there was no time to; it was something I just had to do. I was the commanding officer, and the hostages were my responsibility. I was in charge."

To the question of whether he should have sent someone else in to face Chen, Hou's reply was equally forthright and reflected the inherent leadership qualities of the man.

"Because I was the commander, I understood the situation the best. If I had sent another person in there who did not understand the situation, they might have provoked Chen."

Hou says he used popular underworld slang to speak to Chen, which enabled Chen to relate to him. Although Hou claims that his entering the house unarmed moved Chen and helped establish a sense of trust between them, I feel that it goes much deeper than this.

Hou You-yi is a brave and dedicated man. His demeanor and his actions manifested this. Not only was he unarmed and alone when he entered the house, but he unhesitatingly ran straight up to Chen, even though Chen held the policeman's life in his hands. Hou spoke to him with authority, with confidence, with sincerity, and with conviction.

Hou succeeded, faced with an impossible situation, in negotiating with Chen on equal terms even though Chen held the guns. Through the sheer force of his personality, reflected by his personal valor, he turned his disadvantage into an advantage.

Even further, Hou displayed an uncanny insight into both human nature and the criminal mind in his quick embrace of Chen when the gunman gave him permission to examine Melanie and me. This masterful application of the techniques of negotiation also revealed a compassion in Hou which identified him to Chen as first and foremost a fellow human being.

Later Hou was reported as saying, "He had been on the run for so long and had no one to trust. He thought the police were all cheaters. I thought if he trusted someone he would relent."

Hou's approach was exactly what was needed. He knew that Chen would only respect strength, though the circumstances militated against him being able to show any strength. He also knew that Chen despised arrogance, as well as rules and regulations. Accordingly, he managed to temper his confidence to the degree that Chen could speak to him without feeling inferior or intimidated. Hou's use of gangster terminology played a considerable part in this.

Finally, Hou knew that Chen also had a gentle side and that he harbored deep feelings of tenderness for his wife and two sons. He knew too that this man craved the love he had once received from his long-dead grandmother. Hou is reported as saying after the hostage drama ended that Chen "needed warm tender feelings." The apparently spontaneous, though brief embrace in the darkened room with the bleeding hostages lying at his feet and two smoking pistols in his hands, with the world outside spewing hatred and baying for his blood, undoubtedly touched a sentimental chord in Chen's confused and suppressed emotions.

Having begun a process to gain the psychopath's respect and even some form of confidence, Hou You-yi was able to evacuate both myself and my injured daughter. At the time, I knew nothing about the man, but I thanked God for his obvious valor and professionalism. Through the pain and confusion, I felt for the first time that here was someone who was doing things the right way.

9

›Wild Dogs‹

THROUGH THE BROKEN GLASS they passed me, and confusions of the moment directed my thoughts away from Chief Hou Youyi. In a daze, I thought the horror must be over—we'd all been released, and soon Melanie and I would receive treatment. Surely the nightmare had passed.

How wrong I was!

Outside, the police passed me along massed ranks of their fellows, down the steps to the front gate, where a wheeled stretcher, surrounded by media persons, waited in the street. Feeling half-conscious, with my leg paining and my arms still numbly cuffed behind my back, I was dumped unceremoniously onto my stomach on the stretcher.

I was vaguely aware of a tremendous hubbub and hands roughly pulling at the handcuffs on my wrists. The police were trying to unlock the shackles. Suddenly my hands were free and my arms dropped limply to my sides, the one falling over the side of the stretcher. The cuffs had been tight, and I had been constrained in that way for more than two hours. The sudden flow of blood caused my arms to tingle sharply and I grimaced in pain, unable to lift them.

Through all the confusion I heard Melanie screaming.

"Where's my Dad? I want my Dad!"

The stretcher began to trundle forward with me on it. The police forced a passage through the multitude of media in the street.

As the circulation in my arms improved, I began to rouse myself to full consciousness. I became aware of microphones shoved in front of my face, cameras flashing in my eyes, and Chinese accents shouting questions at me in English.

"How do you feel?"

"What does Mr. Chen want?"

"How many people are in the house?"

"Has anybody been killed?"

Jacolene was close and trying to talk to me. Then the stretcher came to a stop. Melanie was rushed through the passage which the police had opened up between the people ahead of me, towards a waiting ambulance.

I turned around and struggled to a sitting position on the stretcher. A babbling forest of figures with cameras and microphones surrounded me, half blinding me with constant camera flashes. Between this unrelenting mass of media I caught a glimpse of my daughter on her stretcher. She was screaming in pain. Mericia and Wouter stayed alongside her, trying to keep the ravenous media at bay, and to reassure her at the same time.

The crowds thwarted police efforts to maintain a passage-way. People broke through and swamped us. Photographers frantically held cameras aloft in their efforts to capture the drama. Melanie's stretcher was facing the wrong way and the stretcher-bearers could not get it into the ambulance. The crowd prevented them from turning it around.

In a trice, my brain cleared. Desperately I looked around for my wife, my daughter Christine, and baby Zachary. Like a hammer-blow, the reality hit me. They were still inside. The crisis was not over.

The situation incensed me. A totally unreasonable anger

arose in me — anger that my family were still inside, that my daughter was seriously injured, that the police had attempted such a dangerous assault and placed my family's lives at risk. I had been unable to prevent all this happening; I had been helpless throughout the crisis. Why had not a senior police officer or government official been exchanged as hostage in place of my family? Why hadn't a doctor been on hand to treat us? Why all the chaos and absence of any semblance of order or control? Why did the unrelenting *papparazzi* seem bent on capturing blood on camera, even if it meant spilling more blood in the process?

As all this flashed through my mind, my anger focused on what was immediately at hand — the media. Camera persons and reporters closed in around us like a pack of African wild dogs — perhaps the cruellest of predators. The wild dogs of Africa tear chunks of flesh from their victim, running along beside the animal as it desperately tries to flee. In this way, they will literally eat an antelope alive.

Hemmed in by these ruthless predators, the ambulance attendants were unable to move a metre. My daughter's life was ebbing away and she couldn't be taken to where she'd receive medical treatment. Yet the media appeared to clamor at will, totally unrestrained. How could the police, the medics, or anyone else do their jobs? A Reuters correspondent, Geoff Parker, described the scene over international radio. He called it, "pure chaos."

My hot anger mixed with deep and fearful concern for my family. Furious, I grabbed the people nearest to me and thrust them aside. Shouting my disdain at the infernal media, I leapt off the stretcher. I don't know what I hoped to achieve, but my bonds were loosed, and I had to do something.

Perhaps I wanted to go back and help my family; perhaps I wanted to get hold of whoever was supposed to be in charge of this mess and wring his neck; perhaps I wanted to take charge myself; or maybe I simply wanted to fight open a path for the stretcher-bearers, cracking the heads of a few of those blood-seeking reporters and camera people, so that my dying daughter could get to medical care.

Whatever I intended to do, it was in vain. But screaming, I tried to spring into action.

"Get my wife and children out of there!" I yelled as my feet hit the ground. My injured leg collapsed under me. I went down as if pole-axed. Police officers and the stretcher bearers grabbed me. They lifted me bodily and pushed me down onto the stretcher. I kicked and fought against them.

This pathetic display of uncontrolled emotion may have had some effect on the media, because they seemed to fall back and the attendants were able to turn Melanie's stretcher around and force it into the ambulance. As they did so, they bumped it hard and Melanie cried out in agony. Mericia Badenhorst climbed in after her. The sirens began to wail. As the vehicle moved off through the pressing hordes, the police slammed the rear door shut.

My stretcher began to move. It bumped along the uneven, tarred street. I sat up, reluctantly resigned to the fact that I was still unable to control the situation and that there was still nothing I could do. The media continued to press around me, but there was no sign of a second ambulance. However, I had seen Melanie driven off in the first one, and that was some consolation.

Still seething at the media, I yelled threateningly at them to get out of the way. The police fast disappeared from my view as the crowds closed in again. Like an enraged, trapped bull I bellowed:

"Just get my wife and children out of there!"

The crowds began to thin out as we moved further away from the house. But the relentless media kept hounding me for a few more bites of flesh. TV camera persons jogged along beside the stretcher, filming me all the way, while a flushed and excited young reporter, clearly unused to such physical exertion, ran along next to me, holding a microphone out to me.

"What did Mr. Chen say?" the reporter idiotically repeated.

Pointedly ignoring his question, I clung to the rails of the stretcher with my bloodied leg extended in front of me, while the two stretcher bearers negotiated their charge between the cars jammed into the street. I expected another ambulance to be on hand not too far away, but we passed the second block and turned into Hsing Yi Road. The ambulance was caught in traffic a long way off.

The roaring flame of my anger began to subside, but it still smouldered. I slumped morosely on the stretcher and glared darkly at the reporter and cameramen pursuing me between the cars. "Blasted vultures!" I muttered.

Hsing Yi Road looked like a bottleneck out of a parking lot at a football stadium after a cup final match. On this busy artery leading from the surrounding mountains, the traffic had come to a complete standstill. Cars blocked all movement. Apparently, half of Taipei had come to watch the notorious Chen Chin-hsing get killed. The stretcher scraped against cars as it weaved between them, squeezing through narrow gaps. Chinese faces of whole families pressed against their car windows and gazed at me in absolute wonder. I hope I did not snarl at them. But I certainly felt like doing so!

As they wheeled me down the hill backwards, I glanced over my shoulder to see where we were going. An ambulance with light flashing stood a full 500 metres from our house, hemmed in by stationary vehicles. The two stretcher bearers negotiated their way with great difficulty. How would we get anywhere in the ambulance with that terrible traffic jam? I thought of Melanie and imagined her ambulance stuck in an impossible traffic snarl-up with her life ebbing away.

Again I was overcome by that feeling of helplessness. Again I prayed, this time asking the Lord to get Melanie to the hospital in time.

Eventually we reached the ambulance. As they pushed the stretcher into it, the back wheels collapsed before properly

engaging the rail. My legs crashed down onto the tar and I felt
a stab of pain shoot through my left leg.

The wretched, young stretcher bearers hurriedly and with
frightened expressions on their faces corrected the mistake
and pushed me and the stretcher safely into the ambulance.
As the doors closed, I had a view of cameras pushing over the
shoulders of the stretcher bearers, their lenses pointed at my
face. Even closed doors did not deter the media. Something
scraped the window next to me. I glanced sideways and saw a
lens pressed against the glass. They were trying to photograph me between the painted sign writing on the pane!

For the media and others waiting outside our house, the
prelude to our dramatic evacuation (all of which was captured by the live TV cameras) had been police with pistols, sub-
machine guns and assault rifles taking up positions around
the house with their weapons at the ready, when suddenly
repeated shooting erupted from the house. There had been
screams and shouting, more shooting, more shouting, police
rushing around in the street with their rifles aimed at the
house, before two bound and wounded hostages had been
carried out, and then stretchers were being forced through the
milling crowd. It was a marvellous scoop for the action-
seeking TV camera crews, and they tried to follow it all the
way to the hospital.

With siren blaring and lights flashing, the ambulance
inched between the packed cars.

▶▶▶▶▶▶▶◀◀◀◀◀◀◀

Melanie experienced her own horrors. Chief Hou apparently
had no knife to cut through the knots in the cord that bound
her wrists behind her back. In the tension of the moment, he
took hold of her wrists and yanked them apart to break the
bonds. He did not know that she was wounded in the wrist.
The bullet, which passed through my knee, then slammed
into her wrist before penetrating her back, had fortunately

inflicted only a flesh wound on the wrist. But the pulling apart of her hands resulted in the severing of two injured tendons, already exposed and weakened from the gunshot.

Hurriedly carried out of the house by Chief Hou, Melanie was passed along the throng of police, down the steps to the street and to the waiting stretcher. In great pain and unable to describe her injuries (she speaks no Mandarin), she could not tell them she had a back injury.

Not knowing she was in excruciating pain, the police and stretcher bearers pushed Melanie down onto her back on the stretcher. There was little external bleeding from her wounds and those attending to her, hampered by clamoring media, apparently didn't even realize that she had a back injury. In fact, they didn't seem to know she was injured at all.

Screaming from pain she tried to sit up, only to be pushed down again, onto her wound. Moaning, she twisted her body to relieve the pressure on the wound.

"Where's my Dad? I want my Dad!" she cried.

Mericia and Wouter tried to reassure Melanie and explain to the stretcher bearers that it was her back that was injured; but to no avail. In the confusion no one was listening and no one seemed to understand English. She was then rushed through the crowd to the ambulance, followed all the way by Mericia, and then she was mobbed by camera people.

It was at this time that I was vainly trying to get off my stretcher and foolishly fighting with an unrelenting media.

Melanie was wheeled with difficulty through the pressing, hysterical crowd to the waiting ambulance. They finally were able to load her into the emergency vehicle and they rushed straight from the crowds into the stalled traffic. After breaking free of the trapped traffic, the ambulance weaved between the cars on its way to the hospital. It bumped and jerked over the uneven streets. Mericia tried to hold the oxygen mask over Melanie's face. The stretcher bearers didn't help her. In Taiwan, ambulances are not fully equipped to deal with emergencies. They merely transport injured people to the nearest hospital. The crew simply load the injured in and out, and drive like maniacs through the heavy traffic, with sirens blaring and lights flashing.

To be in the safety of the ambulance should have been a relief; instead it was the start of yet another ordeal with very little that was safe about that hair-raising ride.

Inside my ambulance, which swayed violently to and fro, my stretcher bearers refused to examine me or touch me at all, other than to hold me steady to prevent my being thrown off the stretcher during the wild ride. My adrenaline was still pumping. I felt unrealistically strong, refusing to lie down but grimly gripping the stretcher's upright side rails.

Inside the ambulance, relieved of the distractions and concerns about the media and my crying daughter, I became conscious of how extremely tight and uncomfortable was the tourniquet around my leg. From my military training, I remembered that a tourniquet needed to be loosened after about twenty minutes. I had no way of telling how long it had been on, but decided it was time to remove it.

I started to undo the knot, but one attendant immediately restrained me, telling me I should leave it. I peered at him dubiously. Perhaps he did know something about first aid. So I shrugged and left it.

I asked him which hospital we were going to, and he told me the Taipei Veterans' General Hospital. I nodded approvingly. That was one of the biggest and best hospitals in Taipei. Taiwan probably has the finest veterans' care of any country in the world.

Once again the media brought confusion to the situation. We later heard that the Yang Ming Hospital had been placed on standby to receive anyone injured in the hostage drama. In fact, Melanie's ambulance, ahead of mine, had arrived at the Yang Ming Hospital, only to find the entrance to the casualty department blocked by hordes of camera crews and reporters. Somehow, they got wind of which hospital was to be used, and they were waiting to get their blood-soaked scoop.

Local Taiwanese- and English-language radio stations, in fact, announced over the radio that we were being taken to Yang Ming Hospital. Most Westerners living in the city were following events on the radio. One of these was my friend and our deacon Brian McLeod. He phoned Pastor Bill Martin to tell him. Then, being an ardent cyclist, Brian jumped onto his bicycle and pedalled at speed through the traffic to Yang Ming Hospital.

He found the hospital teeming with reporters and other media people. He wondered how Melanie and I were going to penetrate this pack of news hounds.

Cleverly though, the Taiwanese authorities rapidly altered their plan. I'm inclined to think they anticipated the media, that from the start the Yang Ming Hospital had been a diversionary tactic, and Melanie's ambulance headed there in order to throw the media hounds off the scent. After all, it seems, at that stage they thought Melanie's wounds were only superficial and that she was in no real danger. Her ambulance then doubled back to the Veterans' General Hospital. Possibly even the announcement they formulated for the media about the hostages being taken to Yang Ming Hospital was specially engineered by the authorities.

In the meantime, when no patients arrived at Yang Ming Hospital Brian became suspicious. Waiting inside, he never saw Melanie's ambulance come and go. When the hospital officials heard that he was a family friend, they told him we had been taken to the Veterans' General Hospital. He then leapt back onto his bike and pedalled through traffic for all he was worth, wondering what the Taiwanese authorities were up to.

Whatever the intentions of the authorities, they succeeded in temporarily avoiding most of the media. I arrived at the Veterans' Hospital ahead of Melanie. As I was wheeled out of the ambulance and into the hospital, I encountered only one camera person and one news reporter. The TV camera was trained on me from the moment the doors opened, and the reporter shoved his microphone in my face.

"How do you feel?"

I glowered at him and growled, "Like someone who's been shot through the leg!"

I refused to comment further as they wheeled me into the casualty room. Not allowed in, the reporter hovered at the door, soon joined by others. I was transferred onto an examination bed, surrounded by doctors and nurses and my clothes were cut off of my body. Whatever the shortcomings of the ambulance men, these people in the hospital clearly knew what they were doing. They exuded efficiency and professionalism. The tourniquet was removed, my wound was cleaned, and then they started sticking needles into my inner thigh, my neck, and the top of my hand, attaching drips. My agitated state of mind made it difficult for them to find my veins, and I cried out as the medical personnel jabbed the needles into me time and again.

Shortly afterwards Melanie arrived at the hospital. Her desperate, extended ordeal at the hands of the excited and enthusiastic but totally untrained ambulance men was finally over. By then the waiting media contingent had swelled and the hospital police had to cordon off the door and keep them at bay from the casualty department. Melanie was wheeled in, still moaning from pain, and placed on the bed beside mine. Mericia, who was with her, had removed her own jersey to bind Melanie's injuries. A separate bevy of medical personnel repeated the cutting, cleaning and jabbing procedure with her. Apparently they also administered some form of painkiller, because she stopped moaning. I called across to ask her how she was and try to encourage her.

"Daddy, I'm sore! It hurts so!"

I was glad to know she was alive and she was receiving the best possible medical treatment.

Matthew arrived and rushed to Melanie's side. His face was etched with concern as he comforted her. Then he turned to me with a word of encouragement.

Over at the door it seemed that the ravenous media had been ejected by hospital authorities. But other people came. I felt a surge of emotion as I recognized several close friends from our church.

One at a time they stole in, between the busy medical staff, squeezed our hands and whispered words of hope and encouragement. Pastor Bill prayed with us. I felt a new peace descend to me as he reminded me that Jesus had died for me and my whole family, that He loved us and would care for us and that He had all things in his control. (I felt a close bond with Bill, a U.S. Air Force veteran of the Vietnam War.)

Suddenly, between all the friends and strangers, I spotted a slight dapper figure moving rapidly to my side. It was Chris Dippenaar, my very good South African friend and missionary to Taiwan, with his blond hair, neat white shirt and necktie. His brow furrowed, his eyes reflected deep concern. He took my hand and spoke to me in Afrikaans.

Another friend who arrived soon after Melanie, was Ilse le Roux, who also lived on Cherry Hill. Unable to get through the traffic jam, she had abandoned her car, flagged down a passing motorcyclist and summarily mounted behind him, then in her broken Mandarin ordered him to follow the ambulance. The dumbfounded man obeyed without argument. As the ambulance sped up, he warmed to the chase, following it first to the Yang Ming Hospital before ultimately delivering Ilse to the Veterans' Hospital just minutes after Melanie was taken for surgery.

Ilse, a trained nursing sister, cast a critical eye on the proceedings and in her forthright manner was quick to point out what she felt should be done differently. To their credit, the medical staff exercised great patience and did not turf her out!

During all this coming and going both Melanie and I had our injuries X-rayed. We were informed that we would both need surgery. Melanie was wheeled to an operating theatre.

I vaguely recall other friends with me. They gathered

around and prayed with me for Anne and the children. In the end it was Chris who accompanied me when I was wheeled off to surgery. The surgeon, Dr. Huang Ching-kuei, in fluent English pronounced that there was no apparent damage to the bone, though he could not understand why not, given the bullet's points of entry and exit.

"This is a miracle," stated Dr. Huang. "I am not going to operate. Instead, we will just keep the wound clean for a day or two, and then we will check it again."

I thought that an excellent idea. I was wheeled out and taken to a ward.

Michael Letts in the meantime, after realizing there was nothing further that he could do at the *China Post* offices had been in a state of great angst. He watched the developments on TV: the two stretchers wheeled from the front gate of our house, the spectacle of myself and my daughter carried from the house and accosted by throngs of TV camera crews and reporters thrusting microphones into our faces.

Michael was just relieved that we were out and that we did not appear to be too seriously injured. He rushed straight over to the hospital, but found that Melanie was already undergoing surgery. So he waited four hours for her to come out of the operating theatre.

Mac's blood on couch and floor, and the clothing Anne used to try to bind Melanie's wounds. (Photo: Jacolene Spangenberg)

After release, Melanie, wounded and in pain, is wheeled on a stretcher through the crowds to a waiting ambulance.

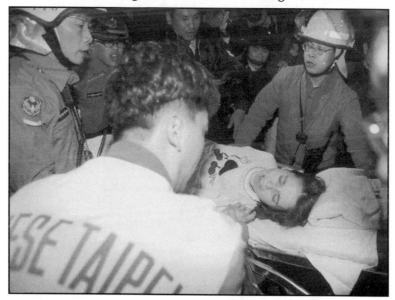

**Bullet holes in the Alexander's front door
after the gun battle.**
(Photo: Jacolene Spangenberg)

10

▸A Mother's Gumption◂

THE SIEGE ENTERED a new phase. As Chief Hou You-yi had carried Melanie out, Chen Chin-hsing had called to him not to re-enter the house. The gunman then grabbed Christine and held her as his shield, while he stood on the sofa from where he could observe Hou's exit below. Quite clearly, this killer had no compunction whatsoever about sacrificing the life of an innocent child in order to get what he wanted.

On the floor, Anne again tried to soothe little Zachary. He was very confused by the goings-on and doubtless longed to be asleep in his cot where he would normally be at that time of night.

Chen was very agitated, and Christine was understandably frightened. Anne reassured her and encouraged her to stay calm. During further shouted exchanges between Chen and the police, they seemed to give him assurances that there would not be another police assault. He relaxed somewhat after that.

He even let Christine go, although each time he thought he heard a suspicious sound he quickly grabbed her again, holding her in front of him while he crouched with his two pistols at the ready.

Once more Chen switched on the TV. He discovered that he was getting the type of publicity he so fervently desired. The wounding of two of his hostages had ensured this. Satisfied, he turned off the set. Apparently he didn't want to be distracted from his state of vigilance.

Showing signs of extreme desperation, Chen agitatedly licked his lips while his eyes darted furtively in turn from the windows to the stairs and to his captives. At one stage, he placed the barrel of one of his guns under his chin, looked at Anne, and informed her that he was going to shoot himself. Anne was horrified.

"Nǐde tàitai gēn nǐde háidze, tāmen aì nǐ (Your wife and your children, they love you)," Anne admonished him. She shook her head vigorously with an expression of deep concern on her face.

Chen lowered the gun and stared long and hard at this strange woman.

When the phone rang again, it was the reporter from *Agence France-Presse*. Using the number he had obtained when the story broke in the newsroom of the *China Post*, he was taking advantage of the lull, as the media concentrated on the evacuation of Melanie and myself. Chen readily spoke to the reporter, making statements and posing demands for the retrial of his wife and brother-in-law. However, tense after the shooting and unsure of the next move by the police, he soon terminated the interview. The reporter then notified the police of Chen's demands.

Chen evidently told the AFP reporter that he would not leave the house alive, nor would he release Anne and the children.

"I will not surrender," he was reported as saying. "I am not prepared to walk out of here alive. I want to cry, but I have no more tears left."

Within half an hour, shortly after 10:00 P.M., *Agence France-Presse* released a report of the interview on its international wire service. Immediately a number of local newspapers and TV stations called the agency to ask for the telephone number of our house. The agency apparently gave the number to all who asked for it. Soon the media began inundating our home with calls.

Chen eventually let go of Christine and she joined Anne and Zach on the floor. Less than a metre away, Chen pointed a gun at them. Christine stared long and hard at the gun, then pointed at it and held her finger like a gun against her head. She made a sound like gunshots.

"Are you planning to shoot us?" she enquired in English.

Chen evidently understood her question. For he smiled nervousy and shook his head emphatically.

"No, no, no!" he repeated, holding up his free hand.

Christine looked at him dubiously, unconvinced after the violence she had just witnessed.

Zachary began to cry, and Anne turned her attention to him. Chen picked up the baby. Like any experienced father, he quickly noticed that the little fellow needed to have his nappy (diaper) changed. Of course Anne knew this, but she thought there was nothing she could do about it.

Chen told Anne to go and fetch fresh nappies. Anne sent Christine upstairs, while she remained with Zachy. Christine returned with the nappies and baby powder. Anne changed the baby.

The shooting had stopped. The tension had visibly eased since Melanie and I had been evacuated. Baby Zachary appeared less disturbed and more contented once he had been changed. Chen calmed down noticeably, though he fingered a pistol constantly. One could only guess at what assurances the police might have given him. It seemed that negotiations of some sort were likely to commence. However, a resolution was obviously not imminent.

Again Chen tried to switch on the TV. It was dead. The police had cut the cable, apparently worried that the media coverage would compromise their deployments by making them known to Chen. Anne felt a link with the outside world had been denied her.

Christine desperately needed to go to the loo (toilet). Why she didn't go when she was upstairs collecting Zach's nappy, only she knew.

"*Hsī shōu jiān* (hand washing room)," Anne said, trying to ask Chen whether her daughter could go downstairs. But apparently her rendering of the Mandarin words were somewhat defective. Incorrect application of the Chinese tones to a word changes its meaning completely.

Chen look at her in bewilderment.

Taking a deep breath and concentrating very hard, Anne tried again.

Still he looked puzzled. Exasperated, Anne thought this was one request she was not going to demonstrate! Once more she tried to say the words, this time with a little more success.

Slowly, an expression of understanding spread across Chen's face.

"WC?" he asked, nodding.

"*Duì* (correct)," replied Anne, pointing to Christine with relief.

Chen readily agreed. Christine scuttled down the stairs toward the bathroom next to the laundry. But as she got to the bottom of the stairs, she froze, wide-eyed.

In the dark, at the laundry door, two figures in black were pointing guns at her. One of them held his finger to his lips, commanding silence. Christine froze. It was the second time that night that a man had pointed a gun at her and made that signal.

Then it dawned on her that they were policemen, so she cautiously approached. Suddenly, next to her, on the stairs leading down to the garage she saw several more armed men dressed in black, wearing bullet-proof vests. In the kitchen stood another three. A whole SWAT team had entered our home.

Silently, they allowed her to pass to the bathroom. They

must have heard the whole conversation between Anne and Chen on the landing just above where they were hiding. I guess they hoped he would venture downstairs, so they could shoot him.

Chen, however, was too shrewd to walk into such an obvious ambush.

When Christine emerged from the bathroom, one of the policemen in the kitchen motioned for her to come. As soon as she entered the kitchen, the policemen quietly closed the door. Two of them could speak some English, and they asked her whispered questions about what Chen was doing, where he was sitting, where the hostages were positioned, and what was Chen's state of mind. They were particularly anxious to hear whether he was angry or not. They then gave Christine advice as to what she should do. They assured her that they would get the family out. They insisted she not give Chen any inkling that they were there.

By this time, Chen became nervous because Christine had been away for so long.

"Come here!" He shouted one of the handful of English phrases he knew.

Quickly the SWAT team opened the kitchen door and let Christine go. She crossed the killing zone and scampered back up the stairs. Chen eyed her suspiciously. At the first opportunity, Christine told Anne about the men downstairs, speaking Afrikaans to make sure that Chen would not understand what she was saying. She had left both the bathroom and the laundry lights on, though this could not be noticed by Chen in the TV lounge.

The phone rang. Chen answered and handed it to Anne. It was Commander Peter Retief of the South African Navy, defense adviser in Malaysia, and our nearest neighbor among South African military attachés. He told Anne that he had been watching the news on television in Kuala Lumpur when he'd seen the report and watched the spectacle of Melanie and me being carried out of the house. He was deeply shocked.

He couldn't believe that he was talking to Anne under these circumstances. Anne reassured him about the three of them, but could give him no news about Melanie and myself. He promised that he would get straight onto Defence Headquarters in South Africa and, after some encouraging words, he rang off.

He was as good as his word.

Peter no sooner rung off than the next person phoned. It was Cheryl McLeod, Brian's wife, a good friend at church. She told Anne that Brian was at the hospital with me and that he'd phoned home to ask her to try to call Anne to tell her I was out of danger and under observation, while Melanie was undergoing surgery to have the bullet removed. The doctors were confident that the operation would go well.

A weight lifted off Anne as she heard this. In those incongruous conditions, the two ladies chatted for a while, almost as if it was any normal evening. With her ready, optimistic laugh, Anne soon had Cheryl wondering whether there really was a desperate gunman next to her. Cheryl also gave Anne the number of Ingomar Lochschmidt's cell phone. Ingomar, the Austrian representative in Taiwan and an active Christian at our church, was at the hospital, and would spend the whole night there. Anne immediately phoned the number without even consulting Chen. She got through to the hospital, and was encouraged to hear about her husband and daughter.

Chen could tell she'd had good news and he asked her about Melanie and me. He seemed pleased when she told him. Anne guessed that he was anxious not to add another notch to his list of killings at a time when he was using the media to gain sympathy for his cause.

Just then the computer fax machine began to receive a message. Anne asked Chen if she could clear it and he said yes. The message came from Anne's Aunt Verlaine Leech, on the KwaZulu-Natal South Coast in South Africa. She had heard of our predicament on the radio and immediately sent a fax in the hopes that it would get through to Anne to find out how we all were. She included her telephone number in the message.

"Can I use the phone?" Anne asked Chen in Mandarin. He passed it to her.

Within seconds she was speaking to Verlaine. Both were relieved to hear the other's voice. Anne asked Verlaine to pass on the news of our condition to everyone she could. Sadly, Verlaine had no means of making contact with Shona. Our daughter had no access to a phone where she worked, and we had no number for the quarters where she lived.

While Anne spoke, Christine looked after Zachary. Every so often Chen would take the little guy and play with him for a few minutes before handing him back to Christine.

When Anne finished speaking to Verlaine, she held Zach for a while. But soon the phone rang for her again. Handing him back to Christine, she picked up the receiver once more. It was her cousin Garth Leech in South Africa.

Briefly, Garth encouraged her to be strong, and then he rang off.

Chen had finished the last of the water in the two-litre bottle. He was thirsty. He handed the bottle to Christine and ordered her to refill it.

Christine trotted downstairs, past the patiently waiting SWAT team and into the kitchen. To the consternation of the policemen, she switched on the kitchen light to see what she was doing. While she filled the bottle, the officers again questioned her. Their imposing black outfits, balaclava helmets, soft boots, and belts festooned with guns and ammunition failed to overawe Christine, as she was becoming increasingly unimpressed with their inability to get the hostages out.

She brought the water up to Chen and he drank greedily. The tension of the evening had drained him. He offered Anne and Christine each a drink of water, and they gladly accepted.

The phone rang again. Anne answered it. It was a reporter from the *United Daily News*, who asked her how the situation was in the house. Anne replied that everything was calm and peaceful at the moment. He then asked her to put Chen on the line, which she did. A long conversation ensued, as Chen seemed to be holding a telephone interview. It was to be the first of many.

By this time Christine was yet again in need of visiting the loo. Now, however, it was quite simple to put the request to Chen when he'd finished on the phone.

"WC."

He immediately understood, and he readily agreed. Anne was surprised, as she was convinced that he was aware of the SWAT team downstairs. She could hear the sound of movements emanating from below the landing every so often. Surely Chen could hear it.

Christine returned. For a while things were quiet. Well past midnight, the situation seemed to have settled for the night. Zachary's bottle was empty, and he began to grizzle and complain. Anne asked if she could go downstairs and make up a fresh bottle.

The goodwill which Chen had felt towards them, probably founded on a strangely warped sense of guilt at having shot Melanie and me, was beginning to wear thin. He was becoming suspicious of these constant visits downstairs. But he could see that the baby needed a new bottle. Reluctantly, he consented.

Because she was expecting them, the still-waiting SWAT team didn't disconcert Anne. First she went to the loo and then she headed for the kitchen. No sooner was she in the kitchen than they closed the door and began questioning her. Producing a pen, they asked her to sketch the layout in the TV room, with the position of each person. There was a frantic flurry to find a piece of paper. Eventually one of them produced some very thin, flimsy tissue paper, and on this Anne sketched the situation as best she could.

The tissue paper had an interesting aside. Two weeks after the crisis, a friend found a bundle of tissue paper on the back balcony, adjoining our kitchen. She found a tin of wax wrapped inside it. This turned out to be an improvised weight to enable the paper to be thrown. On the paper was a carefully-written message in Chinese calligraphy, saying "We need radios. Please get them to us urgently." I can only assume it was a message from the SWAT team, directed at the police outside.

Upstairs, where Christine was cuddling Zachary, Chen was unable any longer to contain all the water he'd been drinking. He turned to a large pot plant and relieved himself in the pot. Christine was disgusted. But he seemed to know that to go to a toilet would mean instant death. He dared not move off that landing.

Back in the kitchen, the SWAT team tried to convince Anne that she should tell Chen the baby was ill and that she needed to bring him down to the kitchen to give him medicine.

Anne smiled wryly at them.

"He'll never fall for that," she said.

"You've got to persuade him," one policemen insisted.

Back upstairs she tried, but not too convincingly. Chen was understandably disbelieving. He could see there was nothing wrong with the child. He told her that if the child needed medicine, she could go downstairs to fetch it and administer the medicine in front of him. Feeling more than a little foolish, Anne left the matter. She found it difficult to understand how the police were underestimating this man.

Chen offered Anne and Christine another swig of water.

To Anne's great consternation, the SWAT team in the kitchen seemed unable to wait quietly. She kept hearing them moving around down there, bumping things or shifting them to different positions.

Inevitably, Chen picked up the sounds. He froze and lifted a gun in each hand. Anne felt a moment of panic as she envisaged a repeat of the earlier shooting. Thinking quickly, she spoke to him in Mandarin.

"*Wōmen yŏu sān gè māo* (We have three cats)," she said,

pointing downstairs.

She was not making it up. Anne has a particular affection for felines and we had always had several cats in our home. She had brought two of them, a tabby called Nuisance and a black-and-white stray called Patches, with her from South Africa. Our third cat was named Snoopy.

As if on cue, just after she'd uttered her words to Chen, Snoopy came up the stairs from where Anne was pointing, strolled through the room, and continued up to the bedroom.

Convinced, Chen relaxed and put away one gun. He ignored the noises. My wife smiled in relief. She quietly thanked God for the timely and miraculous intervention.

The situation between the police and the gunman had reached stalemate. It promised to be a long night. Anne, always intensely practical and not one to easily be deprived of her sleep, asked Chen if they could go upstairs to bed.

Quite taken aback at her presumptuous request, Chen slowly and incredulously shook his head while he pointed his gun at her suspiciously.

Anne discerned that she may have pushed her luck a bit. She was not in a position to argue with him. Changing her track, she modified her request. Could Christine go upstairs and fetch blankets and pillows so that they could sleep here on the floor?

At this more reasonable request, he acquiesced, but he insisted that Anne and the baby remain with him while Christine was gone. He was decidedly suspicious.

It took but a few minutes for Christine to scramble over the barricade and up the stairs so that she could retrieve a baby blanket for Zach, a duvet, and three pillows. Upstairs she saw subdued lights and heard whispering on the floor above the master bedroom. She deduced that there must be another SWAT team up there.

While Christine was gone, the phone rang again. The time was twenty-five minutes past midnight. Without thinking, Anne picked it up. It was TTV News anchorman Tai Chung-jen. He asked Anne what the situation was inside the house.

"Everything is calm and peaceful," replied Anne, evenly. Tai asked if he could speak to Chen. Anne handed the phone to the gunman.

On Christine's return, she and Anne arranged the bedding close to the computer on the floor, at Chen's feet. Cuddling the two children to her, Anne settled down under the duvet, determined to get some sleep.

Chen sat facing them with a pistol pointed in their direction. Anne's feet felt damp and uncomfortable.

"The carpet is sopping wet under my feet!" she exclaimed.

"That was me," said Christine very sheepishly, "when the police were shooting."

Shifting their position on the carpet, Anne sent Christine downstairs to get her a pair of socks from the laundry. Chen probably came close to throwing his hands in the air, his patience sorely tried. Would these women never settle down? Fortunately he was engrossed in his telephone conversation with the TV anchorman, that was being broadcast live across Taiwan.

Christine returned, Anne put on the socks to keep her feet warm, and again they tried to sleep—all except Zachary, that is. The little guy was over-tired and right now he was not going to sleep. He began to perform, instead.

When Anne decides it's time to sleep, she brooks no interference from anyone. She was certainly not going to take any nonsense from Zachary now. All her children will testify that she deals unhesitatingly with a recalcitrant child. Picking up Zachary she gave him a vocal piece of her mind and backed it up with a sharp smack on the buttocks.

Zach let out a howl.

Chen Chin-hsing looked horrified. He might have been the most violent man in Taiwan, but he was deeply imbued with the Chinese practice of never lifting a hand to a child.

"No!" he admonished Anne, interrupting his conversation to shake his finger at her.

Mothers do not take kindly to strange men telling them how to treat their children. She gave him a contemptuous and withering glance, then turned over and covered the wailing Zach with his blanket. His crying soon turned to sobs as he cuddled into the arms that had disciplined him and within a few minutes he was asleep.

For Anne, sleep did not come quite as easily, though. The talking on the phone and the excitement of the events kept her awake for hours yet.

Chen, who had been taking regular swigs from the water bottle and had finally concluded his interview, now felt the need to relieve himself again. The pot plant could take no more, so he pulled over a tin waste paper bin.

"I'm sorry," he muttered as he bashfully turned away from Anne and proceeded to half fill the waste bin.

The phone rang again. Anne felt a twinge of annoyance as she was just beginning to doze. Chen spoke animatedly to whoever had called. Anne could not quite make out who he was speaking to, as he sounded as though he was alternating between Mandarin and Taiwanese.

This pattern continued right through the night. He would no sooner switch off the cordless phone, than it would ring again. Then he would start another rambling conversation. On occasion, he seemed to talk for several hours with the same caller. Anne dozed between the calls.

Once she heard him softly singing a song over the phone. The tune was that of a popular children's song, known all over the world and called "*Vader Jakob* (Father Jacob)" in Afrikaans back in South Africa. Sleepily she surmised that he was speaking to his children and singing them a lullaby. At times, he even broke into laughter as he spoke.

In fact, he was speaking to television anchorwoman Chou Hui-ting on STV, one of Taiwan's largest cable stations. She had been questioning him on his ability as a singer and they had ended up singing together the song known in Chinese as "*Liǎng Chīh Lǎo Hū* (Two Tigers)." His words (and his song) were being broadcast live all over Taiwan.

But this really did not interest Anne at the time. For her, it was more important that the children should get some sleep after all this excitement and, if possible, so should she. Who knows what lay ahead tomorrow and they all needed rest now.

How could Anne be so philosophical yet down-to-earth in those circumstances? After all, she was alone with two children in a besieged house, held hostage by a ruthless, brutal criminal, known to be the most violent man in the country, who had just shot and wounded her husband and daughter in front of her.

People who know her well would have no difficulty providing an answer.

They would tell you that Anne has explicit trust in the Lord Jesus Christ. She is a woman with a wide experience and understanding of life. She is a military wife who has learned to survive on her own for long periods, developing her independence and an ability to cope with emergencies. And she is a mother who, putting her children's interests first, knows the importance of keeping them calm in a crisis.

Mac Alexander as a colonel commanding 44 Parachute Brigade. "I had several thousand people under me. When I issued an instruction, it was carried out. I was accustomed to being in control. I had fought in wars, had been under fire, had led paratroopers in battle. I had recourse to some action in times of danger...Until now. Never had I felt more helpless in my entire life."

11

›A Long, Lonely Night‹

FROM MY BED on the eleventh-floor ward I looked out the
window across the rooftops toward Cherry Hill, and saw the
flashing blue and red lights from the police vehicles between
the blocks of flats. Somewhere over there were my wife, my
daughter and little Zachary, held by a desperate gunman.

The compassion and concern in the eyes of my visitors
brought a lump to my throat. I was so emotional, I had to
consciously take a grip on myself. It was confusing, as I saw
so many faces pass by the stretcher and later the hospital bed.
Nurses fussed around me, and in the background familiar
friends hovered anxiously nearby, their expressions telling me
that they wanted to do something to help but that there was
nothing they could do. Somebody told me that Melanie was in
the operating theatre undergoing surgery. I felt peace about
her. She was in good hands, and I knew that God would take
care of her.

While the nurses settled me as comfortably as they could,
a couple of technicians installed a TV set opposite my bed.
Soon I was watching the media coverage of the crisis, with the
well-known façade of my house appearing almost constantly

on the screen in front of me, illuminated by the flashing police lights. It must have been close to midnight.

As a soldier, I had often been separated from Anne for lengthy periods, sometimes away for as long as six months at a time on active service. When the insurgency war in Southern Africa was at its greatest intensity and I had commanded a company of paratroopers, Anne and I once endured four years during which I was at home not more than a total of eighteen months. Yet not one of those absences seemed as long as this night.

On the television I could see that the police had finally got control of the media around our house. The eerily empty street had been cleared of all except the besieging police. The camera crews had been banished to the roofs and balconies of surrounding apartment buildings. Every so often on the TV there would be an interview with a government or police official, or there would be comment by some self-appointed expert. The TV showed important people arriving on the scene and disappearing into the command post. And of course they showed regular flashbacks of the rather melodramatic evacuation of Melanie and myself. My anger flared again every time I watched it.

Dr. Huang came to see me and told me that he would be giving me an injection.

"What for?" I demanded.

"To calm you down and relax you a bit. It will make you feel better and enable you to rest."

My eyes narrowed and I looked at him suspiciously, probably even accusingly.

"You're not giving me anything," I stated unreasonably. "You want me to sleep and I'm not going to sleep until my wife and children are safely out of there."

Dr. Huang was a good-natured and understanding gentleman. He smiled patiently and tried gently to convince me. I stubbornly refused to let him come near me.

A South African doctor would probably not have put up

with such nonsense, but the gentle courtesy demanded by the highly civilized Chinese culture prevented this man from being rude to me. I was exploiting this in my desire to regain some degree of control over my situation, and I suppose I was somewhat intimidating at that stage.

Ina van der Schyff, a South African missionary friend who is a nursing sister, intervened. She talked rapidly in Mandarin to the doctor. Then she turned to me, speaking Afrikaans. She confirmed that what he wanted to give me would not put me to sleep but would only relax me. As a compromise, she suggested that the dosage be reduced from 75 mg to 50 mg, then I would certainly not go to sleep.

Both Dr. Huang and I had great respect for Ina's competence and experience as a nursing sister. I saw that I was going to have to accept a compromise but I was not in much of a compromising mood.

"Twenty-five milligrams," I growled reluctantly.

"Don't be ridiculous," Ina laughed. "That won't have any effect on you at all. That's what they give to children!"

I had reached the end of my willingness to bargain. I was in no mood to quibble. "Twenty-five or nothing," I retorted stubbornly. "*Ek het klaar gepraat!*" (Afrikaans for "I have finished talking!")

She spoke to the doctor in Mandarin rapidly, to make sure that I could not follow. He looked at me resignedly and I suppose he could be forgiven for thinking "Some diplomat this!"

He drew 25 mg into the syringe, pointedly showing me that he was conforming fully to my demand. While he injected me through the drip, I admonished him.

"Doctor, if I fall asleep before all this is over, I'm holding you responsible. No way that I am going to sleep while my wife and children are still in that house with that man."

The long-suffering Dr. Huang looked at me with a twinkle in his eye.

"Of course," he said kindly. "I understand."

My concerns were partially soothed when Chris told me that the ROC cabinet had given instructions to the police that there was to be no more shooting and that the lives of the hostages were to be given top priority. Apparently Premier Vincent Siew had returned post haste to Taipei from one of the provincial cities to chair an emergency cabinet meeting on our crisis. The cabinet gave their undivided attention to the hostage-taking for most of the night.

I did not fall asleep, though. At one stage, Dr. Ke Dun-jen, the chief surgeon of the team who operated on Melanie, came into the ward and triumphantly held up a plastic bag containing the bullet. Proudly he announced that they had safely removed the bullet from Melanie's abdomen, and that they had found no damage to her organs. She was out of danger and they were now busy with a second operation to repair the damage to the tendons in her wrist.

"I want that bullet as a souvenir," I called after Dr. Ke as he turned to go.

"I'm sorry," he returned, stopping to look back at me. "I must give it to the police. They need it for evidence."

I shrugged.

Friends stayed with me through the night. And so many visitors came, I find it difficult to recall everyone. But two stand out especially in my memory.

Carol Lee, my secretary, and Jimmy Chuang, my driver, arrived in the ward together. Jimmy had been at home in Taoyuan, a town some thirty kilometres outside of Taipei, when a neighbor brought his attention to the drama being enacted on television. Horrified at what he saw, Jimmy immediately phoned Carol. By this time, Melanie and I had been evacuated and it was common knowledge that we were being treated at the Veterans' General Hospital.

"We've got to go see the Colonel now!" he told Carol. Then he drove straight through to Taipei while Carol took a bus to the hospital.

They met at the hospital entrance and when they walked

into the ward I experienced a surge of emotion. They were both such loyal and willing workers who showed constant dedication and friendliness. I felt a deep affection towards them and I could see the concern in their eyes.

Because of people like Jimmy and Carol I held the Chinese people and the Chinese culture in high regard. I worked closely with them every day. They both displayed such commendable qualities that one was compelled to respect them and what they represented — the ordinary people of Taiwan, honest, hard-working, friendly, helpful, polite, proud yet modest, and caring. I knew that without these two understanding people I would never have been able to do my job in that country with a culture and ethos so different from my own.

Jimmy and Carol stayed with me in the hospital for some time. In the morning, Carol opened my office at the embassy and manned it for me all alone for the next ten days.

Jimmy left the hospital and went straight up to the house on Cherry Hill. Though the police would not allow him to get close to the house itself, he was on hand to assist Jacolene and Wouter, who constantly talked to the police on the scene and phoned back situation reports to the ambassador, to Jaap le Roux at the embassy and even directly back to the Department of Foreign Affairs in Pretoria.

During the four hours Melanie was in surgery, a crowd of people, our friends and the ubiquitous media, gathered in the waiting area. The Christians drew aside, joined hands, and prayed.

One woman whose husband worked at the embassy and who did not share our religious convictions gave them a scathing look.

"There go that bunch of holier-than-thous again!" she commented in Afrikaans.

Mericia and Ina, who could understand her Afrikaans, looked at each other. They could see that this woman was deeply concerned for Melanie but frustrated that she could do nothing for her. Her skepticism seemed to make her resentful that these Christians did have something they could do — pray.

There were many others praying too for our family, for Chen, for the police, and for the peaceful resolution of the situation. One friend put it very succinctly:

"The Christian community rallied around them and God reigned."

Melanie emerged from the operating theatre after 2:30 A.M. accompanied by Dr. Ke, and was taken to the recovery room. The doctors permitted those waiting outside to see her, two at a time, then the nurses said no more visitors. Melanie was quite exhausted. But she was not yet to rest.

When Melanie was ready to be moved to a ward, Ina and Dr. Ke accompanied her. Waiting outside in the corridor was Michael Letts, who immediately leaned over to speak to her. But the media were also waiting: cameras flashed as Dr. Ke tried to keep them back. It was only at the entrance to the ward, where a policeman had been stationed, that they were halted and restrained. Melanie was wheeled into the ward to be with me.

Still very groggy, she looked better than when I had last seen her, but she was still in considerable pain. She had been given morphine and was barely conscious for the rest of the night and the next day. She slept on and off. All night Mericia was at her side seeing to her needs.

Ambassador Nikki Scholtz arrived for a brief visit shortly after I had been settled in the ward to give me some words of encouragement before he had to leave to once again face the media, the ROC Ministry of Foreign Affairs and the South African Department of Foreign Affairs. He must have been the most sought-after man in Taiwan that night and really should have looked severely harassed. Yet he was remarkably calm and I found his visit reassuring.

At 2:20 A.M. (8.22 P.M. on the 18th, South African time) the South African Department of Foreign Affairs released the following media statement:

> The South African Government is concerned about
> the events in Taipei where the house of the military
> attaché was occupied by a Chinese assailant. The
> military attaché and his family were held hostage.
> We realise that the Government of the Republic of
> China is doing its utmost to resolve the matter. We
> hope that the matter can be resolved speedily with-
> out loss of life. The South African Government is in
> constant contact through diplomatic channels with
> both the ROC authorities and the South African Em-
> bassy in Taipei. Further details will be made avail-
> able as soon as they can be confirmed. We would
> like to express our good wishes and a speedy
> recovery to those injured.

Out of concern for us, although he was due to leave
Taiwan in a few days, cousin Matthew spent the night in the
hospital. Going up and down between the eleventh-floor
ward and the first-floor restaurant, he drastically reduced the
latter's stock of Coca-Cola! At one stage, a horde of media
persons cornered him. They probably recognized the South
African flag on his cricket cap. He found himself exercising
his newly-acquired Mandarin language proficiency when he
was called on to make a statement on behalf of the family.

As the night wore on, Matthew unfolded a hospital chair
which opened into a bed, and curled up on it in a corner of the
ward to grab a few hours of shut-eye. He was exhausted by
the tension and rushing around. Visitors stared in disbelief at
the scruffy, dishevelled young man stretched out there in
fitful slumber, dressed in boots, blue denim jeans, and a check
shirt, with glasses awry and cap fallen off, exposing his un-
combed, blond hair.

A telephone was installed next to my bed. One of the first
calls I received was from my superior officer, the Defence
Force's Chief of Foreign Relations. The commodore was very
quick to tell me that they had everything under control in

South Africa and that there was nothing I needed to worry about over there.

I had only one concern in South Africa: my daughter Shona, who had by then joined the South African Air Force. I wanted her kept informed, I wanted her to be reassured that we were thinking of her at this time and I wanted her to know that we were not injured badly.

The commodore went to great lengths to allay my fears. He told me that she had already been contacted and that she would be kept fully informed at all times.

I was told that I had enough to worry about in Taiwan; I was not to worry about a thing in South Africa because he would sort everything out there for me. Satisfied and grateful, I thanked him profusely. It was good to know that I had a system manned by concerned individuals who were backing me in this time of crisis.

I was making a mistake. The system and the individuals were to let me down.

In South Africa, Anne's brother Arthur Leech, a commercial traveller, had been on his way home to Cape Town from Worcester. As he approached the Huguenot Tunnel through the Du Toitskloof Mountains he heard a news report on the radio saying that the South African ambassador in Taiwan had been taken hostage. Breathing a sigh of relief that it was not his brother-in-law, he entered the tunnel and lost radio reception.

In the meantime, his wife Carol heard a similar report on *Cape Talk Radio* while she was busy at home. But she caught the name "McGill Alexander." She immediately phoned the radio station and they confirmed to her that it was our family who had been taken hostage. She explained to them that I was the military attaché and not the ambassador. They wanted to interview her, so she gave them Arthur's cell phone number.

As Arthur emerged from the tunnel, his phone rang. It was *Cape Talk* and he was on the air. He was thunderstruck when they told him that it was our family who were being held hostage. So much so that he was almost incoherent during the interview and unable to provide the interviewer with any information. Arriving home, he contacted his sister Vonnie and later received a call from the commodore in Pretoria, assuring him that everything possible was being done. He then spoke to Telkom, the telephone company, and through them he obtained the number of the Veterans' General Hospital in Taipei. Persistent efforts on his part were eventually rewarded, and he was put through to me.

It was indescribably gratifying to hear the voice of my brother-in-law. He was overcome with concern and I was able to allay at least some of his fears. He told me that Anne's mother, who was visiting her sister in Johannesburg, was being protected from the full impact of the crisis as they were concerned about what effect it would have on her. Just two weeks earlier her husband of fifty-one years, Anne's father George Leech, had died. Anne and I had been to South Africa for the funeral, and we all knew that Anne's mom Judy was in a fragile state.

After Arthur rang off, my attention again focused on the television. Nothing seemed to be happening at the house. My heart ached for my wife, my youngest daughter, and little Zachy. As the hours ticked by, I prayed fervently for their safety. I knew God was with them, and yet—doubts plucked at my mind as persistent thoughts entered my imagination of what could happen if the police did something foolish. There was not a shadow of uncertainty in my thinking that Satan was causing me these doubts, and I had to consciously rebuke him.

I turned to the window. The grey dawn was breaking and I could make out the imposing, traditional shape of the Chinese Culture University on Yang Ming Mountain. It was a typically overcast day as the polluted city of Taipei came to life again.

12

▸Christine's Drawing◂

THE GUNMAN SQUATTED on the floor, pointing a pistol at his hostages. The house was dark. Lights from police vehicles flashed intermittently from outside. Under these conditions, a twelve-year-old was hardly likely to sleep, despite all Anne's efforts. Maybe her mom and baby Zachary could sleep; but not Christine.

For a while she lay on the floor and cuddled up to the dozing Anne, while Chen continued his rambling harangue on the telephone. Eventually she sat up and looked around. To one side of the room she saw her school bag where she had dropped it the day before. Reaching for the bag, she rooted around inside, and pulled out a pen and notebook.

Chen ignored her, engrossed in telling the media his story.

Christine felt an urge to draw or write something which would persuade Chen to "stop being mean." At the same time she was deeply concerned about Melanie and myself. She had watched us being dragged out, obviously hurt, but she did not know how badly. And in the house she had seen nothing which gave her confidence that all would end well. Something was wrong. TV dramas didn't turn out this way.

So often when our family had faced a crisis in the past, whether concerning finances, relationships, careers, school, or anything else, we had come together in prayer. Now Christine found herself alone, the only one awake with this hardened criminal.

To focus her feelings, she decided to express her prayer on paper.

"I felt that God was with me," she later told her school's student newspaper. "I just felt that He was there, and it felt pretty special."

While Chen squatted on his haunches on the floor, talking on the phone, he watched Christine by the wan light filtering through from the study.

Though Christine didn't know it at the time, Chen was talking to a television news anchor and all of Taiwan was listening to the conversation. The commentator was urging Chen to keep the hostages safe.

Christine began drawing a picture in the middle of a blank notebook page. She drew a large Christian cross. Then she drew a heart around the cross, completely enclosing it. Above the drawing, she wrote a brief prayer.

Christine didn't know who the gunman was talking to or what he was saying. But she knew he was bad. She thought to herself, "If this man would really understand the love of God, he wouldn't do bad things again." So in the darkened room, she reached over to show him the picture.

Still talking on the phone, Chen set down his gun and took the notebook from Christine. He turned it around and studied the drawing. Then he began describing the drawing to the TV anchorman.

"Let me tell you something," Chen said in Chinese (the transcript was later translated.) "This girl, who is probably over ten years old . . . She drew me a picture of Jesus. Around it is a big heart shape. I have been very touched throughout the whole time. They never stopped praying—the father, the mother, the two sisters. Praying over and over again. I was really touched. But there is nothing I can do."

All of Taiwan listened as he told about our family's faith and what this little girl had drawn. Though he could not read much English, he knew that the cross indicated *Jesus*; and evidently the message was clear to him. Tears welled in Chen's eyes as he stared at the picture. It was yet another spiritual encounter for the hunted man.

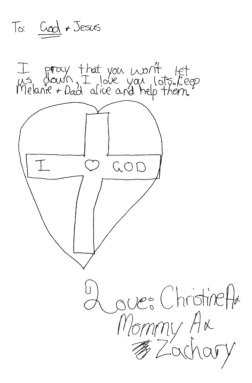

The interviewer asked Chen about his own religion.

"My whole family are Buddhists," he replied. "Sometimes I believe, and sometimes I don't."

He handed the notebook back to Christine. Shaken up, Christine sat for a long time watching Chen speak on the phone. She wanted to tell him that he didn't have to live the life of a criminal, that he could have God in his life.

Chen shifted nervously, wilting under Christine's steady gaze. How foolish for him to be pointing his gun at this child with her penetrating blue eyes. He was later to admit that he felt somewhat embarrassed then to be holding these people at gunpoint.

Eventually Christine tried to sleep. It was in vain and she was barely able to doze. But in any case, the night was almost over. Dawn crept through the windows, grey and foreboding, and Anne roused herself after a restless night.

Anne stared at Chen, still busy on the phone and squatting on his haunches. It seemed to her that he had remained in that uncomfortable posture all night. Shaking her head at what she regarded as senseless, self-inflicted discomfort, she attracted his attention, then she showed him the baby's empty bottle. He nodded. His all-night conversations seemed to have left Chen somewhat complacent. Anne trotted down the stairs and saw that the SWAT team had withdrawn during the night. It was later claimed in the *United Evening News* of 20 November that the SWAT team passed up six opportunities to kill Chen, because they did not want to risk the lives of the hostages.

Downstairs, Anne paid a visit to the loo, made up a fresh bottle in the kitchen, and collected tubs of yoghurt from the fridge. Then, wryly grinning to think that the house was again empty but for the hostages and the hostage-taker, she returned to the TV lounge. Giving Christine a tub of yoghurt, she offered one to Chen, but he declined. After Anne and the children had breakfasted, she left Zachary in the care of Christine and seated herself behind the computer. Chen didn't seem to object, so Anne perused her e-mail.

Footage of Melanie's and my evacuation appeared on television screens in almost every country around the globe. Anne found anxious messages on e-mail from friends and relatives in South Africa, New Zealand, and England.

Chen interrupted Anne. The cordless phone which he had been using constantly through the night was experiencing battery failure. He asked Anne whether she could recharge the battery. She explained that the charger was in the bedroom upstairs. He did not want to go up there. Anne took the phone from him and handed it to Christine, telling her to take it upstairs and place it in its cradle so that it could recharge.

Chen asked whether there was a phone downstairs. Anne replied in the affirmative and offered to show him where it was. He agreed, and then held his hands out towards Zachary who was in Anne's arms. One hand still gripped a pistol.

"Come to Poppa!" he said in English. Anne handed the baby to him. The situation seemed so anomalous, with this hardened killer showing affection towards this child.

As Christine rejoined them, they all descended the stairs to the lounge, Anne leading the way and Chen bringing up the rear, holding Zach in one arm and his pistol at the ready in the other. Anne showed him the telephone, and he quickly handed Zachary back to Anne and began telephoning. He crouched on the floor as he talked, but Anne and Christine sat with Zachary on one of the couches, surveying the scene in the brightening daylight.

The walls were pockmarked by slugs, a chandelier light had been shot out, the front door was riddled with bullet holes, windows were shattered, and the long lace curtains were ripped and torn. They flapped lazily in the breeze that blew through the jagged windows. The CD player which had sat on the windowsill now lay on the floor, surrounded by soil spilt from knocked-over pot-plants, and a CD rack lay on one side, two bullet holes showing conspicuously as the splinters of wood stuck out, and CDs lay strewn over the floor.

Everywhere empty cartridge shells lay scattered around where they had fallen from the balcony above, while from the stairs to the window ran a repulsive trail of blood. Our home had become a battlefield littered with debris.

For about half an hour Chen spoke on the phone, but it was obvious that he felt vulnerable and exposed down there. He showed increasing signs of nervousness.

Eventually he put down the phone and herded everyone back upstairs. Christine went to the bedroom and retrieved the recharged cordless phone. Chen immediately phoned out again. He was still talking to the media.

Even when not speaking on it, Chen held the phone, so Anne could not get hold of it. He seemed to evidence an air of despondency with the dawning of the new day, perhaps because his desperate efforts had yielded nothing. Catching Anne's eye, he held her gaze for a long while. Then, slowly, he again lifted one of his pistols and placed the barrel under his chin, as he had done the night before. The look in his eyes told Anne that he was close to the end of his tether and deadly serious in his intentions. As a vision of the blood-spattered scene her children would witness flashed through her mind, she anxiously held out her hand in protest and again repeated her plea of the previous night that he should remember his wife and children.

Once more Chen looked long and hard at this wife and mother before again lowering the gun and turning his attention back to the telephone.

Frustrated, with no idea what was going on outside and no further news concerning Melanie and myself, Anne and Christine decided to retrieve my cell phone from my car in the garage. Interrupting Chen, Anne explained to him what they wanted to do.

He appeared to understand and agreed to allow Christine to go downstairs. But first he warned the girl, getting his meaning across with threatening gestures. He pointed to her, then aimed the gun at Anne and made a popping noise. Obviously, he was saying that if Christine ran away, he'd kill her mother. Wide-eyed, Christine nodded.

She headed down the stairs and into the garage. She wanted to know what was going on outside – what plans had been made to rescue them. She marched right past my car and straight to the roll-up garage door. It was the same door through which the police assault team had entered the night

144

before, and through which they must have retreated, closing it after them. Pressing the electronic control button, Christine waited for the door to slowly roll up. In the street outside lay the special jack that the police had used to force the door open.

The street had emptied of all except police. The officers on duty heard the garage door opening and hastily sought cover behind walls and parked cars. They nervously pointed their weapons at the ever-widening gap. When the door was about half way up, Christine stepped out into the street, blinking in the bright light after the inside darkness. She found herself confronted by an array of automatic pistols, shotguns and assault rifles, all pointed at her by wide-eyed and totally-surprised policemen.

For a moment she looked around, taking in the scene. She was becoming accustomed to people pointing guns at her.

"When are you going to get us out of here?" demanded my daughter, without losing her composure. "He's been holding us in there for twelve hours now and all that you've done is shoot and make him angry. Why don't you do some-thing without shooting?"

The officers appeared taken aback by her scathing tirade.

"Don't worry, we do have a plan," called one policeman cautiously from behind one of the cars. He spoke in English. "We are busy with it now. But you must very quickly come over here where you will be safe. Don't go back inside there."

The events of the past night had hardly enhanced the credibility of the police in Christine's view. She was skeptical of anything they said.

"No!" she replied shaking her head very emphatically. "I'm going back. If I don't, he'll kill my mother. I'm not leaving her." Then, putting her nose in the air she added, "And you'd better move it and do something about getting us out of here."

With that she ducked back under the garage door and closed it, leaving the flabbergasted policemen out in the street shaking their heads in wonder and looking thoroughly perplexed.

The camera crews and reporters perched on the roofs and balconies of the surrounding buildings watched this little episode from a distance, unable to hear the exchange of words. Quickly the the media spread a story that Chen had sent Christine out to deliver a message to the police, but that she had refused to leave her mother when she had the opportunity. At this time, the little heroine began to grip the imagination of the Taiwanese public.

"Come here!" the agitated voice of Chen shouted from upstairs.

Hurriedly Christine retrieved the cell phone from my car and scampered back up to the TV lounge. Chen glowered at her suspiciously, but she just smiled at him and handed the cell phone to Anne, who was sitting in an armchair, playing with Zachary.

Chen had placed his gun on the floor in front of him and was gesticulating animatedly while he spoke on the phone. The moment Anne would let go of the now wide-awake Zachary, the little tyke would crawl across the carpet like a flash and reach for the pistol. Chen would snatch it up and gently chide the baby in heavily-accented English.

"No! Bad! Bad!"

Anne would haul Zach back, but as soon as he got the chance, he would beetle off to try and grab the gun again.

Cell phone in hand, Anne dialed the hospital number given her the night before. She got straight through to me, and I could scarcely contain my emotion.

We reassured each other. She sounded so cheerful and in control that I was quite overwhelmed at this wonderful wife of mine. She handed the phone to Christine and I heard an excited daughter who couldn't wait to share her adventures with me.

"Dad," she said in a low, conspiratorial voice. "I've been playing the detective."

146

13

‣No Tears To Shed‣

BROUGHT FROM HER PRISON CELL in the night, Chang Su-chen, the wife of Chen Chin-hsing, arrived at the police command post in a mini bus about half an hour before midnight, with a woman who was apparently her mother. The police negotiators, it seems, wanted her on hand for the negotiations.

The media monopolized the telephone right through the night and most of the next morning, delaying the start of negotiations. While one newspaper and at least six different TV stations interviewed Chen, the police couldn't reach him.

Virtually all television stations in Taiwan cancelled their scheduled programming and broadcast the drama live. The state-run Taiwan Television interviewed Chen for more than two hours. He told them that he would be willing to negotiate with Police Chief Hou You-yi.

On the phone, his words airing all across Taiwan, Chen admitted guilt for various crimes and said that he was willing to accept punishment for these offenses. He apologized to all his victims, to Pai Ping-ping the mother of the murdered girl, and to all those who had suffered as a result of his actions. He confessed to the rape of a number of women in the greater

Taipei area over the previous months and admitted that he and Kao Tien-min had been responsible for the triple murder in the plastic surgery on 23 October, though he denied having pulled the trigger.

Chen Chin-hsing's long and rambling interviews over the telephone with TV and newspaper reporters didn't present a very structured, coherent case for the people of Taiwan to assess.

"I deserve to die," he admitted. "Society will never accept me."

"Don't come in, or I will get nervous," Chen warned the police through the media. "I have no intention of turning myself in. I won't hurt these people I have here, but it is difficult to say what will happen if the police burst in." He said that he might become irrational and shoot someone.

At one stage while he was speaking, Zachary could be heard cooing and gurgling in the background. The interviewer asked Chen about his own children.

"I miss my children," he replied. "I know these foreigners are innocent, but I need them as hostages because the authorities will not listen to me. My family are innocent too." He claimed to have deliberately targeted foreigners as hostages in a move to generate the most publicity possible.

"I'm waiting for police authorities to negotiate with me, though I don't know how they will deal with it," he told the media. "I'm not going to surrender. I'm not prepared to go out alive. I want to cry, but I have no tears to shed."

From his rambling and vague statements the media deduced the following: that he had, since his childhood, mistrusted the police and those in authority; yet, if he could turn the clock back, he would himself have "studied hard to become a high official"; that he admitted to being guilty of numerous heinous crimes for which he deserved to die and for which he was prepared to die; but that innocent people (his wife, brother-in-law and friend) had been dragged into the situation and that if he did not stand up for them, "some-

day what happened to me could happen to you all."
He contradicted himself often. Yet he was in fact skillfully
manipulating the Taiwanese viewers and listeners by harping
on issues with which they could identify: questionable police
procedures and bureaucratic bungling and indifference. The
spotlight of center-stage which he had achieved as an ordinary and down-trodden member of the masses placed him in
a unique position to gain unwarranted sympathy and understanding from the public.

Well aware of the antagonism he had generated in the
hearts of many Taiwanese because of the gruesome death of
Pai Hsiao-yen, he claimed that she had died from choking on
a moon cake while heavily drugged. Moon cakes are a popular Chinese confection which tend to be dry and crumbly.
This dubious explanation seemed to be directed at television
audiences with the specific intent of gaining more sympathy.
Days later, under police interrogation, Chen was to change his
story, saying that the girl had died from choking on a handful
of sleeping pills which his accomplice Lin had forced her to
swallow. The pills, he said, included the drug FM2.

Each television station that interviewed Chen seemed to
be trying to outdo the others in their efforts to extract ever
more shocking admissions and revelations from the infamous
criminal. Chen disclosed details of his movements over the
past seven months. He revealed that many sightings of the
fugitives reported in the media had been true. One news
anchor asked Chen whether he was going to kill himself.

"Yes," he replied. "That's what I'm here for." But he
reacted with annoyance when asked when he intended doing
it.

The police outside abruptly interrupted the interview by
shouting at Chen to commence negotiations. Angered by their
attempts to pressure him, the hostage-taker shouted back.

"All these media keep calling me. What do you expect me
to do?"

However, as soon as he'd rung off, Chen yelled out the

window to any reporters in earshot. "I'm waiting for your calls." His desire for publicity seemed to far outweigh his desire to negotiate.

In the immediate vicinity of our house at least 400 police officers hid behind cover in the streets, on the rooftops of surrounding buildings, peering from behind shrubs in neighboring gardens, peeping over balconies, carefully aiming their weapons through windows from nearby apartments, manning road blocks on the streets of every block, and keeping the journalists, camera people, and curious inhabitants of Taipei at bay.

Apparently the Panchiao chief prosecutor, Chang Chenghsing, succeeded in getting through to Chen, and at about 7:20 A.M. Chen requested that Chang investigate what he considered to be unacceptable treatment of his wife by the police. Chang agreed, and asked Chen to release a hostage to show his good faith. Negotiations had begun.

Again, Chen was too shrewd to fall for this one. He insisted that the agreement be set down in writing. Chang agreed, and Chief Hou You-yi and another prosecutor both added their assurances to Chen that this would be done. It seems that Chen also demanded at this time that the cable television be reconnected so that he could watch a media briefing by the prosecutors in which they would explain the agreement.

At one point Military Police senior officers arrived at the command post. Shortly afterward, the highly-trained Military Police Special Task Force moved into the area. However, they kept their distance, waiting for the civilian police to accept that they could no longer handle the situation and resort to calling them in.

Inside, Chen, calm but angry, lay on the floor waiting.

At about 10:00 A.M. the police again called and told Chen that his wife was outside and wanted to speak to him. He agreed to see her. This started negotiations proper. It had taken over fourteen hours to bring him to this point.

Thirty-six minutes later Chang Su-chen, dressed in a check shirt and red track suit pants was seen walking down the street towards our house, escorted by a helmeted, flak-jacketed Chief Hou You-yi. In her hands the attractive but apparently confused and uncertain woman clutched a packet containing some bread rolls for her husband, as well as a small tape recorder.

Hou led her to our front gate and showed her the steps. Hesitantly, she made her way up to the front garden, while TV viewers watched her emotional pain and fear on their screens. Her frightened face was etched with heartache as she called out to Chen with a wavering voice.

"You can trust me!" she said.

Chen answered her, strongly and with self-assurance, and bade her enter.

Cautiously she climbed through the broken window and disappeared from view of the TV cameras. It was 10:39 A.M..

Another woman, a mysterious fortune teller known only as "Madame Chen," and apparently a close friend of Chang Su-chen, followed her into the house and Anne recalls the simultaneous arrival of both women in our TV lounge. They both greeted Anne as they entered the room. To Anne's surprise, "Madame Chen" greeted her in fluent English.

Chen Chin-hsing sat cross-legged on the floor with his pistols. The reunion with his wife was at first unemotional. The two women sat cautiously on the edge of the couch close to him. Chen and Chang Su-chen spoke to each other quietly, and she took out the sandwiches and pastries from the packet she carried.

They offered food to Anne and Christine. Each took a sandwich and ate it, while Chen himself unenthusiastically ate some of the food.

As the husband and wife conversed, they gradually relaxed. Chang moved off the couch and sat beside Chen on the floor, putting her arms around him and snuggling closer into him. She cried, and the hardened criminal who was her husband bit his lip. His eyes began to swim with tears. Anne could almost tangibly feel the surging emotions being experienced by the disconsolate couple.

"Madame Chen" had with her a document. She read it out to Chen, then seemed to explain its contents. Anne thought the document must be a proposal from the authorities. Later the minister of justice reported in the media that this document was a written copy of the agreement police made with Chen over the telephone—that if Chen released a hostage, his wife's treatment by the police would be investigated.

Chen and his wife then began to talk animatedly while "Madame Chen" sat to one side. Unable to follow the conversation, Anne amused Zachary while Christine exploited the sudden distraction to slip upstairs to her room. There she gave vent to her intense curiosity to see what was going on outside. Her bedroom had a balcony which looked out on our front garden and the street below, so she opened her sliding door and stepped across to the edge of the balcony wall. She peered over.

The street below looked deserted; but then she saw that the police had barred access further up the street and they were holding hordes of people away from the house. She could see the occasional police looking out from behind cover, but all appeared very quiet. Then she saw rows of photographers and camera crews lining the tops of apartment buildings all over the neighborhood. Perched precariously on the flat rooftops, they were all aiming high-powered lenses straight at her.

Feeling suddenly very self-conscious and shy, Christine drew back behind a pillar, then slipped back inside. She made her way back down to the TV lounge and saw that Chen, who was still talking to his wife, had not even missed her. He had taken one or two more bites from the bread rolls, then tossed the rest on the floor. Obviously, he was not thinking of his hunger.

She took Zachary from Anne and began playing with him.

"Madame Chen" talked to Anne about Chen and his wife. As the morning wore on and Chen told them more about how he had come to enter our house, "Madame Chen" interpreted the details to Anne. She looked at Anne sympathetically.

"You look tired," she said.

"I am tired," Anne confessed. "I didn't get any proper rest last night and I'm stiff and sore from lying on the floor."

"Here, let me massage your neck," said the woman, getting up and moving behind Anne. As Anne sat on the armchair she began to work on her neck and shoulders.

"Mmm, that feels good!" murmured Anne with her eyes closed.

"Wait a minute!" retorted the woman, pointing at Chen's wife. "She's a trained masseuse. Let her give you a proper massage."

By this time Chen was again busy on the phone, presumably talking to the police. "Madame Chen" spoke to Chang Su-chen, and the latter's woebegone expression changed to a sad smile. She indicated that Anne should lie down on the floor and when she had done so, the two women proceeded to give her a very thorough massage, from her neck and shoulders right down to her feet and toes, while Chen spoke heatedly to negotiators and Christine played with Zachary. Anne groaned in pleasure and relief as her body relaxed. A bizarre scene indeed!

When they finished, Chang Su-chen took Zachary, who had begun to grizzle and be quite miserable. She asked Anne for a nappy and then deftly changed him. He cheered up, and she played with him and cuddled him. Always an affectionate and responsive baby, Zach gurgled with glee, grabbing her hair and touching her face. The woman smiled the doleful smile of a mother who had been imprisoned and deprived of her own children. When Chen finished on the phone, she talked to him very seriously, clearly focusing her conversation on Zachary. Perhaps she was reminding him of their own sons. He grew pensive, and made a phone call, apparently to the police, while Chang rocked Zachary to sleep in her arms.

"Madame Chen" turned abruptly to Anne.

"He has agreed to release the baby," she stated. "Collect some diapers and a bottle to go with him."

Anne scurried upstairs to Zachary's room to pack a small bag for him; then downstairs to the kitchen to make up a fresh bottle of formula. Returning to the TV lounge, she handed all the stuff to Chang Su-chen. Then she took Zachary and gave him a kiss and a hug. The two mothers smiled gently at one another as the child who was neither of theirs was handed with love and care from the one to the other.

Chang Su-chen carried the baby and his things down the stairs. Chen shouted to someone outside. When his wife got to the broken window, Chief Hou You-yi was waiting outside for her. The expectant horde of photographers on the rooftops got their second chance for a dramatic picture as the wife of the country's most notorious criminal gently and carefully handed the infant through the smashed pane into the out-stretched arms of the helmeted policeman. It was 11:53 A.M..

Zachary's release came as an immense relief for Anne and Christine. They had both become increasingly concerned for his welfare and felt that he needed to get out of that volatile situation as soon as possible.

Awkwardly Chief Hou carried little Zachary down the stairs and emerged into the street. A young man in civilian clothes, presumably also a policeman, quickly approached. Hou handed the child and his little bag to him and the man turned and started back up the street towards the command post. Cameras clicked and whirred, and the man began to run. With outstretched arms, the little fellow bounced up and down with a confused expression of discomfort on his face.

In the hospital my heart leapt with joy as I watched them carry the little boy that I loved so much to safety.

154

**Baby Zachary carried to safety
by Taipei police chief Hou You-yi.**
(AP Photo/Eddie Shih, PictureNET Africa)

14

›Hospital Vigil‹

IN ATTEMPTING TO GET the authorities to take note of his demands, Chen Chin-hsing could not have done better than to take hostage South Africans.

The imminent termination of official diplomatic relations between South Africa and Taiwan, scheduled for the end of December, meant that negotiations regarding the further status of the new relations between the two countries were at a crucial stage. Taiwan stood to lose a lot of face unless the final agreement was seen to bring them some benefit despite the withdrawal of official recognition by South Africa.

For a South African diplomat and his family to be killed by a crazed gunman in the capital of Taiwan at this sensitive point in the process would surely jeopardize Taiwan's position in negotiations. It was thus not surprising that the ROC Premier and his cabinet issued the urgent instruction that the police were not to place the lives of the hostages in any unnecessary danger. Though this instruction arrived at the scene too late to prevent the rash police assault which resulted in Melanie's and my being shot, it did stop all further efforts to resolve the issue by violence.

As the crisis dragged into the second day, a further emergency cabinet meeting was held the afternoon of Wednesday the 19th.

Because of the diplomatic sensitivity of the situation and the notoriety of Chen Chin-hsing, the media had a field day. Taiwanese viewers saw front-page headlines from South African newspapers splashed across their TV screens.

In hospital, I tried hard to follow developments on TV, but a constant stream of high-level Taiwanese visitors made this very difficult.

First came Vice-Premier Mr. John Chang and later the Director General of the National Police Administration, Ting Yuan-chin. Both apologized. Though I appreciated their concern and told them so, and though I assured them that I attached no blame to anyone in government, I was in no mood to simply mouth pleasantries and engage in diplomatic doublespeak.

These men attempted to convince me that the police had never returned fire when Chen opened up on them. I made a point of telling them exactly what I had experienced, and I insisted that they not send any police teams into the house until my family had all been released.

No doubt I would have had far more to say had I known that the police SWAT teams had been inside the house all night. At one stage, the TV had shown police officers laying a ladder between the roof of my house and the house next door, and crawling across to our house. I had become very worked up, raising myself up in my bed.

"Are you crazy?" I yelled at the TV. "What do they think they're doing? They'll get Anne and Christine killed!"

Chris Dippenaar had gently pushed me back down.

"Relax, Mac. They had cut the TV cable and Chen is demanding that they repair it so that he can see them broadcast his demands. No technician will go near the place, so the police have to do it."

This succeeded in calming me, but it was a ploy. Chris

was perfectly correct about the demands to have the cable repaired, but that is not what the police shown on TV were doing. They were trying to enter the house! Chris was fearful of my reaction should I learn of this.

I shouldn't have believed him, because the TV cable did not go near the roof. That didn't occur to me at the time. But I remained suspicious of the police activities, particularly as the TV showed intermittently a police sniper on a roof, a group of police officials at the entrance to the command post talking heatedly on cellular phones, and dishevelled SWAT teams running out and fresh ones moving into the neighborhood.

As I fretted helplessly in the hospital bed, Chris wrote a few words on a card and handed it to me. I read it in silence:

> *The Lord has chastened me severely,*
> *But he has not given me over to death.*
> (Psalm 118:18)

Chris smiled at me. I felt a reassuring warmth as my friend squeezed my shoulder. Those words of scripture gave me a boost and I felt strong enough to face the continuing crisis once again.

Of the visits from senior military officers, I was particularly pleased to see Lieutenant General Huang Yung-dea, the Deputy Chief of the General Staff for Intelligence. Although we had at times experienced differences which had led to confrontation, our relationship was frank and direct. I had great respect for his professionalism.

This Air Force general with a fighter-pilot background had an unbelievable capacity to party. He hosted many dinners which we attended, and with his fine voice he would lead us all in some rousing singing before the party was over.

General Huang had a burning desire to persuade me to consume some of the fiery, clear spirits known as *Kao Liang*, distilled from sorghum on the island of Kinmen. He never succeeded, though, and I eventually departed Taiwan the same teetotaler I was when I arrived.

During his visit, Huang told me the armed forces had deployed their Military Police Special Task Force which had been trained to deal with hostage situations, who would remain on standby in the area until such time as the civilian police requested their assistance. In my own career as a soldier, I had frequently worked with the police in South Africa under similar arrangements.

General Huang, dressed in civilian clothes, asked me if I'd mind if he was present when the Director General of the National Police Administration came in. I assented. During the stormy visit (I became very angry when the director general intimated that the police had done no shooting), General Huang remained inauspiciously in a corner of the room, listening to everything with an amused smile. After the director general left, Huang grinned and told me that I'd handled the policeman well.

The ward rapidly filled with huge bouquets of flowers and boxes of fruit from well-wishers. They came from cabinet ministers, general and flag officers, government officials, schools, businesses, clubs, associations, colleagues and private individuals. A huge bouquet which included a king protea (South Africa's national flower) arrived from a general in Singapore. I was deeply touched.

In addition, I received messages and cards from many people I did not know, and from distant parts of the world. I was astonished by the show of support from many sources. And all the while, our friends in Taipei streamed in to bring encouragement.

A delegation from the Taipei American School arrived and handed me a card which the students had made, with Christine's picture on it, and they expressed their solidarity and support. I really choked up.

Perhaps one of the most emotional visits was from the Chinese staff at our embassy. They arrived *en masse*, with reticent and worried faces. One by one they came forward, taking my hand and saying something encouraging or just looking at me with tears in their eyes. They all knew Anne well. The one day a week she came to the embassy to do my classified typing and filing, she would breeze into each one's office, cheerfully greeting them and chatting with them about the ordinary things in life. They all loved Anne for her unpretentious and down-to-earth ways. Now she was a hostage in a terrifying, life-threatening situation. They didn't know what to say; but their eyes said it all to me.

The only one who was not there was Jimmy—he was at the house, waiting for the release of Christine and Anne! Not for one moment did Jimmy waver in his steadfast vigil.

One particularly moving visit was by Dr. Kao Yu-chi, our family doctor in Taipei. A Chinese Christian who bubbled over with joy in the Lord, he had a close association with Anne, treating her for asthma, occasional high blood-pressure, and various minor ailments. He burst into my ward in a great state of consternation, clutching a paper packet. His face was streaked with tears. He rushed to my bed and took my hand.

"Colonel Alexander," he cried out with a pained expression. "I'm so sorry. I must help Mrs. Alexander. I've brought her some antidepressant tablets and sleeping pills. Can't we persuade the police to let me go in and give them to her? Perhaps I can help to get her out!"

It was my turn to calm someone down and I assured him that the police were doing all they could. We just wanted him to pray.

"I am praying," he replied. "My family and I have been up all night praying for all of you." Touched, I took the packet from him and promised to get it to Anne somehow.

Hordes of reporters tried to get in to interview Melanie and me. Fortunately, the hospital authorities and our friends kept them at bay. So the media phoned me.

I cannot even begin to recall who all called me as I lay in the hospital that day. I just never seemed to be off the phone and I found it difficult to follow what was happening on the TV with all the attention that the telephone demanded. From time to time there was a very graphic and comic diagram presented on TV of how the media envisaged our shooting having taken place, with myself in a contorted position to get my knee in line with Chen's gun, while Melanie was bending over almost double so that her back could align with my knee. It prompted a little amusement which broke some of the tension in the ward.

Many calls came from friends and well-wishers whose supportive sentiments boosted me immeasurably. Those from the media were less edifying and often quite trying as they persistently probed to try and glean the tiniest bit of new information.

The people around me tried to protect me by grabbing the receiver when the phone rang and screening the calls. I insisted on speaking whenever I heard that it was someone from the South African media. News could be twisted by journalists who were more concerned with deadlines than they were with accuracy. I knew that many people in South Africa who cared very much for us would be hungry for any news. It was therefore important for me that the facts were made known in my own country.

Slowly, with measured tones and selecting my words with care, I conducted these phone interviews with South African newspaper and radio journalists. I listened later with amusement to my sullen enunciation on a recording of one such interview, broadcast on the station *Cape Talk*.

Just when I began to feel despondent about the apparent absence of any progress, the phone next to my bed rang for the umpteenth time; but this time it was Anne! How wonderful it was to hear her voice.

15

▶A Heavyweight Arrives On The Scene◀

SHORTLY AFTER ZACHARY was released, Chen received another message over the telephone. Apparently investigators were willing to consider taking another look at their accusations that his wife was involved in the Pai Hsiao- yen kidnap/murder.

Chen then agreed to release another hostage at 4:00 P.M.. About this time, a new character in the drama appeared on the scene—famed lawyer and politician Frank Hsieh.

Hsieh Chang-ting (his Chinese name) had long been an implacable foe of the ruling Kuomintang Party in Taiwan, and had been imprisoned for his opposition during the days of political intolerance. With the coming of democracy to Taiwan he became an active member of the largest opposition party, the Democratic Progressive Party (DPP), which advocated a Taiwan separate and independent from mainland China.

He established a solid reputation as a human rights law-yer and was once elected to the country's legislature. In fact, he was often referred to as "the human rights lawyer." At the time of our hostage-taking he was practicing law in his home city of Kaohsiung in southern Taiwan, while still serving as chairman of the DPP Central Advisory Committee.

Like so many other Taiwanese, Hsieh apparently arrived in our neighborhood on the morning of 19 November. At about 9:00 A.M. he appeared on the scene, when Anne, Christine and Zachary were still inside the house with Chen Chinhsing. Hsieh's arrival would spur much controversy. What were his motives? It is true that as an opposition heavyweight politician he stood to gain political advantage from his involvement in the crisis. Yet it cannot be denied that as an acknowledged human rights lawyer he must have had a sincere concern for the human issues at stake.

Another factor gave Hsieh a personal stake in the whole affair. The letter which he had received from Chen after his announcement on 8 November that he would be prepared to offer legal assistance to Chang Su-chen, had placed a moral obligation on his shoulders. By his own admission, Hsieh had only read the letter when the hostage crisis exploded the night of 18 November. Hsieh was later to acknowledge with what could have been a twinge of conscience, that had he read the letter earlier and complied with Chen's request, the kidnapper may never have taken hostages.

Whatever his reasons, Frank Hsieh approached the command post and asked to be allowed to enter our house and talk with Chen. But it seems that the National Police Administration Director General turned down the request, so Hsieh left the command post. However, he apparently spoke to some of the reporters outside, telling them he would be prepared to serve as Chang Su-chen's defense lawyer in her pending appeal case to the High Court in Taiwan, aimed at contesting the twelve-year prison sentence she had received— on the condition that Chen release his remaining three hostages. Hsieh then left the scene.

In the meantime, according to what "Madame Chen" later related in a letter published in the tabloid *Liberty Times* on 23

November, Chen told Chang Su-chen that the hostage-taking had been carried out because it was all that he could do for her, his wife, who was now being arraigned because of his crimes. He could not afford to provide a lawyer for her, and his reputation was so bad that no one would dare to take her case which was so badly tainted by his actions.

Anne recalls that both Chen and his wife became very emotional, and Chang Su-chen wept wretchedly. She told her husband that if he would just surrender, Frank Hsieh would come forward to be her lawyer. He found this too unlikely to believe. Hsieh, after all, had never responded to his letter.

Then police repaired the cut cable for our television, and Chen was again able to watch the media coverage of his escapade. During discussions and media conferences on the TV, Chen listened intently to what was said. It was probably in this way that he learned of Hsieh's offer. He suddenly became very excited, jumping up and talking animatedly.

"Madame Chen" told Anne that a famous lawyer had agreed to take on Chang Su-chen's case. Everyone smiled. Anne's hopes of getting out with our daughter began to rise.

Chang Su-chen called the police to say that her husband wanted to see Hsieh; but she was told that the discussions would have to take place on the phone.

When he heard this, Chen became angry, snatched up the spare magazines of ammunition that he'd laid on the carpet, shoved them into his pockets and picked up his guns, cursing as he stood up and looking frighteningly aggressive.

"Madame Chen" then telephoned Director-General Ting Yuan-chin and told him that it was essential that they allow Hsieh into the house to prevent further violence. At first Ting said it would be dangerous for Hsieh, then reluctantly agreed. (Ting subsequently claimed that Chen had by then already agreed to surrender, and that Hsieh's actions merely delayed his inevitable release of the hostages.) The police chief later claimed that they did not want outsiders such as Hsieh influencing the outcome and that they only agreed to his involvement because of the pressure they felt from the media.

For Anne, it did not seem as though Chen had any intention of surrendering at that stage. In fact, suicide still appeared to be his preferred option for climaxing the crisis, and quite conceivably, he could decide to take them all with him.

She recalls many telephone calls, some of them very animated, but she had no idea what was being said. What she does recall is Frank Hsieh being escorted into our house to the bottom of the stairs by someone, then coming up on his own.

It was about 12:40 P.M. when Hsieh, not wearing any protective gear, was escorted by the police to our house. Cameras at the ready, everyone waited with bated breath.

Chen was still squatting on his haunches on the floor next to his wife, but as Hsieh appeared at the top of the stairs he placed his two pistols on the floor and bowed down on his knees with his hands out in front of him towards Hsieh. Hsieh himself later admitted to being speechless at this show of acknowledgement as Chen thanked him for coming to speak to him and for offering his services as legal representative of his wife. He hadn't expected this, Hsieh later said. His heart had been thumping in his chest as he had entered the house and approached Chen.

Chen remained on the floor and Hsieh sat on the couch to one side of him. Anne didn't know what they discussed, but she did notice a calmness in Chen while they spoke, and she was grateful for Hsieh's presence. Until then, all negotiations with the authorities had been conducted only by telephone. Other than during the brief appearances of Chief Hou You-yi, no one with any authority had spoken face to face with Chen. Anne really didn't know who Frank Hsieh was, nor who he represented; but to her it was obvious that he had been sent into the house to negotiate with the hostage-taker, and that boded well for the outcome. At last she could see someone was doing something.

Hsieh later recounted that his exposure to the cut-and-thrust of debate in the Legislative *Yuan* (Parliament) contributed to his success in negotiating with Chen Chin-hsing. His experiences as a political dissident and defender of his own wife in a court of law gave him empathy for Chen's feelings.

"I was a political prisoner before," Hsieh was subsequently reported as saying. "So I knew exactly how Chen felt about the law. And I decided to sneak religion and karma into the discussion," added Hsieh, a practicing Buddhist. He said that this was part of the tactic he used to break down the psychological defenses of the armed criminal.

Hsieh's wife You Fang-chih had been accused of accepting fraudulent payments in a shady Buddhist cult scandal, but Hsieh had successfully defended her in court and cleared her of all charges. After the hostage crisis had ended, Hsieh was reported as saying that as a man whose wife had been wrongly accused, he could relate to Chen Chin-hsing's agony.

While the earnest discussions between Chen, Chang and Hsieh progressed, "Madame Chen" noticed that Christine looked bored. She suggested that they pick up the empty cartridge cases littering the house.

Christine got a bag, and the two of them collected shells. First they moved around the little group of negotiators and then they looked behind the couch and chairs, inside the flower pots and in the corners. Unaware she was tampering with evidence, Christine steadily and systematically filled the bag. Then they moved down the stairs and into the lounge, picking up the brass casings as well as flattened, spent, lead bullet heads. When they were finished, Christine sat down to count them. There were seventy-six cartridge cases in the bag.

The conversation between Chen and Hsieh was conducted with little emotion. However, at one stage Chen asked his wife to say something. She began describing, with graphic demonstrations, treatment she alleged she had received at the hands of the police (translated to Anne by "Madame Chen"). She showed how they had kicked her in the vagina, administered electrical shocks to parts of her body and forced her to sit naked on a block of ice as well as on a chair with protruding nails—to get her to confess that she had been an accomplice in the kidnapping of Pai Hsiao-yen.

Her words and actions incensed Chen, apparently hearing these details for the first time. He jumped up and waved his pistols about threateningly. The infuriated criminal shouted and grimaced as if in physical pain. Hsieh restrained him, talking earnestly and calmly to reassure Chen. Anne, frightened by Chen's sudden display of anger, was very grateful for Hsieh's presence and his firm, calm actions.

Chen quieted down, as Hsieh continued speaking to him in an earnest tone. Hsieh later said that he told Chen that he needed to stay alive in order to face his adversaries. Chen's dark countenance brightened. He fell to his knees in front of Hsieh and again bowed himself to the floor.

The hostage-taker's behavior perplexed Anne and Christine. Why such great reverence for someone who must surely be representing the hated authorities in these negotiations? The fortune-teller explained: Hsieh was one of the country's foremost lawyers who championed the oppressed, and he had promised to represent Chang Su-chen at her appeal trial.

Anne understood then, but she felt a vague uneasiness. This explanation implied that Hsieh was not speaking on behalf of the authorities. So what had happened to the negotiations? Anne could hardly ask Hsieh or this "Madame Chen." And she did not want to alarm Christine by sharing this nagging doubt with her.

It was time to pray again and ask the Lord to restore peace to her mind and lay the doubts at rest. Jesus was in control of the situation, and He would carry us all through. Silently, as she sat in front of the computer on one side of the room, Anne prayed. Then she felt a warm assurance spread throughout her being.

Frank Hsieh was leaving. She looked up and said goodbye to him. It was after 3:00 P.M.. Hsieh had talked to Chen for nearly two hours.

Anne and Christine again found themselves with Chen,

his wife, and the enigmatic fortune-teller "Madame Chen." Just who could this strange but friendly woman be? Why had she been allowed by the police to enter the house with Chang Su-chen?

Frank Hsieh subsequently explained that the *nom de plume* "Chen" was used because it was a very common Chinese surname and he wanted to keep her identity secret. This indicated that she was known to Hsieh. Yet, the police allowed her to enter the house with Chang Su-chen. Apparently she was known to them also. She was rumored by some newspapers to have high contacts with the police, and Frank Hsieh himself described her as someone who has "a very good relationship" with the police. Other sources described her as a friend of Chang Su-chen, and this was how she introduced herself to Anne. Just whose confidante was she, though?

In her letter to the *Liberty Times* on 23 November 1997, "Madame Chen" claimed that her husband had approached the Criminal Investigation Bureau and the Police Administration to request that she be allowed to accompany Chen Chin-hsing's wife into the house. Her husband believed she would be able to save the situation. She explained that she and Chang Su-chen had agreed on a secret code to use during discussions, and that their whole purpose for entering the house was to bring about the safe rescue of the hostages.

"Madame Chen's" role remains unexplained to us. She said in the newspaper that from time to time during the negotiations, she would contact the Director General to keep him abreast of the situation inside and to request that they not do anything outside to raise Chen's suspicions.

She also confirmed that Chang Su-chen had not discussed her alleged torture at the hands of the police before Frank Hsieh arrived in the house. She said that before Hsieh left the house at 3:00 P.M., Chen had said to him, "After you came in here, I made a decision. I am going to come out and face judgement by the law." At this, Chang Su-chen broke down and cried.

This was a measure of the confidence, reverence and gratitude Chen held for Hsieh, but it did not reflect a final commitment on the part of the criminal. Events were to show that he needed more assurances before he would be willing to surrender.

Nevertheless, according to "Madame Chen," the very fact that the authorities had allowed Frank Hsieh to see him when he had requested it, had restored to Chen a measure of faith in the authorities. He expressed his wonder that after all the bloodshed and terror of which he was guilty, people would still listen to his requests.

When he emerged from our besieged house, Frank Hsieh was met by Chief Hou You-yi, who escorted him along the empty street to the command post. Hsieh crossed the police barrier, then addressed the media in the street.

Inside, Chen and the women again turned to the TV set to watch the coverage which virtually every channel was giving the crisis. Occasionally, the cameras homed in on a motor scooter parked near our house and the commentator would explain how Chen had used it to get to our neighborhood.

Chen laughed out loud and said that, although they had got the story right, they were looking at the wrong scooter. He said he had actually parked the scooter some distance away. They were right that he stole it though, he chuckled.

A short time later, Frank Hsieh returned to the house, this time accompanied by prosecutor Yeh Chin-pao, head of the investigation into the Pai kidnapping and murder case. Once again, they were escorted by the tireless Chief Hou. While the two walked up the steps and climbed into the house through the broken window, Hou waited outside the gate in the street. He looked bored with all these negotiations.

Clearly, he was a man of action. Another policeman sidled up to him and they chatted for a while. The street looked deserted and the neighborhood unnaturally quiet.

Intense discussions took place inside the house. Hsieh later said Chen "was behaving just like an ordinary guy as we sat down and reasoned, but when his hostages were out of sight, his face would change in a flash." The lawyer said these sudden changes starkly reminded him that the man he was dealing with was antisocial and had an extremist personality.

But Anne was encouraged to discover that the man Hsieh brought with him was an official. The tense talks became formal and focused. Surely matters were coming to a head.

Suddenly, Frank Hsieh asked Anne for a packet in which to place Chen's guns. *This is it,* she thought. *He's surrendering.* She went to my study and came back with a carrier bag.

But when she saw that Chen handed over only two of his guns with some ammunition, retaining one gun, her heart sank again. Prosecutor Yeh took the bag and he and Hsieh left, going downstairs and out the lounge window.

The crisis was not yet over.

Together, Hsieh, Yeh, and Hou walked down the street to the command post, conversing seriously as they went.

The dapper, neatly-clad Hsieh rubbed his hands together as he spoke and looked as though his mind was working in a deliberate and concentrated manner with his expression reflecting the direct gaze of a lawyer who knew where his argument was leading him.

Yeh Chin-pao looked glum, grey, and concerned like a good civil servant.

Hou You-yi, wearing his bullet-proof vest, but carrying his helmet in one hand, appeared remarkably fresh in his white, long-sleeved shirt and tie. A faint smile played across his features, and like the outstanding commander that he was, he exuded confidence.

What were spectators to make of this? Both Hsieh and Yeh addressed a clamoring crowd of reporters and photographers beyond the barrier and gave them vague assurances that negotiations were progressing as well as could be expected.

Hou let them speak. For him and his special task force, it was vital that Chen be taken alive; so talking was essential, even if the talking was done by politicians to the media.

Hou's task force was following a lead claiming that the Pai kidnapping had been connected to a powerful Chinese triad criminal group. When Chen's accomplice Kao Tien-min died in the brothel shoot-out, police had found 40,000 New Taiwan dollars (US$1,430) in his pocket, indicating he had received financial backing even while on the run from the police.

A police spokesman told the media that Chen's surrender could help them solve a number of crimes. "All the information would vanish if he died," they said. "That would be a big blow to our anti-crime campaign."

At this time another voice was added to those pleading with Chen to surrender. TV celebrity and mother of the murdered girl, Pai Ping-ping, in a surprise move, now made public an open letter to Chen Chin-hsing. In it she said that the international scale of the hostage crisis made her feel terrible, and she urged Chen to "stop hurting the land in which he had grown up." She also promised to help him receive a fair and open trial by volunteering to work with the media and by keeping an eye on police and prosecutors if he released the hostages. Whether these promises had any effect on Chen is not certain.

Back in the house, Christine was by now beginning to feel the effects of almost two days and a night without sleep. She found the negotiation process tedious and boring. It did not involve her. She gathered the blankets and pillows pushed to one side on the floor, and made up a bed for herself. With Zachary gone, she had no one to play with, so she lay down and slept.

Later, Frank Hsieh returned alone to the house. He sat in the TV lounge speaking to Chen for some time, while Anne kept herself busy at the computer. Eventually, Hsieh came across the room to Anne and told her that Chen had agreed to let Christine go. He explained that she would also be released, but that there were some technicalities which Chen wanted clarified, and that she could only go when these had been ironed out to his satisfaction. Perhaps a further thirty minutes or an hour would be required.

With mixed feelings, my wife went over to Christine, who lay sleeping on the floor. She was immensely relieved that Christine would be able to get out and felt excitement at the thought that her whole family would now finally be safe. But would she see them all again?

She woke Christine and told her to dress warmly – she was being released!

"What about you?" Christine asked, without hesitating.

"I'm not coming with you right now," Anne replied. "They want to sort out a few more things, and I'll come as soon as they are finalized."

Christine, totally unconvinced, gave a typical response. "I'm not leaving if you don't come with me. I'm staying right here with you!"

It took quite some talking on Anne's part to persuade Christine. Only when Anne and Hsieh gave her the strongest assurances that it would be half an hour, or at the most an hour, and then her mother would rejoin her, did she reluctantly consent to go. Christine slipped upstairs and put on a warm windbreaker. On her return to the TV room she said goodbye to Anne and, her spirits now rising at the thought that it was all but over, she was escorted by Frank Hsieh down the stairs and to the shattered lounge window. It seems that Hou had been waiting downstairs in the main lounge, because he followed Frank Hsieh out the window. Finally, Christine climbed through and was helped to freedom by Hou You-yi. It was 4.30 P.M..

Outside, there was an audible buzz from the media on the surrounding rooftops and balconies. There was no mistaking who this was, climbing out through the broken window. Ever since her drawing of the heart and her decision to return to her mother after talking to the policeman in the street, all of Taiwan was talking about "Ku-lis-teen" (as the radio and TV commentators pronounced her name).

Now the cameras clicked and whirred as the commentators excitedly told their expectant audiences of the little heroine's release. As Hou accompanied her out into the street, they were met by other police, smiling broadly, and the whole group began the walk up to the command post and the clamoring crowd of reporters.

I think this was the first inkling Christine had of the literal overnight-celebrity status that she had achieved. As they walked, the police officers asked her how she felt and congratulated her on the courage she had displayed. Smiling and a little bemused at all the unexpected attention, she chatted to them with the normal self-confidence she always showed when speaking to strangers.

A few paces behind came Hou You-yi and Frank Hsieh, talking earnestly.

Suddenly, three figures moved forward from the street in front of the command post. First came Wouter Badenhorst, then Jacolene Spangenberg, and behind them came my faith-

ful driver, Jimmy Chuang. Wouter spread his arms as he approached. Christine recognized him, she rushed into his arms. As they embraced, my daughter's emotions spilled over and the tears began to flow. She was free and alive and with friends! The two of them held each other tightly, and continued walking down the street. Christine wiped her eyes. Jacolene was there. Jimmy came up to join them and walked along calmly beside them with a serious expression on his face.

Christine's release.
(Photo: Fan Lee, *The Journalist*)

173

Outside the command post, a minibus waited. One of the policemen herded Christine straight into it and got in with her. Wouter and Jimmy joined her, while Jacolene remained behind to be on hand should Anne be released. As the bus drove off, it had to move through the crowd of waiting reporters and photographers beyond the barrier. They mobbed it, and pursued it along the street as it moved away. Looking out the windows, Christine got her first taste of the *papparazzi*.

As the bus disappeared into the traffic, the media people turned back to the barrier where they spotted Frank Hsieh and accosted him. He gave them an impromptu interview, skillfully combining his experience as a lawyer with that of a politician to provide some tantalizing insights into what was happening. He repeated Chen's demand that his wife and brother-in-law be guaranteed a fair trial by the government, adding that Chen had said he would not release Anne until he had received such a guarantee. Hsieh also told them that he had agreed to represent Chen and his family in litigation.

About this time an over-enthusiastic spectator among the hordes in our neighborhood that day met with an accident of his own. The young man, apparently very anxious to get a ringside view of the release of the hostages, or perhaps even a final gun-battle, clambered onto a high wall outside one of the nearby houses. He slipped, lost his balance and tumbled to the street below, breaking his left leg on impact. Looking embarrassed, he was evacuated by the stretcher-bearers who were waiting in case more hostages should be injured. He ended up on the same floor as I, a few wards down the hall, in the Veterans' General Hospital.

Watching the TV in the hospital, we all gave a cheer when Christine emerged. But I felt a stab of fear in my heart. Where was Anne? Why had he not released my wife? By then, our pastor Bill Martin was sitting next to me. Chris Dippenaar interpreted what Frank Hsieh was saying during his interview, explaining that Chen had agreed to let Anne go, but he needed a few more assurances first. My heart went cold and my faith began to waver. Would I never see my wife again?

Bill took my hand and began to pray to Jesus. He prayed for Anne, for Chen, and for me. I sensed the power of the Holy Spirit in the room with us. My doubts seemed foolish now as I again rested in the will of my Saviour.

Mericia left her faithful vigil at Melanie's bedside and hurried to the casualty entrance downstairs, where she met Christine, Wouter and Jimmy as they de-bussed. Mericia and Wouter grabbed our little girl and formed a protective screen in front of her as they marched through the press of media people who surged forward to photograph and interview her.

They only partly succeeded in shielding her. Microphones and camera lenses were thrust at Christine, and she was asked interminable questions. She warmed to this sudden fame, though, responding with a smile and telling them that Chen "was really nice to us" and that "he didn't want to hurt us."

When asked about her mom, she confidently replied that she would be out within half an hour, and told them that Anne was amusing herself by playing computer games!

Wouter tried in vain to keep the media at bay, smiling at their persistence. Eventually he, Mericia and Jimmy got Christine into an elevator and brought her up to the ward. I was overjoyed to see her, and she rushed in to my bedside and hugged me. We chatted for a while. She reassured me about Anne, bubbling over with naïve confidence that it would very soon all be over. Then she greeted all the other people in the ward who she knew.

Christine and her friend Lindsay then prayed and sang Christian choruses together as they rejoiced over her release. Matthew took them down to the Burger King restaurant in the foyer of the hospital. Inevitably, she was recognized. People spoke to her, and Matthew noticed microphones being surreptitiously sneaked closer. He quickly whisked the girls away and back up to the lounge next to the ward.

Inside the ward, once all the excitement over Christine's release had subsided, Jimmy spoke to me. He had safely delivered my daughter to me, but his task was not yet over.

"Okay, Colonel," he stated. "I go back now to wait for Muflow." That was his linguistic corruption of the Afrikaans word "Mevrou" (Madame or Mrs), and the name by which he always respectfully but affectionately addressed Anne. Tears sprang to my eyes as I handed him Dr. Kao's packet of medicines, telling him to give it to Mevrou when he saw her. As he walked out, I shook my head. I was incredulous at his calm constancy in this crisis. Wouter too, returned to the house to await the release of Anne.

Downstairs, at about 6:12 P.M., Matthew had again tried to slip out for a Coke. It was his great addiction which he was satisfying, and having bought a tin of the soft drink, he turned back to the lift. But he was spotted by lurking media and cornered in the corridor. He found himself again giving an interview to several TV stations as spokesman for the family, Coke in hand.

While Matthew fielded the questions of the media on my behalf, I witnessed a heart-wrenching scene on television. Pai Ping-ping, the vivacious mother of the murdered Pai Hsiao-yen, was interviewed and asked to give her opinion of the hostage crisis. Sobbing and weeping, the bereaved mother expressed her continued aversion towards the hostage-taker and condemned his actions in strong terms. The television station showed flashbacks of her lovely daughter before the kidnapping and brutal murder, as well as shots of her flower-bedecked, Chinese Buddhist funeral.

I shuddered. These images brought home afresh the fact that the man holding my wife was a cold-blooded murderer.

16

▸Armed Only With Love◂

CHRISTINE HAD BEEN WRONG about Anne playing computer games. She was in fact conversing with the outside world through e-mail. Anne sat at the computer somewhat awkwardly, as she had to sit in the low, soft armchair because Chen had put her computer chair into his barricade of the stairs leading up to the bedrooms.

She found a message from Johan Schronen, crime reporter at the *Cape Argus* newspaper in Cape Town. Somehow, this enterprising journalist, a stranger to us, had managed to trace our e-mail address. She told him that Christine had been released, that Frank Hsieh had assured her she would be escorted out within the next hour, and she confirmed that she had spoken to me on the phone and that Melanie and I were doing fine. She ended off by assuring him that all had been calm and relaxed for most of the afternoon.

Schronen phoned the local radio station, *Cape Talk,* with the news, and as he read her e-mail message over the air, Anne's brother Arthur heard it. He immediately contacted Schronen, delighted by the news, and asked him to send Anne an e-mail greeting from her family. The message cheered

Anne at a time when she was beginning for the first time to feel despondent.

Almost two hours after Christine's release, despite all the promises, it still seemed that Anne was no closer to following our daughter to freedom. But my wife's practical, optimistic nature soon rose above the circumstances. Recalling that her cats had not been fed since the previous day, she informed "Madame Chen" that she intended going downstairs to the kitchen to see to the needs of her pets.

The fortune teller looked surprised. This could hardly be a priority in these circumstances, and she must have found the request somewhat incongruous, but she interpreted it to Chen. She showed even greater surprise when the gunman nodded understandingly. He was no longer taken aback by the unusual behavior of this inscrutable Occidental woman he had captured. This captive had her own ideas and refused to be intimidated by his reputation or his actions. He accepted this and developed an odd form of trust and confidence in her.

Nevertheless, he was taking no chances, so he insisted on accompanying her to the kitchen, and watched with a mildly puzzled expression, gun in hand, while she called the cats and set out their food and some milk and fresh water on the floor. Two of the cats responded, the third seemingly still too frightened by the previous night's shooting to put in an appearance. The chore completed, Anne and Chen returned to the TV room where his wife and Madame Chen were talking.

Frank Hsieh arrived back in the house at 5:50 P.M.. He immediately began discussing matters with Chen. Anne paid little attention to the talking which she could not understand. But it was later claimed by Hsieh that this was when he had placed a new cassette into the tape recorder which Chang Su-chen was using to record Chen's conversations, and that he kept the tape which he had replaced. Hsieh used this tape later to counter accusations made by some authorities that his involvement had delayed the conclusion of the crisis.

While Hsieh was inside the house, Chief Hou, who must have accompanied him to the window, walked slowly back down the street to the command post. His demeanor revealed nothing—no concern, no agitation, no frustration. With the renowned Asian patience he was waiting for the drama to play out, not allowing himself to get into a frenzy over things he could not control. As he entered the command post, he passed Wouter Badenhorst in the street. Night had fallen. Wouter paced slowly to and fro under the street lights, hands in his pockets and staring at the ground. He too could do nothing but wait. The drama entered its second night.

In the hospital, I was far less calm and collected. An announcement came on the television that Chen would be surrendering in thirty minutes. I counted the minutes to my wife's release, only to hear that the surrender had been delayed by another twenty minutes. This pattern continued from about five o'clock in the evening for almost three hours. The tension built up steadily and I found it difficult to lie still. The nurse brought in a machine for exercising my bandaged leg. But I couldn't take my eyes off the TV. Chris Dippenaar interpreted the reports and the writing in Chinese characters that appeared on the screen.

The document containing Chen's agreement with the authorities was shown to all of Taiwan, so that Chen could himself see that it was being publicly aired on television. The prosecutor had promised that he and his colleagues would probe deeper into all evidence relating to the alleged involvement of Chen's wife and others. Chief Hou You-yi had agreed to reinvestigate the charges against Chang Su-chen, her brother Chang Chih-hui and Chen's friend Chou Huo-jung. It had also been agreed that they would be retried in the light of whatever new evidence might emerge from these investigations. Frank Hsieh announced that Yeh Yao-peng, a member of the Control Yuan (a parliamentary body), would investigate the alleged police torture of Chang Su-chen.

The agreement was not what concerned me. I just wanted

to see Anne set free. Bill Martin prayed with me again, and I sank back onto my pillows calmer, but not yet at peace.

Sometime after seven o'clock, Chen demanded to speak to TVBS general manager Lee Tao. In the course of the telephone conversation, Chen apparently railed against the endemic corruption of the police in Taiwan.

"We need to change the entire police system," Chen is said to have fumed at one stage, "because they cannot be allowed to torture innocent people."

It would appear that he announced his readiness to surrender and come out, but only if he was met by Hou You-yi, whom he said he "could trust."

During this time, Hsieh had left Chen and he came across to where Anne was sitting at the computer. He told her that Chen had not yet decided whether to give himself up or to commit suicide. He said that Chen and his wife wanted to discuss this matter and that he would be leaving for a short while in order to give them the opportunity to do so. He then went downstairs and, it seems, again went out through the window.

Anne did not take this news well. So many times now her hopes had risen; she would just begin preparing herself to walk out of the house and join her family in safety, finally putting this nightmare behind her; but then her hopes would be dashed again. Now, as Frank Hsieh left, she felt the tears spring to her eyes. For a moment, she felt lonely and deserted. But she knew that this would not do. The Lord was still with her. She could not allow circumstances to get the better of her.

"Don't be so stupid!" she muttered to herself disdainfully. She wiped her tears with the back of her hand and turned to the computer in a supreme act of will.

Just then "Madame Chen" came over and explained that Chen had not seen his wife in seven months and that they wanted to be alone together for a few minutes, because they did not know whether they would ever see one another again.

However, because of Anne's importance as a hostage, she would have to remain with them, although she herself would be leaving for a while. She asked Anne to please grant them as much privacy as possible under the circumstances; then she followed Frank Hsieh downstairs and out of the window.

Anne understood, and turned back to her computer. She was not going to let this be another setback to her morale. She had taken a grip on herself now, and she was ready to see this thing through to the end. Behind her she heard Chen and Chang conversing in low tones in the darkness. She concentrated on her screen, checked her e-mail, and read about our crisis on the Internet.

Anne received a fax from the president and president-elect of the "Welcome to Taiwan International Club," a club for wives of diplomats. It read:

> *Dear Anne,*
> *We all love you and pray for you. Keep your faith and*
> *courage. Romans 8:28. 'And we know that all things*
> *work together for good to them that love God, to them*
> *who are the called according to His purpose.'*
> *Love, Athenia Kuo and Shirley Hu.*

The message buoyed her spirits immensely. She wondered why she had allowed herself that momentary lapse of control. There were clearly so many people praying for her, the whole situation simply had to be safely resolved very soon.

A few minutes later, Chang Su-chen called to the people outside, and Anne heard them entering through the window downstairs. Apparently, Chen's wife had told them that he was now ready to surrender.

In the hospital we did not know this. On TV a time had again been announced for Chen's surrender—7:30 P.M.. Again the hour had come and gone with no sign of captor or captive. I was beginning to feel almost beside myself. Then we saw four people on the screen, climbing through the lounge window into our house. The second one appeared to be a woman, and the last one was Chief Hou You-yi.

Coming up the stairs into the TV room were Hou, Frank Hsieh, "Madame Chen", and someone else whom Anne assumed was another police person. The crisis had reached its finale.

As the group approached, Chen and his wife turned to Anne. Chang Su-chen put her hands together and both she and Chen thanked their hostage. Anne looked at them for a moment in bewilderment.

"Why on earth are they thanking me?" she thought. Then it dawned on her. They were thanking her for respecting their humanity; for granting them a few moments of intimacy.

In that instant Anne saw them for the first time for what they were—two lost sinners whose lives had been ruined by their sin and whose sin had ruined the lives of many others. She saw them as God saw them—a pathetic, frightened pair, held in the unrelenting grip of sin. Chen Chin-hsing, the merciless killer who had terrorized a nation, had flaunted the law, and who had defied both police and politicians, now stood before this gentle mother whose husband and daughter he had shot and whose family he had held at gunpoint for a night and a day, but who was armed only with love—the love of Christ.

Anne saw in her mind's eye a picture of Jesus sitting down to eat with tax-collectors and harlots and she knew that He would have also invited these two to join Him.

Reaching out to Chang Su-chen she gave her a hug. Then she turned to the somewhat pungent Chen.

"Whatever happens," Anne said to him, "remember that God loves you."

Then she took the dirty, dishevelled and dumbfounded ruffian in her arms and embraced him. When she released him and stepped back, Anne saw tears running down the cheeks of Chen and his wife. Her words, and this scene, were what greeted the disbelieving group which had arrived to arrest Chen. At least one of the four was so incredulous at what they witnessed that this person subsequently told the story to the media. Every TV channel, radio station and news-paper in Taiwan took up the story and repeated it all over the island.

The fortune teller "Madame Chen" stared at Anne aghast. She could not comprehend Anne's act of love, and blurted out at her: "You are the God!"

"No," replied Anne. "I'm just the messenger."

But, there in our TV lounge, the harsh reality of the law dealing with a criminal now had to take its course. Chen turned to Hou and handed him his remaining gun. Hou asked Anne for a packet. She quickly retrieved another plastic car-rier bag from my study and Hou placed the gun inside it. Chen emptied his pockets of the unused ammunition with which they were still bulging and this was also thrown into the bag. It was later reported that he still had 157 rounds on his person.

Hou then snapped a set of handcuffs onto Chen's wrists as the captor-turned-captive held his hands out in front of him. Hou wanted to leave, but Anne now pulled a stunt on him which I could have warned him would happen.

"Hold on a minute. I need to fetch something," Anne said, and she darted upstairs to our bedroom. "I won't be long."

So, while the world waited with baited breath for the notorious rogue to emerge, Anne delayed everything in order to powder her nose! Practical to the end, Anne did not want to face cameras unnecessarily scruffy. She slipped on a clean jersey and combed her hair. And since it might be a while before she could return to the house, she collected a handbag and quickly filled it with a few items. Then she rejoined the group downstairs.

However, if Chief Hou and his entourage thought that they could now emerge from the house, they were mistaken. With a disarming smile, Anne delayed them yet again.

"I need to see to my cats," said Anne quite nonchalantly and slipped downstairs into the kitchen to set out an extra supply of cat food and fresh water in their bowls.

"Okay," she called out cheerfully. "All set. We can go now."

That there were hundreds of reporters, photographers, and government officials waiting tensely outside the residence concerned Anne not a bit. No moment was too great for my wife. Perhaps some of the married men in the group understood!

At last they were able to move down the stairs and to the front door. It was the first time that the door had been used since the crisis had begun. Anne was the only hostage who walked out the door; the rest of us had been carried or had climbed through the bullet-riddled window. Camera crews on the rooftops and balconies sprang into action. The door, pockmarked with bullet holes, began to swing open. Unable to restrain the media at the barriers in the streets the police shouted in vain as people surged through. Police cars were parked, together with an ambulance, one behind the other, outside our gate. A massive police motorcycle escort had been formed up in an adjoining street for the previous two hours or

(Photo: Fan Lee)

more. Now, just before our front door opened, the police donned their helmets, mounted their machines, pressed the starters and revved the engines.

TV viewers all over the world saw Chen emerge onto our porch, his wrists handcuffed in front of him, his wife, with bowed head, clinging to his left arm. They were flanked by Hou and another policeman. Behind them came Frank Hsieh and "Madame Chen," while right at the back was Anne.

But in my hospital ward I was watching another channel. They only picked up the group as they came down the outside steps and through the gate, and they focused on Chen and his wife.

Chen Chin-hsing and his wife Chan Su-chen are led out of the house by Chief Hou (left) and other officers, after Chen's surrender. (AP Photo/Yao Chih-ping, PictureNET Africa)

I saw no sign of Anne. While there was a general hubbub from the people in the ward with me when they saw Chen, my only concern was for my wife.

"Where's Anne?" I called out, lifting myself almost out of the bed and craning my neck ridiculously as if I wanted to see behind the TV set. "Why can't I see Anne?"

Bill restrained me, and Chris answered that she must be there, just out of sight. The crowds of photographers pressed around the police who attempted to hold them at bay in front of our house.

Camera flashes illuminated the gateway in the dark as Chen walked out, his head held high and looking straight ahead. Hou, still wearing his helmet and with his left hand on Chen's shoulder, held the packet containing the gun and ammunition in his right hand.

As the police and others crowded around, Chang was taken away from her husband and he was quickly and firmly placed inside the back seat of the nearest police car, flanked on both sides by a policeman. Chang was similarly guided into the car behind him. Still I could see no sign of Anne. That sense of frantic helplessness again rose within me.

The lights on the police cars flashed as they moved forward. First a car full of policemen; then another, with Chen's poker face visible in the back; next a third, presumably with Chang Su-chen in it; fourth was an unmarked civilian vehicle; and bringing up the rear was a minibus. The cavalcade of cars moved along the street and around the corner, sirens blaring, to where they linked up with their waiting police motor cycle escort before disappearing into Taipei's terrible traffic. It was all so quick and smooth, almost an anticlimax.

As they left, a crowd of media milled in the street in front of our house and the ambulance moved through them towards our gate. Then, quite suddenly, the cameras homed in on Anne. There she was, moving through the crowd toward the ambulance and smiling broadly. My heart leapt with joy.

"There she is!" I yelled, in unison with the others in the ward. "She's okay! Praise the Lord! Oh, thank you, Jesus!"

It was 8:54 P.M.. She had been held hostage by Chen Chin-hsing for twenty-four hours and forty-four minutes.

Struggling through the crowds, Anne climbed into the ambulance, helped by Jimmy. They were followed by the ubiquitous Wouter and Jacolene who now finally felt they could leave their post. As the doors closed behind the four of them, photographers literally mobbed the ambulance. Slowly the vehicle drove off, leaving the crowds wandering aimlessly around the street and lots of police standing in our tiny garden. Then the crowds began to thin and the TV showed the police starting to withdraw and the command post being evacuated by officials.

Everyone gathered around, some holding my hands, others laying hands onto my back as I bowed my head in that hospital bed and gave thanks to God for delivering my family from that dreadful experience. My friends—my Christian family—joined me in praise to God for His faithfulness.

In my mind, all I could see was that radiant smile which Anne had displayed as she emerged from her ordeal of almost twenty-five hours. It was the smile she had been smiling the first time I saw her. It was the smile I had fallen in love with more than twenty-six years earlier. I sank back onto my pillows to await the arrival of my wife. I felt like I was waiting for our first date.

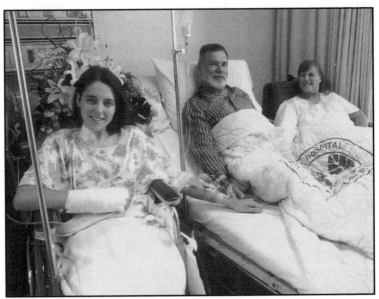

Melanie, Mac and Anne (still smiling) in hospital the day after Chen's surrender. (AP Photo/Hsieh San-tai, PictureNET Africa)

17

‣After Shocks◂

WHEN ANNE AND I AWOKE on the morning of Thursday 20
November 1997, our story and our pictures were splashed
across every newspaper on the island. The drama had elicited
such interest, that some papers produced whole editions with
no other news in them. Reporters everywhere in Taiwan
clamored to get interviews with us and well-wishers queued
in the hospital corridors to see us.

The hospital and our friends kept the media at bay for a
few days until we had worked out the many personal issues
that needed attention. Later, when we did grant interviews
with police and media, Chris and Johanna Dippenaar, as well
as the ever-present Ina van der Schyff, interpreted for us. Ina
moved into the hospital and personally nursed us throughout
the time that we were confined.

When Jacolene brought my briefcase, I pulled out my
business diary and telephone book, glad to finally have the
phone numbers to contact family and friends in South Africa.

It was early morning in South Africa and our call woke
Shona. Anne and I were overjoyed to be able to talk to her, but
it was immediately apparent she felt resentful because it had
taken us so long to contact her.

Only then, with growing horror, did we learn what an ordeal our child had endured because of the failure of my superior officer to keep her informed. In the months ahead, this oversight was to strain our family relationship like it had never been strained before. Already, we could sense the deep hurt in our daughter's voice between the sobs of relief. She was so grateful that we were safe, but why had we ignored her through all of this? Her resentment was understandable, particularly in view of the fact that the media in South Africa was giving major coverage to all of us who had been held hostage and even to Anne's mother, sister and brother, yet no one seemed to acknowledge Shona's existence.

The commodore did call from Pretoria to inform me that we could all come back to South Africa to rest and recover from our ordeal. I laughed at this. Reminding him that I had to close down my office in the next six weeks and terminate South Africa's official military relations with Taiwan as tactfully and inoffensively as possible, I turned down his offer. How he thought I would be able to take a holiday at that crucial stage was beyond me.

The question of psychological treatment arose. During the war in Angola, we had introduced a program of psychological "defusing" for soldiers who had come under hostile fire for the first time. No such program existed during my first years in combat, but I survived many years of intermittent war, without noticeable psychological damage. My concern now, however, was for my family. They weren't trained for terrifying gun battles.

Though the hospital had psychologists, they didn't speak English. They produced an American IQ test for each of us to do. I didn't think that made much sense.

Then Chris Dippenaar told me of a Christian psychologist named Wendell Friest who was a Lutheran missionary from America. His services were used by the missionary community. He offered his services free of charge. He was a jovial, relaxed man who allowed us to talk through our experience without frequent interruptions. He was quick to tell us that he felt we had all come through the ordeal remarkably well, and as a Christian he understood when we gave the glory for this to God. He did warn us, though, that sometime in the future we could experience delayed reaction to what we'd gone through. The most positive sign he identified was that we were all willing to speak about what had happened and were not attempting to block it from our memories, despite Melanie's reluctance to open up to a stranger like him.

The missionary community had again come to our aid.[1]

Mericia came to see me in the hospital. "If anyone tries to tell you that you didn't lose a lot of blood, let them come and talk to me," she said, pulling a wry face. "It took me ages to clean up that mess." She got the job of cleaning blood off the sofa, the floor, the carpet, and under the carpet.

Christine's original bag of seventy-six spent cartridge cases were supplemented by almost as many recovered by the forensic experts. Jacolene found a further twelve and when Anne and I finally packed up all our belongings a month later, we found ten more. All in all the police subsequently admitted to us that they estimated that Chen had fired about 160 shots inside the house. They were not as willing to tell us how many they had fired back at him.

We were relieved to hear that the fancy CD player we had bought in Hong Kong had not sustained any bullet "wounds" when it was toppled onto the floor. However there was one bullet hole through the back of a sofa and another through one of the carpets. Bullets had pockmarked the lounge walls and riddled the front door. The aluminum window frames were bent, twisted and jagged. Virtually every window in the lounge, TV room and study was shattered. Police bullets which had holed three study windows had gone on to penetrate the roof. Overturned pot plants had left soil scattered everywhere. One of the chandelier lights had been shot out. My exercise rowing machine had two neat holes in it.

People were calling our house the "house of horror."

Eyebrows were raised after Anne was discharged from hospital, and she, Christine and Zachary simply moved back in without any qualms. Anne's strong sense of realism, absolute rejection of superstition, and unwavering focus on her home made her decision quite understandable.

Relief spread across the island that the crisis had been resolved and the man who had terrorized Taiwan had been apprehended.

Then, like the after-shocks of an earthquake, recriminations began, and we were caught in the middle.

Pai Ping-ping, the grieving mother of the victim of the tragic kidnapping and murder had made her feelings clear throughout the hostage-taking. Interviewed often on television, through a veil of tears and a voice choking with emotion, the popular entertainer Pai had urged the authorities not to submit to the demands of the criminal. Later it became clear that they were doing just that. The authorities had secured Anne's release and Chen's capture only through agreeing to revise the case against Chang Su-chen, her brother and his friend. Pai called it "the kidnapping of justice."

In an open statement to the press, Pai denounced the way the crisis had been handled. Saying that Chen's "directing" of the drama could trigger a series of such crimes in the future and that it served as a very bad example for ROC citizens, she claimed that it was actually the people of Taiwan and the judicial system that had been held hostage.

"Who is the real victim in the whole episode?" she asked. Chen's trial had not even begun, but according to her, the public had already "lost half of it."

Pai's supporters castigated the authorities for making concessions to a self-confessed murderer. Many people felt that the deal officials made with Chen had set a precedent. They feared other criminals would follow suit and press their demands in similar fashion. Pai Ping-ping said that the deal conveyed "the most negative message" to society.

"The judicial system's dignity has collapsed overnight,"

railed the actress.

The media launched their own tirade of criticism. The *United Daily News* concluded that the lack of internal stability epitomized by Chen's crime spree and culminating in his international hostage-taking would cancel out all of Taiwan's diplomatic efforts. The *China Post* felt that, because South African diplomats had been involved, obstacles could arise in future relations between Taipei and Pretoria. A *Reuters* story depicted the media in Taiwan as news-hungry and insensitive to the ordeal that the hostages had been suffering. Some analysts thought the media's unscrupulous coverage of the hostage drama further damaged Taiwan's image abroad. Even Foreign Minister Jason Hu reportedly admitted that the events around the hostage taking "will certainly affect our national image."

Others were quite scathing about the manner in which the police had been slow to take charge of the situation, allowing everybody to mill around and get in the way. Police credibility took a further knock when the Director General admitted that there had been major shortcomings in the force during the investigation of the case. Reports of police cover-ups shook the public. Conflicting reports abounded. While some police sources told the media that Chen might have been involved in as many as thirty robbery and rape cases in the Chungshan District over the preceding seven months, the precinct itself denied any knowledge of most of those cases.

The sensational claims of Chang Su-chen that she had been tortured by police during interrogation continued to fuel speculation in the media. Officials remained adamant that there was no indication that Chang Su-chen had ever been tortured and that she had never mentioned it during earlier questioning by prosecutors, even when she had been specifically asked about it.

Chen's claim that Pai Hsiao-yen had choked to death on a moon cake was rejected by the Panchiao prosecutors who said that the autopsy revealed that there had been some kind of pressure applied to her neck, but her stomach was found to be empty. They had found no evidence that she had been raped.

Prosecutor Shou Chin-wei scorned accusations that the police had retarded negotiations with Chen during the crisis and thereby jeopardised the lives of hostages. He claimed that Chen had been ready to surrender at 4:00 P.M. to the Chief Prosecutor and Chief Hou You-yi; then he suddenly requested to speak with Frank Hsieh.

As for the accusations by Pai Ping-ping and her supporters that the judicial system had been prostituted by the deal made with Chen to gain the release of the hostages—even Chen Chin-hsing, who may have committed many heinous crimes, still had certain rights as a citizen of the ROC. Just like any other member of the public, Chen was entitled to request that the case against his relatives be reviewed. Since new evidence had come to light, there was nothing unusual about granting permission for the case to be reopened.

The head of the Taipei District Court, Liu Jui-tsai, pledged that all suspects in the murder case would be given a fair trial. Public Prosecutor General Lu Jen-fa also later confirmed that Chen's petition and its granting were perfectly legal and would not bias the outcome of any trial.

The expatriate community expressed understanding that this had been a one-off occurrence and that in comparison with most countries around the world Taiwan was a pretty safe place to live. Taiwan could not, however, expect to be isolated from the rest of the world when it came to violent crime. Many saw this as part of a world-wide phenomenon. Most of the people in Taiwan were relieved just to know the notorious Chen Chin-hsing was finally behind bars.

Nevertheless, some elements in the expatriate community evidenced a very deep anger. Perhaps the feelings of helplessness and outrage that something like this could happen to foreigners living in this country were too much for some people to contain.

An American living in Taipei wrote a letter to the *China*

News saying he was repulsed by the trend of blaming society for a criminal's actions. He saw it as a typical example of embracing the criminal and ignoring the victim. This would convince criminals to blame society rather than face responsibility for their actions. He claimed that America's crime rate was caused in part by viewing crime as justified because of the criminal's hard life.

Others complained that the press had depicted Chen as being good to his hostages. One bitter correspondent railed against my family for "perpetuating the myth that this man cared for them and their lives," explaining our delusion by saying that we had to convince ourselves that he was decent because the alternative meant admitting that we were held by a crazed, maniacal killer. This, she conceded, would have been tantamount to giving up all hope of survival. But other people should not be fooled.

I wondered whether she thought that we had been fooled by the gunshot wounds that Melanie and I had suffered?

"This man is no hero," one correspondent wrote. "He has no shred of decency in his character. Chen Chin-hsing is a cold-blooded killer and rapist. That's all. He is not a hero. He deserves no sympathy, no good wishes, and certainly no good press." Harsh sentiments these, and ones which I could understand. Yet their simplistic tone indicated that the writer in her anger had completely missed what was being said about Chen. What he had done was not being lauded. Rather, the system that had produced him was being questioned.

Anne and I knew Chen was evil. We also knew that Christ had died that evil people might be saved from their sin. We knew we had not been able to do anything to earn the grace of God. Neither could Chen. But he could accept Christ's sacrifice, just as Anne and I had done; and his heart and life could be changed. God loved Chen Chin-hsing, though He hated his evil deeds. Could we as Christians do any less?

Some newspapers reported that we had established a special bond with the man during those few hours of terror, and that we were in fact condoning the wicked acts of which he had been accused. It was almost as if some people felt we had come under the spell of this man and had been brain-washed by him. The fact that Anne hugged him just before he left the house, was cited as evidence of this.

When I found out about this disturbing tendency among our detractors, I went to great pains during subsequent media interviews to set the record straight. Aware of the extreme reluctance of the popular media in South Africa and else-where in the Western world to publish anything pro-Christian for fear of offending people of other faiths, I had little hope that my explanations would appear in print.

I was wrong. Both newspapers and television happily repeated what I told them, verbatim. A front page article in the *China Post* quoted:

> 'Christ died for our sins. So we know that God hates sin, but loves sinners,' Colonel Alexander said. 'Even this man (Chen), God loves him too. Our family hates the sins he committed. But that doesn't mean we don't love him. God loves him, so who are we not to love him.'

The *China News* front page article quoted my words as follows:

> 'All we were trying to do was show the love of Christ for him. In Christ, you don't hate the sinner, you hate the sin. And God hates sin. Christ didn't die for the good guys, Christ died for the bad guys. Christ died for harlots and tax-collectors, he died with the criminals and granted them eternal life on the cross. People here seem to have difficulty understanding this concept.
> 'Throughout it all we saw him as a bad guy. Our concern was for him as a sinner. The man must bear the consequences of his actions. . . . But that doesn't make him any less of a human being.'

The *China News* described Chen as neither a celebrity nor a monster, but rather as "a product of the system, and there are many other examples of the system's unwanted residue likely to empathize with his plight."

Certainly an element of Taiwanese society was strident in its condemnation of "the system." Barely minutes after Chen Chin-hsing and Chang Su-chen had been hurried away from our house in a convoy of police cars, a team of activists had converged on the street in front of our gate. Wielding a megaphone, they had loudly proclaimed that Chen was merely the victim of an increasing decay in society and its schools. The gradually-dispersing crowds of onlookers took with them these thoughts, leaving behind them the littered streets of Cherry Hill.

The head of a group advocating educational reform was reported as saying that society was forcing people like Chen Chin-hsing to commit crimes, that he was a victim of the failure of families and schools.

At a press conference in Pretoria the day after Chen Chin-hsing surrendered, ROC Ambassador Loh I-cheng said, "The case (involving Chen Chin-hsing) was probably the biggest crime case Taiwan has had in forty years. It's the first time in our history that people went to the streets to protest about a crime."

While some of the media condemned "the system," others blamed the authorities. The Chinese-language *United Daily News* of 20 November strongly criticized the treatment meted out to Chen by the ROC government. Many innocent victims of crime, the editorial claimed, rarely receive the kind of special attention and exceptional treatment focused on Chen, thus raising doubts about the impartiality of the judicial system.

Others commented on what they regarded as disturbing tendencies by the authorities to use Chen's claims for their political gain, as a way to boost their sagging images. It was almost ironic that the media had so much criticism to level at others, since their role during the hostage crisis was the most controversial of all.

TVBS General Manager Lee Tao argued that the media had complemented the police efforts rather than interfering in their actions. The controversial TTV anchor, Tai Chung-jen vindicated his two-and-a-half hour interview with Chen by stating that he saw himself as under an obligation to extract as much as possible from the criminal so that both the police and the public could have access to the information.

While my view of what had happened was deeply subjective, I gained the impression that the safety of the hostages had been a very low priority for the media and that it was almost as if they were bent on manipulating the situation to increase the chances of a spectacular climax to the crisis. That, after all, was what would sell copy! Doubtless the media would regard my cynicism as unwarranted and bigoted.

An officer with the Taipei Criminal Investigation Division said, "Chief Hou You-yi had to call the media and plead that they stop using the line so that he could talk with Chen." He also criticized the media for turning Chen into a folk hero. "There is no such thing as a criminal hero," he said.

Of course, the Robin Hood image has always been a popular one with the public who could readily identify with a renegade who represented the oppressed and who was forced to do bad things though he retained pure motives. Certainly the media seemed to be fostering such an image of Chen despite the fact that many of his victims had been every bit as oppressed as he claimed to be.

One lawyer pointed out that the media appeared to be confusing "the people's right to know" with "freedom of the media." The former, he said, should have limitations set so that society does not end up paying too high a price for this privilege. "The key," he said, "is social responsibility; the media needs to understand the rules of the game."

Hsiung Chie, news department director of the World College of Journalism and Communication blamed the rapid, almost overnight, liberalization of the media in Taiwan for the free-for-all which had taken place. The transition from a tightly-controlled media in a military dictatorship to a free media in an open democracy had caught the news people unprepared and immature. Chie felt that many reporters hadn't enough experience or training to talk to a criminal of Chen's perfidious character.

Others raised questions. What if the media had prevented negotiations by monopolizing the line? What if they had angered Chen, causing him to take drastic action?

Within a few days, the National Press Council in Taiwan organized a forum to urge the media to voluntarily refrain from what it described as "irresponsible" journalism. The council, a private group, drew up a pledge which contained restrictions on activities by media persons which might harm hostages and kidnapping victims or inhibit the actions of the police.

Most reporters were prepared to sign the pledge, though some doubted their publishers would accept a code of ethics. Others remained defensive and adamant that the police had contributed to "inconsiderate" coverage by the media because they had neglected to provide clear guidelines for the media.

Still others offered thoughtful self-examination. Richard R. Vuylsteke, senior editor of the *Free China Review*, writing a guest column in the *China News*, struck such a pensive note. He referred to a seminar held in Hong Kong three days before Chen had burst into our home. The seminar was attended by two dozen foreign correspondents, bureau chiefs, editors and journalism professors from the Greater China region.

Examining the future of the media in Hong Kong and on the mainland, a stark picture emerged of increasing control of the media, of less and less access to government officials and of declining professional and ethical standards in journalism.

In comparison, Vuylsteke pointed out, Taiwan had shown a commendable progression of its media towards a democratically acceptable standard since the lifting of martial law only a decade ago. Taiwan's media was in no danger of being again subjected to censorship, and government officials seemed to crave as much media coverage as possible. However, Vuylsteke warned, the hostage crisis had shown that the media in Taiwan were still giving insufficient attention to responsibility and matters of professionalism and ethics. Gently chiding his fellow journalists he wrote:

> A free (and freewheeling) media is essential to the health of a democratic society. But that freedom also entails tremendous responsibilities, including high standards of fairness, accuracy and, yes, common sense. Access to leaders — and to criminals — should not be abused. And a carefully measured degree of self-censorship should be imposed, especially when safety, propriety, and common decency are involved. . . .

His words of wisdom reminded me of the lectures I gave my children — after they had committed some misdemeanor. I had a sneaking feeling that the Taiwanese media would pay about as much attention to his lofty words as my children did to my lectures!

Not all that emerged from the crisis resulted in recriminations. There was universal praise for the role of Police Chief Hou You-yi. Certainly Hou's performance improved the tarnished image of Taiwan's police.

Hsieh told the media that Anne's loving attitude towards Chen Chin-hsing was one of the deciding factors in bringing about a peaceful resolution of the crisis.

The media also complimented the government for its avowed intention to get rid of the guns circulating in the underworld in an effort to "wipe out crime." In Taiwan there had always been a ban on the ownership and employment of firearms by all except the police and armed forces. This ban had been effective during the years of draconian control under martial law, but more recently this had changed. Democracy, a growing human rights awareness, and an apparently corrupt element in the law enforcement agencies had contributed to this change. Criminals seemed to have little trouble obtaining guns and were increasingly using them in their unlawful activities, sometimes shooting quite indiscriminately. To me, this was a clear indication that the banning of controlled, licensed firearms had little effect on gun-related violence. The Chen Chin-hsing case was a classic example of this.

The wave of public sympathy for Chen Chin-hsing which was apparent after his surrender produced its own recriminations and accusations. The media reported that Chen's long telephone interviews and his apparent concern for his wife had aroused many people's support. Junior high school students were writing essays on his valor and gallantry, and intellectuals were comparing him to traditional tiger-killing folk heroes.

This outraged the authorities. Minister of the Interior Yeh Chin-feng whose predecessor had been forced to resign as a result of the perceived breakdown of law and order of which Chen Chin-hsing's antics had been a significant part, was offended at the fickleness of the public.

"I hope people in society at large can get a clear understanding about Chen Chin-hsing," she reportedly said. "That kind of behavior is not worthy of sympathy and should be condemned by society."

Chief Hou You-yi made it known that he wanted to demythologize the mystique of heroism that had come to be associated with Chen. "Actually, Chen Chin-hsing isn't a real man," he was reported as saying. "He only knows how to rape women."

Human rights groups saw Chen's exchange of hostages for a guarantee that his wife would be given a new, fair trial as an indictment of the country's "barbarous" legal system.

Many accusations had been thrown at Taiwan in the past for alleged human rights abuses. These were said to have been perpetrated on political dissidents during the decades of martial law on the island. The last such dissident had been freed in 1990, some years after the lifting of martial law. Now, however, it was increasingly being alleged that suspected criminals held in detention were continuing to be abused in the same way. Chang Su-chen's allegations gave impetus to these claims. Some went so far as to say that torture was regularly countenanced by the judicial authorities and was not restricted to the police.

Lawyer and human rights leader Chiu Huang-chuan stated, "My organization has received too many complaints about torture to take it lightly. Most have come from those under a life sentence or death sentence, as they are the ones unable to publicize the abuse." These human rights abuses in the criminal justice system, he said, were an enduring legacy of martial law.

The human rights groups felt that Chen's many years of experience at the hands of the police and judicial system had left him with no faith at all in being treated fairly by them or in obtaining fair treatment for his family. To his mind, his only chance was to force their hand through an act of terror.

Lawyers were never present during police interrogation of a suspect. Ultimately, it was the word of the suspect against the word of the police interrogators, and judges invariably believed the latter. Bent on emphasizing that Chang Su-chen's case was not the only one in which forced confessions had been elicited, the human rights groups produced an elderly man who described himself as "the father of Hsiao Yang-jen," a prisoner. His voice quivering with emotion, the old man told how his son had been tortured into making a confession.

"I tried to take the police to court," wailed the old man. "But the case kept getting overturned. What can an ordinary person like me do?" His plight, perhaps more than anything else, explained why the "ordinary person" in Taiwan could identify with Chen Chin-hsing. It was not that they approved of the criminal's deeds; but rather, that they knew what he was up against.

Chan Wen-kai, a lawyer and official of the Association to

Reform Civil Law, admitted that some legal guidelines did
exist to protect the rights of suspects held in police custody,
but that these were often simply ignored. These practices were
encouraged by the public's hard attitude towards criminals,
claimed Kuo Hung-chih, of the Humanistic Education
Foundation.

"There is a consensus in society that it is okay to hit a bad
guy," he said.

Taiwan might be a democracy, but it seemed to have a
long way to go before it would embrace a culture of human
rights. Again, as these things sank in, I thought of my own
country's bad record in this regard.

Women's groups, too, reacted to the Chen Chin-hsing saga
now that the horrid bogeyman was safely in police custody.
On 25 November, women legislators and representatives of
women's organizations came out strongly at a press conference in support of those women who had been rape victims at
the hands of Chen. Various speakers emphasized the fear in
which many women lived and condemned the government's
failure to implement policies to protect them from people such
as Chen.

Tai Mei-yu, the wife of the secretary-general of the ruling
party, lamented that women did not feel safe anywhere,
whether at home or at work, during the night or the day. She
complained that the government should regard the safety of
women as a priority.

One traditional Chinese practice which did nothing to
prevent the perpetration of these violent crimes, but at least
eased the financial repercussions they had on victims, was
that of awarding the victim some recompense.

"Consolation money" is a concept which is common in
Taiwan's society. For someone who has suffered damage or
loss, even though that loss cannot be necessarily replaced by
money, it is customary for the authorities to present some
financial token of consolation as a gesture of sympathy. On 23
November the Interior Minister met with the parents of the

nurse who had been murdered by Chen and Kao in the triple homicide in the plastic surgery. Yeh handed over an envelope of consolation money from the government to the grief-stricken mother.

The envelope contained a check for 200,000 New Taiwan dollars (about US$7,000). The next day, the Kuomintang's Department of Cultural Affairs Director handed the family a second check for 100,000 New Taiwan dollars (some US$3,500). The murdered girl's mother, Huang Ying-tsai, made it known that although they were not well off, they regarded the consolation money as more than what they needed and that they wished to donate part of it to some charitable organization.

Some people told us that as foreigners injured in a violent crime in Taiwan, we were entitled to "consolation money." Melanie, who was the most traumatized by the hostage-taking, felt quite strongly that we as a family should be entitled to some form of recompense for what had happened to us. She went so far as to say that we should lay claim to the reward which had been offered for Chen's capture.

I differed with her, saying that as diplomats I did not see how we could be offered "consolation money" because our experience was no more than an occupational hazard. As for the reward, I felt any number of people had a greater right to it than we did. I also felt it would be inconsistent with our Christian witness and both vulgar and mercenary for us to make noises about money. Lastly, as a diplomat I would not be permitted to accept foreign money without the permission of the South African Department of Foreign Affairs.

Nevertheless, I told Melanie that she was not a diplomat and that she was entitled to approach the authorities if she felt that strongly about it. She was in two minds, as she saw any financial recompense as a means of paying the considerable debt she owed on her studies at university. Eventually she decided to leave it. We were never approached at any time by anyone from the authorities regarding "consolation money."

18

▸Celebrations◂

Overnight, our home on Cherry Hill became a tourist spot for the people of the city. Our normally-tranquil residential area was jammed with cars full of visiting Taiwanese anxious to see the "house of horror" which had featured so prominently on their TV channels.

While Jacolene Spangenberg busily assessed the damage inside the house the day after Anne's release, she came downstairs to find a Taiwanese family absorbed in examining the lounge and taking photos of one another posing in front of bullet holes! This, despite the presence of a police guard at our front gate. Jacolene chased them out of the house.

Even as much as two weeks after the crisis, we would encounter families arriving in the street outside our home on a Sunday afternoon, equipped with plastic deck-chairs. Setting up their seats in the road, they would recline in comfort as they pointed out to one another the various parts of our residence and discussed the events of our night of terror. An innovative form of weekend recreation and celebration!

It hardly seemed coincidence that only days after the hostage-taking we had the opportunity to celebrate our thanks by observing with American, Taiwanese and international friends the traditional American holiday of Thanksgiving.[1]

In the hospital, every one of the hundreds of letters of support which we received prompted us to again give thanks to God for using this event as a testimony of His love.

The Governor of Taiwan Province wrote to express his shock and regret. He said in part, "As events unfolded, it was impressive to observe the strength that you and your entire family displayed. . . . You are an excellent model of a Christian family contributing to the community, displaying courage and faith in God, and forgiving the wrongdoer."

Even the higher echelons of government in Taiwan acknowledged the role of God in our experience. It did concern us that the perception was still that *we* had shown strength. What strength we had we drew from Christ, but at least this Source was being given credit, however indirectly.

The commanding general of the ROC Sixth Field Army, Victor Teng stated, "I think that you and your family have taught a lesson to all the people of Taiwan, let(ting) us know what is courage and what is the true love of Christianity."

We were surprised to receive messages from people we had never met. A United States citizen from Hsinchu wrote, "Your calmness and clear testimony for Jesus Christ have inspired me. I praise God for your faithfulness! God is glorifying Himself through this and you are His instruments."

Canadian missionaries Dr. Nicholas G. Krushnisky and his wife assured us that their churches had been praying for us and that they would "continue to pray that our Lord Jesus Christ heal you and restore you to complete health."

A Baptist missionary, Andrew Peat, working on the outer island of Penghu in the Taiwan Straits, made contact with us. He served with the local Prison Fellowship Ministry. He saw an opportunity for us to use what had happened to us as a witness for Christ, encouraging us to speak in churches and to make a gospel video. Both of these we did.

The Good Shepherd Sisters Social Welfare Services in

Taipei wrote, "This is to tell you that we are very proud of you. . . . Many people are touched, especially by Christine offering the Heart of Jesus and the drawing 'Jesus loves you' to Mr. Chen. . . "

A message reached us through several Chinese Christians about a Zimbabwean missionary in Hong Kong, the Rev. Peter Anderson and his wife Geralyn, who had written to friends in Taiwan:

> You know, Geralyn and I were moved that day to specially pray for the South African family. Somehow we felt the Lord was working and we prayed that if they were believers the Lord would keep them safe and use them to be a testimony to the man, still at that time holding the wife, foster child and daughter. We were relieved all ended peacefully. It was so good to get your e-mail and indeed the Lord had moved us to pray when He did. Probably many others were praying.

What particularly touched us was that we learned that Geralyn Anderson was very ill at the time from chemotherapy treatment for cancer, yet she found time to pray for us.

A heart-warming letter arrived from a Christian family in Kaohsiung who told of how they had prayed for us right through the night of the hostage-taking and how they believed that it was the love that our family showed towards the kidnapper that dissolved his ferocity.

A girl called Lina told how she had been praying for Chen's soul for a long time before he had taken us hostage. When she and her co-workers heard about the hostage-taking they prayed for us, interceding with tears through the night. Lina thought that perhaps God allowed our ordeal to take place so that Chen's soul could be saved.

We stood in awe of what He was doing, yet we knew that we didn't deserve any of the praise that people were heaping on us. We were profoundly humbled that God should have chosen us as a means to accomplish His will. And we were beginning to see something of what His will was for Taiwan.

One Taiwanese family wrote, ". . . We ask God to forgive us, for we judged instead of loving. . . .Your family are a real miracle to our society (which needs to be healed by the Gospel). I believe your words have influenced our people so much — they are the best witness for God. . . ."

A former ROC diplomat, Lee Yu-tang, wrote,

> . . . on this Thanksgiving Day that Americans in their exemplary way annually observe world wide, I wish to express my deepest thanks for your Christian testimony. . . . As official ties between our two countries come sadly to a close, you have rendered an indelible contribution, not only to the friendship that has existed between our peoples, but you have also demonstrated the peaceful role that the military can play. Above all, you have given magnificent witness to the truth and reality of Christ Jesus' teachings.

Cosmic Light, a Christian missionary and publishing organization wrote to tell how they had prayed for us and for Chen Chin-hsing in tears and how they knew that the Lord loves him too. They wrote in anguish of their continued prayers for the salvation of Chen, for the comfort of the mourning families of those who had perished at his hands, for the voices of rage raised against him to be quieted. They were waiting, they said, for the soul of a prisoner on death row to turn to God.

My heart was wrenched by a hand-written letter from a young boy called Paul. He wrote of his unhappy home life, of a father who was seldom home and who was a stranger to him and his brother, never speaking more than three words to them. He told of an embittered mother whose life was filled with anger and resentment at her unfaithful husband. How lucky we were, he felt, to be the sort of family that we are; his family was terrible, and he had always wanted to have a dad like me.

It began to dawn on me that the media were portraying us as an ideal family in which the relationships were perfect. The thought frightened me. We were so far from perfect. Indeed, our family experienced all the stresses and strains of normal domestic life. Anne and I had our occasional disagreements; Melanie could be single-minded and manipulative to the point of producing friction; Shona was sometimes headstrong and determined to the point of causing a family uproar; Christine's strong personality clashed almost daily with Anne's rigid sense of right and wrong; my own dedication to soldiering and obsession with my vast personal library and books in general often made me a distant figure to my family, and my periodic outbursts made me quite unreasonable. Yet here was a young boy who imagined that all was sunshine and roses in the Alexander household. This made me feel awful.

Yet, as I pondered this I realized that when our family faced a domestic upheaval or disagreement, we would pray together. We conducted family prayers and Bible reading in the evenings as often as possible. Our custom was to observe these short, quiet times together, listening to what God had to say and concentrating our thoughts and prayers on others.

Quite clearly the young boy Paul did not experience these things in his family life.

Like a revelation it came to me that we were not perfect in any way, but our roughness was smoothed out by the love of Christ, which gave us a great peace despite our imperfections.

Even as we celebrated answered prayer, loving friends and family, how very important it was to remember people all around us who are hurting and oppressed and don't feel that they have anything for which to be thankful.

Finally, we were heartened by the many messages from military attachés around the world. Colonel Dirk Hanekom, wrote from Bonn, Germany, quoting one of the South African women working in the embassy there as having commented about Anne: "*Now there is a woman with characteristic South*

African pluck — our own modern Racheltjie de Beer."[2]

Koos de Wet, a very correct military man, faxed a letter from Lilongwe, Malawi, with the understated heading: *"UNPLEASANT EXPERIENCE WITH CRIMINAL."*

The message that told me the crisis was over, was the one I received from Colonel Malcolm Kinghorn, South African High Commission Defence Adviser in Ottawa, Canada. Malcolm and I had parachuted together on many occasions, including an historic jump from a Second World War German Junkers Ju-52 trimotor aircraft. For several years we had made an annual pilgrimage together to watch a schoolboy rugby tournament in Johannesburg at which we would cheer our respective schools. His brief fax message to me now held a significance which he knew only I would understand. It read simply:

"Dear Mac. Bravo Zulu[3]. Malcolm."

Chief Hou You-yi visiting Anne, Christine, and Mac in hospital.
(Photo: Chris Dippenhaar)

19

▶Confusions◀

On Saturday 22 November 1997 police chief Hou You-yi surprised us with a visit. Neatly dressed in a suit and tie, smiling broadly, and brimming with friendliness and quiet confidence, the likeable Hou breezed into the hospital ward and greeted Anne and me with a polite handshake.

Speaking through an interpreter, he enquired after our welfare and expressed his satisfaction that we all appeared in good health.

I thanked him very sincerely for the role he had played in the drama, telling him I regarded him as one of the bravest men I had ever encountered.

Chief Hou smiled disarmingly and made light of the compliment, quickly steering the conversation in another direction. He displayed the attributes of a true gentleman.

For about twenty minutes we chatted affably, and after photos had been taken, he bade us goodbye and paid a brief visit to Melanie in her ward.

Melanie was still rather dopey from the drugs, but was able to pose with a smile for a photo. I began to realize that Hou was not averse to a little publicity.

His visit was followed by one from a number of junior police officers who wished to take statements from Anne, Melanie, and me.

The next day, Sunday 23 November a Chinese tabloid in Taipei, the *Liberty Times*, published an article about Melanie that purported to be based on information obtained from an authoritative source. Someone brought me a copy in the hospital.

I read it and became very angry. The headline stated: "MELANIE: 'CHEN ATTEMPTED TO RAPE ME.'" Reporter Lu Ping-yuan then proceeded to claim that Melanie had told police the day before that Chen had tried to rape her after he had broken into our house. The report then quoted "medical attendants at the Veterans' General Hospital" as having revealed that early on the morning of 22 November Melanie had woken from a nightmare screaming uncontrollably and that she had been rolling hysterically on the floor.

It was claimed that she "had something to tell the police," and that as Chief Hou You-yi was "coincidentally" visiting our family in the hospital at the time, he urgently called two policewomen to take Melanie's statement.

Meanwhile, Anne and I were reported to have told Hou that after Chen had tied us up, he had taken Melanie to the third floor of the house where he had attempted to rape her. However, the police unexpectedly arrived on the scene "just seventeen minutes" after Chen had contacted them. They opened fire to stop Chen carrying out his barbaric act.

This unbelievably speculative account then went on to say that the police believed that when our family "knelt down to pray, Chen might have mistaken the shadows of the trees for the police" and opened fire, accidentally hitting Melanie and me. It also claimed that Melanie had described to hospital psychiatrists how Chen had seized her by the throat after tying up the rest of us; then taken her out of the living room and tried to rape her. The arrival of the police, however, had prevented him from doing so.

The whole report was utter rubbish; but what concerned me was that the reporter had been able to "quote" police and hospital sources with absolute impunity. Though no hospital psychiatrists had seen any of us, Melanie's surgeon, Dr. Ke Dun-jen had been present when a policewoman had taken a statement from Melanie.

I had agreed to a police request that Anne, Melanie, and I would each give them a statement.

A number of police officers visited us. Anne recognized one of them as a member of the SWAT team who were inside the house during the crisis. Chris and Johanna Dippenaar assisted us as interpreters while the police took down what we told them. The police had made some serious mistakes and I was very anxious that these should not be suppressed, otherwise the next such crisis would be handled no better. But the guys who made the mistakes were not going to record anything incriminating.

My fears proved justified. When I insisted that Chris read what the policemen had written, he confirmed that they were not including everything and that some vital points were being omitted. Johanna, too, confirmed that some of what Anne and Melanie were telling them was being twisted.

Annoyed, I gave the police officers a quick and heated lecture on ethics, refused to sign the statement unless it was written in English, instructed Melanie and Anne not to sign anything and told the policemen and women to remove themselves before I became really angry. Clearly disgruntled, they all departed to report to their superiors.

A day later the fictitious report appeared in the *Liberty Times*. Either the hospital authorities had told the reporter about the police interviews, or one of the police, peeved at my lack of cooperation, was trying to embarrass my family. I consulted with my ambassador, Nikki Scholtz, and he suggested that we discuss the matter with someone from the ROC Ministry of Foreign Affairs. He made an appointment for us to see Mr. Timothy Yang Chin-tien, director of the Ministry's

Department of African Affairs.

When Dr. Ke heard why I wanted to go to the Ministry, he became very agitated. He tried very hard to dissuade me, saying that it would place the hospital in a very bad light. I waved the newspaper article at him, asking him what about the bad light in which my family was being portrayed? He looked very distressed and gave me the assurance that the hospital had had nothing to do with it.

"Put it down in writing then," I exclaimed. But my mind was made up about going to the Ministry.

So it was that on Monday 24 November I sallied forth[1] from the hospital in uniform with my cane, in the company of my ambassador. After hobbling along the long, imposing corridors of the Ministry of Foreign Affairs building on Jen-ai Boulevard we arrived at Mr. Yang's office. The consummate diplomat and an absolute gentleman, it was impossible to be angry in the presence of the erudite, knowledgeable and charming Timothy Yang.

Nevertheless, I proceeded to express my feelings strongly, albeit politely. First I thanked him for all that the Ministry was doing for my family and me as well as for the outstanding medical attention we were receiving at the Veterans' General Hospital. Then I told him that the police had been guilty of certain mistakes during the early part of the crisis and that I had told the highest authorities who had visited me, including the Director General of the National Police Administration what these were.

Next, I gave him the same assurance that I had given the others, that it was not my intention to discuss these mistakes with the media. However, I went on to tell him that I had been highly dissatisfied with the police efforts to manipulate our statements and I was unhappy about certain press reports which seemed to me to have been leaked and which were blatantly untrue. I also expressed strong reservations about the political pillorying of Frank Hsieh which was taking place (he was being accused by the ruling party of political oppor-

214

tunism in his involvement), and that we as a family had no doubts about the critical role he had played in securing the release of Christine and Anne.

Yang knew about the *Liberty Times* report, and agreed with my view, making all the right noises, but explaining that he could not prevent newspapers from writing what they wanted to. I accepted this, but in turn I pointed out that it was not so much what they had written as it was the strong suspicion that I had that the police had fabricated the story and then leaked it. This meant that I no longer had any confidence in the police or in their confidentiality.

When he assured me that the police were doing their utmost to investigate every aspect of the case, I produced what I regarded as my trump card—a plastic bag full of spent bullets, empty cartridge cases, and some unfired 9mm rounds.

"These," I proclaimed dramatically, "were found in my house, under the cushions of the sofa I was sitting on when I was shot, *after* the police forensic experts had completed their examination of the house. I regard such inefficiency as extremely unprofessional and there is no way in which you can expect me to have confidence in such a police force."

Impassively, Mr. Yang accepted what I said, but when he looked enquiringly at the bag, I told him that I would deliver it to the police personally, in my own time, and returned it to my pocket. He accompanied Nikki Scholtz and I back along the corridors to the front door and bade us goodbye.

On my return to the hospital, Dr. Ke presented me with a sheet of paper. I read: "I and all the medical staff and nurses including psychiatrist do not tell any things about the family to the press media. — Dr. Ke Dun-jen, MD."

I felt like a heel. But later I was reminded of the words of the queen in Shakespeare's *Hamlet:* "The lady doth protest too much, methinks."

I was finally discharged from the hospital on Saturday 29 November 1997. We were able to make it a low-profile affair, with Jimmy bringing Anne to fetch me, and with me hobbling down the corridors, leaning on my ash cane. A few hours after my arrival back at home, a reporter from a popular South African magazine (called *You* in English and *Huisgenoot* in Afrikaans) arrived at our home to interview us. There was to be no rest for our family and his visit was a portent of things to come. Franz Kemp, however, was a pleasant and friendly man who wrote a pretty accurate article on our experience.

He was particularly taken by the plaque given to us by Anne's grandfather, which we display prominently wherever we live. Its bold letters proclaim:

> . . . as for me and my house,
> we will serve the LORD.
> (Joshua 24:15, KJV)

In his article, Franz Kemp made much of the fact that, despite the walls of the house having been peppered with bullets, the plaque had remained untouched, spelling out its message above the scene which had unfolded in the house.

▶▶▶▶▶▶▶◀◀◀◀◀◀◀

In preparing the case against Chen Chin-hsing, investigators pieced together the parts of the puzzle as best they could. Chen himself was repeatedly interrogated, as were all the suspected accomplices. Early in the process, Chen denied vehemently the charge that he had cut off the little finger of Pai Hsiao-yen's left hand. He placed the blame on Kao Tien-min, who had died in the gun battle with police the day before our hostage-taking, saying that it was also Kao who had sent the severed digit with the ransom demand to the girl's mother.

Chen was adamant that he did not know the alleged mastermind behind the kidnapping, though he admitted having once met him through Lin Chun-sheng, the first of the kidnappers to die. Police began to question Hsu Chia-hui, alleged to have been Lin's girlfriend and who had hidden the fugitives in an apartment. Nothing was obtained from her, as it eventually transpired that she had in fact been Chen's girlfriend. Chen, it seems, had been quite a philanderer, even while ostensibly happily married to Chang Su-chen.

A number of police precincts in the city and county of Taipei were beginning to connect the notorious criminal to deeds of violence in their respective areas. Other families had been held captive, some for as long as a week at a time, in their own homes, by hoodlums now believed to have been Chen and Kao, during their evasion of the police.

Most of the families had been women and children where no man was living in the house. They had been powerless to resist the heavily-armed thugs, who had broken into their homes demanding food and shelter. Adding to the wild speculation in the media were claims in several Chinese-language newspapers that the trio of gangsters had been responsible for several other kidnappings. Suddenly, Chen Chin-hsing seemed to have been guilty of almost every crime committed in Taiwan in recent months, as well as several which had never even been committed!

Two days after the hostage crisis ended, Frank Hsieh announced that he was preparing to defend Chang Su-chen, as he had promised during negotiations with Chen. He also said that he would form a team to defend Chen's brother-in-law and other defendants implicated in the Pai Hsiao-yen case.

On 29 November, Taiwan had scheduled important local elections throughout the island. Law and order had become a key issue; and it was inevitable that the hostage crisis and the surrender of Chen Chin-hsing would have some impact on votes. The question was, which way would it sway them? The ruling National Party (KMT) could benefit from the peaceful resolution of the crisis and the capture of the country's most-wanted man; but on the other hand, the opposition Democratic Progressive Party (DPP) could receive a boost in voter confidence because of the significant intervention by one of their leaders, Frank Hsieh.

In the election, Hsieh's Democratic Progressive Party

scored an upset victory, gaining many positions from the ruling KMT. It was clearly a backlash reaction to the perceived decline in public safety. But it is in the nature of politics to sway back and forth. There were other issues which lingered darkly below the surface, giving rise to postulations.

Frank Hsieh had returned to his office in Kaohsiung in the south of Taiwan, where accolades were heaped on him for the part he had played in ending the stand-off. Hsieh himself played down his achievements, saying that he only did what was expected of a member of society and that he was responding to Chen's appeal to him for help. But Hsieh was quite clearly a major political asset as a result of his role in the highly-publicized crisis. He had created a very favorable impression on the people of Taiwan.

Hsieh was reported as saying that the police had been hoping for a situation to unfold during the crisis in which the hostages would be released before Chen Chin-hsing turned his gun on himself and committed suicide. "They wanted it that way. Otherwise so many stories would come out: police relationships with the Mafia, gun trafficking, crimes that police have not recorded. I really believe that the police did not want Chen Chin-hsing to live."

As for the statements by Justice Minister Liao Cheng-hao and police chief Ting Yuan-chin that Hsieh had not been needed in the crisis and had in fact delayed its resolution, Hsieh was now quite scornful in his reaction.

"If the police could have handled it themselves, they wouldn't have asked me to go in," said Hsieh. "If I had refused and things went wrong, they could have blamed me. If I went in and somebody died, they could say it was my fault. They needed a scapegoat in case the situation turned sour. It turned out okay, so they said my having been there was unrelated to the success of the negotiations. I knew that I was being used as a convenience by them, and it placed me in a difficult situation. But I did what I did to protect people's lives and for no other reason."

Anne believed him; and so did I.

He next proceeded to rekindle some sympathy for his client, Chang Su-Chen. Marrying a bad guy did not automatically make her a criminal, he said. There could have been all kinds of motives producing her actions of protecting her husband when the police came looking for him. Chang, he said, was currently not being permitted to have a lawyer present during police questioning, and she was still being held in isolation.

"Those in the law stand together and mutually protect each other," he was reported as saying to the media. "It's like that in traditional Chinese culture. Everyone reads daily in the papers that she (Chang Su-chen) has a legal judgement against her, but investigators are not releasing any details, so everybody thinks she is a demon. Any lawyer who defends her will be questioned by society."

Prosecutors announced that they were looking into the possibile involvement of a large gun-running organization. The market value of the firearms and ammunition traced to the three suspects amounted to NT$5million (US$178,572). It seemed highly implausible that they would have acquired such an amount of money unless it had been through some criminal activity, or that they would have acquired the arms unless it had been through a gun-running organization.

Historically, the Western mind has considered Chinese society, with its intrigue and secrecy, mysterious. The role of shadowy crime bosses in government, in business, and even in the armed forces is a matter of constant conjecture. Though I could not prove or disprove any of the stories which tend to circulate about the issues, I find it highly hypocritical to ascribe them to the "mysterious Oriental." Considering the amount of speculation around the alleged roles of the Sicilian Mafia, the Illuminati, the Freemasons and other secret organizations in the West, one wonders what gives Westerners the right to point fingers at the Chinese in this regard.

20

▸Visit To The Prisoner◂

P ASTOR H UANG M ING, National Director of Prison Fellowship Taiwan sent me a letter while I was in hospital. He raised a startling possibility. He suggested that we visit Chen Chin-hsing in prison. His organization was affiliated with Prison Fellowship International, which was founded by Chuck Colson, the fallen — and later born-again — former White House special counsel under President Richard Nixon of the U.S.A..

Anne and I were under so much pressure from the media and various officials, that we had very little time to respond to the hundreds of items of correspondence we received. Close to exhaustion and struggling to keep things together, we did not respond to Pastor Huang's letter. However, his suggestion started Anne and me thinking.

▸▸▸▸▸▸▸▸◂◂◂◂◂◂◂

After Chen's surrender on that fateful 19th day of November, the large convoy of cars carrying Chen and his wife had departed from our house and quickly disappeared into Taipei's teeming traffic.

Chen was apparently taken for questioning either to the Panchiao prosecutor's office or the headquarters of Hou You-yi's special task force at the Taipei County Security Police office in Chungho. Chang Su-chen was returned to Tucheng Detention Centre. The media reported that Chen was immediately interrogated and that the session was recorded on video tape. He was said to have displayed no signs of aggression or agitation. At 1:45 A.M. on Thursday 20 November, Chen was apparently transferred to a single cell at the Taipei County Police Headquarters where he was kept under heavy guard.

At 9:15 A.M. he was photographed when he emerged, handcuffed and wearing a white motorcyclist crash helmet with a face visor, apparently to protect him from any would-be assailant. It seems that he spent the rest of the day in the task force headquarters undergoing further interrogation by Hou You-yi's team. At 5:40 P.M. he was removed to the Panchiao office, and at 6:17 P.M. he was taken to the Tucheng Detention Centre, where his wife was being held. They were now both in prison, awaiting the grinding of the judicial system's wheels.

On Thursday 4 December the wheels began to grind as Chen Chin-hsing's case got under way at the Panchiao District prosecutor's office. Chen was indicted on a string of criminal charges, some of them together with his deceased fellow gangsters, for which the prosecutors recommended the following sentences:

1. Kidnapping and murder of Pai Hsiao-yen in April: death.

2. Motorcycle theft on 5 May: three years in prison.

3. Kidnapping of Taipei County Councillor Tsai Min-tang and extortion of five million New Taiwan dollars (US$178,500) on 6 June: death.

4.   Kidnapping of businessman Chen Chao-yang and extortion of four million New Taiwan dollars (US$150,000) on 8 August: death.

5.   Abduction of three women at gun point and nonfatal shooting of a police officer on 11 August: ten years in prison.

6.   Motorcycle theft and threatening a police officer with a gun on 22 September: three years in prison.

7.   Various counts of robbery: eight years in prison.

8.   Eighteen counts of rape: eighteen years in prison.

9.   Murder of plastic surgeon Fang Pao-feng, his wife and nurse Cheng Wen-yu on 23 October: death.

10. Forcible sexual harassment of Cheng Wen-yu on the same day: seven years in prison.

11. Abduction of two women in central Taipei on 18 November: eight years in prison.

12. Hostage-taking of South African embassy's military attaché and four family members on 18 and 19 November: life imprisonment and life- long revocation of civil rights.

Other charges were added later, but on these main charges alone the prosecution was requesting four death sentences, one of life imprisonment and a total of another 57 years in prison.

The prosecution produced medical evidence that Pai

Hsiao-yen had been beaten to death, and that her stomach had contained no trace of moon cakes or tablets. Chen's brother-in-law, Chang Chih-hui, was also indicted for having sexually harassed Pai as well as for having assisted in her kidnapping and murder. For him, too, the prosecution recommended the death penalty.

At a news conference, Panchiao chief prosecutor Shih Po-liang told reporters that Chen had committed his crimes with "an abhorrent cruelty" which displayed "a total absence of human nature."

The next day, 5 December 1997, Chen's trial began in the Panchiao District Courts.

▶▶▶▶▶▶▶◀◀◀◀◀◀◀

Several members of our church told us they felt the Lord wanted our church to be responsible for taking the gospel to Chen Chin-hsing in prison. One dear friend told us that she felt very strongly that it was Anne and I who needed to bring the message of Christ to the criminal.

At that time we were inundated with requests for interviews by radio, television, and newspaper; two Christian organizations in Taiwan wanted to make documentary videos about our experience; and there were only a few weeks remaining before we would have to leave the country. Anne was preparing for our move back to South Africa, and I was frantically trying to finalize the closure of my office.

We did not realize that many people were praying about our taking the gospel to Chen. One man who was not content to just pray was our friend Ingomar Lochschmidt. He was the unofficial Austrian ambassador, a member of Calvary, and he had a good grasp of Mandarin.

On Monday 15 December 1997 Ingomar phoned me at my office to tell me that he had managed to arrange the visit. The judge who was trying Chen would be holding a hearing the next day and she had agreed to let us speak to him for a few minutes at the court before the hearing began. Would Anne and I be prepared to go along? Chris Dippenaar was willing to accompany us as the interpreter.

Until then, I had thought vaguely how wonderful it would be if the gospel could be brought to Chen. But, knowing the role which bureaucracy played in the Taiwanese government system, and aware of the concept of revenge so prevalent in the society, I did not seriously believe it would be possible for victims to visit such a high-security prisoner. Now, confronted with the real possibility, I was thrilled at this opportunity to show Christian love and forgiveness. At the same time, we didn't know how Chen would receive our visit.

And admittedly I was filled with a strange trepidation — almost a revulsion at the thought of again coming face to face with the perpetrator of so many heinous crimes.

Hiding my fear, I told Ingomar that I was quite happy to go, but that Anne would have to make her own decision about facing the man again. Then Ingomar said that he and Chris felt because Anne had spent the most time with Chen and was the one whom he knew best and seemed to trust the most, that she should be the one to speak to him.

How would Anne react to this request to take the message of the love of Christ to the man who had shot her husband and daughter and terrorized her and her family? The next day, the day of the scheduled visit to Chen, was Anne's fiftieth birthday. She certainly had not planned to spend her birthday in this way. I phoned her at home.

Without a moment's hesitation Anne agreed to the visit. I could hear the excitement in her voice. For Anne, the prospect of anyone with whom she is personally acquainted going to a lost eternity without Christ is always a matter for deep concern. She and I had discussed the whole hostage-taking over the past month and we were convinced that it had been divine intervention that had led Chen to our home. As such, it placed a divine responsibility on us. With an interpreter, Anne would gladly talk to Chen. In two weeks' time we would be leaving Taiwan, so this would probably be our first, last and only opportunity to speak to the man after his arrest.

The next day (Anne's birthday), Ingomar's driver took Ingomar, Chris, Anne, and I to the Panchiao District Courthouse. Ingomar brought a Chinese Bible for Chen, and Chris brought him some Christian literature and a box of Swiss cookies baked by Johanna.

As we travelled, Ingomar explained to us that it was not going to be as simple as we had initially thought. Only the judge of the case could grant permission for someone to see the prisoner, and she first wanted to question us about our motives for wanting to speak to Chen. She would, in any case, only grant us a very brief visit.

We wanted to avoid publicity, and for the visit to take place quietly, without the media knowing. In Taiwan, however, this was a forlorn hope. The TV cameras and journalists were waiting for us at the courthouse. The official with whom Ingomar had made the arrangements had warned that he could not be blamed if the media found out about our visit. They mobbed us as we got out of the car. Fielding the barrage of questions with a terse "No comment" we pushed our way through the media gauntlet.

With my ash cane, I hobbled into the building. We were all ushered up the stairs and the media followed, only restrained with difficulty by the justice officials. I wagged my finger at a particularly persistent TV camera man, angry at the ever-intrusive media. Predictably, that is what was shown on the news that night!

We entered the privacy of a Chinese-style reception room with its large, carved wooden chairs and low tea tables. We were introduced to several judges and other officials, and served tea. Soon Judge Tuan Ching-jung, Chen's judge, arrived. I was taken aback. She was so young.

Once the usual pleasantries had been exchanged we got down to business. With Chris doing the interpreting and Ingomar occasionally interjecting to clarify a point, we explained that we wanted a brief visit with Chen in order to tell him about Jesus and give him a Bible, some literature, and the cookies. They were not particularly concerned about the Bible and the literature, but showed grave suspicion at the cookies. Many questions were asked about them. Evidently they worried that we might be planning to poison him.

Eventually the attractive young judge revealed that the visit we were requesting would be extremely difficult to arrange. However, it would be simpler to do so if Anne and I would be willing to testify in open court. It now dawned on me that we were involved in negotiations. Allowed here on the pretence that we could see Chen, we now understood that a *quid pro quo* was involved. This is an ancient diplomatic principle, and we should all have known better than to expect anything else.

But to testify would mean waiving our diplomatic privilege which could lead to other difficulties in these last two weeks of changing our country's diplomatic status. I knew that the police and the prosecutors had masses of evidence against Chen. Our testimony would hardly make any difference to the final sentencing and I did not want to subject my family to the stresses and rigours of such a high-profile court case on the international stage.

Speaking Afrikaans, Anne and I discussed the matter with Chris Dippenaar. I told Chris that I would not waive our diplomatic immunity. Chris, who had understood all the Chinese discussions, told me in turn that the court representatives would not be prepared to come away from this meeting with nothing. Ingomar was clearly more than a little upset. He felt that the official with whom he had dealt had not been wholly honest with him. The man had never intimated that there would be a return gesture required.

Chris, who had been living and working with Chinese people for ten years, was not surprised by the request.

I remained adamant. We would not testify in court. Chris conveyed my feelings to them, and after some discussion among themselves, they asked if we would then consider being video taped as we answered questions about the incident, so that the videos could be used as evidence in court. I was incredulous, and refused this point blank, as well. What about them audio taping us then?

Again I refused. Anne made it clear that she would go along with whatever I said, as this affected my professional diplomatic status.

The young judge looked across at me. She said something to one of the others and he translated it into English.

"It is with regret that the judge has to tell you that it will not be possible for you to see Chen Chin-hsing. He is a very dangerous criminal and she could not guarantee your safety."

During the course of my military career I had once been sent for "negotiation skills training" which I had more than once put into practice during heated debates with the leaders of stone-throwing mobs. It was time to draw on these rusty skills again. I stood up.

"Tell them that I did not come here to negotiate," I said to Chris in English. "I came to speak to Chen Chin-hsing. If the judge is not prepared to grant me permission to do so, then I have been wasting her time. Please apologize to her on my behalf. We'll be leaving now."

Then I walked towards the door. Anne and Ingomar also stood up while Chris translated. There was a fleeting look of alarm on the young judge's face and she and her colleagues spoke rapidly to each other. Chris called me back and the Chief Justice told me in English that they wished to discuss the matter further. Wasn't there some way we could assist them, even if it was just by recounting to the judge what had happened? It was time for a concession on my part.

"Of course," I replied. "We will gladly tell her anything she wants to know. Provided that there are no tape recorders, video cameras, or court appearances involved."

The judge, who was also standing now, readily consented. Her whole demeanor had changed. For the first time she smiled as she motioned for me to sit down. She sat beside me as I wondered what had happened to the report which I had sent to the Public Prosecutor. Perhaps Taiwan law did not allow him to show it to the judge. Whatever the case, it became apparent that the judge knew none of the details of what had taken place inside our house on 18 and 19 November.

Leaning on the low tea table, I drew a sketch of the house plan on a sheet of paper, and on this we described the events. She listened very attentively, made copious notes and asked many questions, all of which we answered quite openly.

We spent over an hour recounting our story, at the end of which the judge appeared very satisfied. She informed us that we would be allowed to see Chen Chin-hsing to give him what we had brought, but that unfortunately she could only allow us a few minutes. I assured her that a few minutes was all that we needed.

We then set off, following her and the others along corridors, down stairs and eventually into a small courtroom. There were police officers and judicial officials all over, especially inside the courtroom.

"Wait here," we were told, and left standing in the middle of the room. Nearby stood five policemen and eight or nine civilians all dressed in dark suits. Next to me, the judge put on and arranged her court robes. As she did so, she turned to me and for the first time spoke English.

"You are wasting your time trying to tell this man about God. He is a hardened criminal who does not believe in anything."

I was surprised at her good command of English.

"Yes Ma'am," I replied. "I know what kind of man he is. But that is exactly why he needs to know about God's love."

I expected to be taken to a cell to see Chen; but then we heard an awful clanking and rattling sound and the next thing Chen, flanked by two policemen, was led in through a side door. He seemed to be wearing the same checked shirt and slacks that he had had on when he took us hostage. The shirt was not tucked in, but he was clean-shaven and his hair had been cut.

What really brought home to us the reality of the situation were his chains. His ankles were shackled together, enabling him to only take short, shuffling steps and his wrists were manacled in front of him. The shortness of his stocky figure was exaggerated by the two burly policemen on either side of him. Glancing around furtively at all the people as he was led towards us, he looked confused and uncertain. "Like a little boy who was lost," is how Anne later described him.

An official explained to Chen why we were there, and for the first time he seemed to see us and recognize us. Putting his hands together he bowed very respectfully towards us.

"*Hsièh-hsieh, hsièh-hsieh* (Thank you, thank you)," he said.

Hemmed in by onlookers we stood, Anne and me in front, Chris next to us and Ingomar just behind us. The judge had moved across to her bench where she was sorting papers.

We had rehearsed what we would say to Chen, and Anne immediately began. We would literally have only a few minutes, so she condensed the message to make sure he would get the gist of it. With Chris rapidly interpreting, Anne told Chen four things:

1. We have all recovered well and we have forgiven you for what you did to us.

2. God loves you and He will forgive you for everything you have done, provided you repent and accept Christ as your Saviour.

3. You only have one life, so you cannot hope to make amends in a next life. You must do it now.

4. There is only one God, and you can only come to Him through Jesus Christ.

Chen listened eagerly, nodding and bowing as each point

was made. Whether he comprehended or was just being polite, we could not tell. But we were merely sowing the seed. It was the Holy Spirit who would open his understanding.

Barely three minutes had passed, but the court officials became agitated. The man who had explained our presence to Chen looked at me and tapped his watch impatiently. Time was up. The hearing had to begin. I glanced at the judge. She was settling herself to commence with the proceedings. I nudged Anne.

"Give him the Bible," I whispered.

Chinese Bible and literature given to Chen. (Photo: Huang Ming)

Taking the Bible and the literature and the cookies from Ingomar, Anne handed them to Chen, briefly explaining what each was. He had no sooner accepted them than one of the guards took them out of his manacled hands. We were given assurances that he would receive them later. Then he was led away to the dock. Guards hurriedly ushered us out, while those attending the hearing took their seats.

During the arraignment which followed, so reported the media, Chen told the tribunal comprised of the pretty young judge and her assistant that he had taken our family hostage without the intention of killing anyone, and that he had told us as much soon after taking us hostage. He apparently insisted that he committed the crime only to draw the attention of the international media to what he believed was the innocence of his family and to how they had been wronged by police and investigation authorities.

A court official told reporters afterwards that this statement matched the testimony we gave prior to the hearing.

Outside we ran straight into a battery of television cameras and an inquisition of reporters. Elated that we had been able to see Chen, I smiled broadly at the media as we pushed through them.

"No interviews," I admonished the reporters affably.

"Did you speak to Chen Chin-hsing?" demanded a particularly obnoxious reporter shoving his microphone into my face. I paused at the car door while the others climbed in. With a smile and a wink I said to him, "If I answered you, that would be an interview, wouldn't it?" With that I swung myself into the car and Ingomar's driver eased the Mercedes-Benz through the crowd of media and into the street.

A buoyant mood lifted us all as we were driven back through the busy streets to Taipei. Animatedly, we debated the merits and demerits of capital punishment. Anne and I felt that it was scriptural and warranted in certain cases. Ingomar was firmly opposed to the taking of life for any reason; while Chris held strong reservations about the death penalty.

It seems that after our departure from the courthouse the media, reluctant to come away empty-handed, had converged on the official who had accompanied us to the car. He was also the man with whom Ingomar had made all the arrangements for our visit and the one who (we suspected) had informed the media of our visit in the first place. Finding himself the main attraction, he willingly rose to the occasion.

He told them how we had assisted the judge in compiling details of what Chen had done in our home, how we had asked to see Chen and been permitted to do so, what we had said to him (he recounted Anne's four points almost word for word) and that we had given him a Christian Bible. All this appeared on television that night and in the newspapers the next day.

Though we had wanted to keep our visit low profile, it became clear to us that God had other plans. The publicity that it received turned out to be a further witness to the grace of God. Contrary to our expectations that it would produce a negative reaction from the Chinese people, we found a general expression of amazement and respect for what we had done. Even if we had not intended it to be publicized, it was seen by many as a practical example of forgiveness, a concept quite foreign to many people in Taiwan.

Nevertheless, the complexity of the human psyche does not allow for unanimity on issues such as these. Other people saw our actions as pandering to a manipulative criminal. Much controversy had been aroused by the effect that Chen's telephone interviews on TV had had on the populace.

Chen Chin-hsing's saga fostered in the public an awareness of the strange dichotomy in the society that produced him. It was the very dichotomy of human nature. Lin Wan-yi, head of the National Taiwan University's sociology department, explained that decades of authoritarian politics and education had made people prone to characterize others in simplistic terms as either all good or all evil. For me, this observation rang a bell, as I extrapolated it to the transformation occurring in my own country of South Africa.

Lin went on to say that people in Taiwan had thought of Chen as only thoroughly evil before the telephone interviews that occurred while he was holding us hostage. Suddenly they heard some good coming from him and were surprised by it. People couldn't understand how he could love his own wife and son, yet go and kill someone else's daughter. Yet Lin saw this wave of admiration for Chen following the interviews as an emotional reaction that would not last long.

By the time we went to see Chen, Lin's words were coming true. The people had begun to harden their attitudes towards the man Chen, as his evil deeds were constantly highlighted. Hence our surprise that our visit was so well-received by many people.

Newspaper reports generally took a subdued tone about our visit. Yet the *China Post* openly described it as follows (which must have been the way the court official described it):

> 'They gave Chen a Bible as a Christmas gift, and through a local priest they told Chen he could seek forgiveness from God for his sins.'

21

▸The Good-Bye Whirlwind◂

THE **T**AIWAN WE WERE LEAVING was not the same Taiwan we had arrived in less than two years earlier. It was almost as if the very fabric of Taiwanese society had been affected. One writer, Father Daniel J. Bauer, described it sadly as "a sense of loss in the air, the loss of something akin to innocence that I doubt we'll ever know again. . . . (It) begins with a realization that with the taking of hostages, on some new level we have now come of age here in Taiwan."

Like our own land of South Africa, Taiwan was a country in transition. In some small way, our traumatic experience had been a part of that transition. But we were unable to fully comprehend this at the time. During our last month in Taiwan the filming of three television documentaries about the hostage-taking required us devoting a great deal of time to being endlessly interviewed for each one. Cameras followed us around at home, at work, and at church. They filmed us eating meals, talking to one another, driving in the car, and walking up the stairs. Having let ourselves in for this, we discovered that no part of our personal lives was sacrosanct.

TVBS, the major network in Taiwan, made and aired a

half-hour program and an hour-long panel discussion of the events by journalists. The Baptist Mass Communication Centre in Taiwan made a video for their *Gospel Profile* series which they intended to use for outreach and as part of their training for missionaries deployed in the Far East. Overseas Radio and Television (ORTV), a Christian organization, produced a half-hour program.

Anne appeared on a live phone-in TV program called *Studio Classroom Call-in Rally*, aired on Christian television in Taiwan, North America, and New Zealand.

Taipei's ICRT radio station's Jeffrey Mindich came to our home to conduct a lengthy interview with each of us which was broadcast in five episodes. Dramatically titled, *A Nation Transfixed – A Family United*, it attracted many listeners.

Our first and most heart-breaking farewell was the inevitable one we had long expected. The time had arrived for little Zachary to go to America and be united with his real family at last. We had only been helping Melanie look after him while his adoption was finalised. Now the paperwork had been sorted out and the children's home had agreed to use an American friend from our church, Myra Stinson, to accompany Zachary on his flight to the U.S.A.. Zach would live with his adoptive parents in Milwaukee.

The day before he left, Anne, Christine and I stayed at home, quietly enjoying Zachary. While Anne worked in the kitchen, he scooted about in his walking ring, poking his fingers into drawers and cupboards, chasing the cats, and eating Oreo cookies, covering his face with crumbs.

Anne wrote Kevin and Rosie (Zach's adoptive parents) a letter as if it were from Zachary saying how much he was looking forward to finally meeting them. It also told about his sleeping and eating habits, likes and dislikes, routines and developmental accomplishments. Together with a photo album of his five months with us and a few favourite toys, the letter was placed in a tiny backpack in the shape of a cow. That afternoon we handed the backpack and a little suitcase of clothes over to our friend Myra, took some final photos, and for the last time hugged the little boy who we loved so much. Our tears flowed freely as Myra carried the confused little mite out the door. (The next year we would travel to Philadelphia for Melanie's wedding, visit the U.S.A. for the first time, see historical sites there, see Zachary again, and meet his new, loving parents.)

For now, we simply stayed too busy to be melancholy. We had to sort out the bureaucratic nightmare of having our cats flown back to South Africa and quarantined. Melanie and I had physiotherapy sessions to attend at the Veterans' General Hospital. Anne had to take delivery of a little Opel Corsa car we had ordered for her to take back to South Africa, and of course the interviews and speaking engagements continued non-stop. The day of our departure loomed ever closer.

But then came a departure we were not expecting. Melanie, who had been deeply affected by our experience with the gunman, was finding it difficult to cope with all the publicity and pressure. She felt a strong need to get away.

The young reporter Michael Letts, who had been seeing her daily since the hostage-taking, had finished his internship and returned to America. Melanie became depressed and quiet. Then she received an invitation to spend Christmas with the Letts family in America.

We were more than a little taken aback. Anne and I had looked forward to spending a quiet, healing time together as a family at Christmas. But we could see that Melanie needed to get away, so once again I dug deeply into my pocket and we said goodbye to Melanie at Taipei's Chiang Kai-shek International Airport on Sunday 14 December 1997. She flew east and arrived at the airport in Philadelphia to be met by Michael's parents and a stunned and disbelieving Michael, who had not been warned of her arrival.

Melanie had an incredible holiday with them, touring Philadelphia, Washington D.C., Gettysburg, and Boston, where Michael would be working. After an exciting and memorable month, Melanie returned to South Africa, flying three-quarters of the way around the world.

Meanwhile, the Chienan Elementary School in Taipei invited Christine to share her experience with Taiwanese school children, to help make children aware of danger and to help them learn to deal with crises.

Christine, a little reluctant and shy from all the publicity, said she wanted her family with her at the event.

"We want to give you each a set of Chinese clothing," they told us, so that we would always remember the Chinese. Two charming young ladies from the King Car Education Foundation met us in central Taipei at an exclusive clothing shop. At this, Christine began to show considerable excitement.

The Taiwanese ladies allowed us to choose from a wonderful variety of colorful and attractive traditional Chinese clothing. Anne, Christine, and I each selected outfits, and were measured, so the tailors could produce perfect fits.

A week later, at the Chienan Elementary School, the principal, as well as officials from the King Car Education Foundation, and the inevitable bevy of media people met us. We climbed several flights of stairs to the school hall, as I struggled valiantly to keep up with my family and our hosts.

In the hall a wildly-excited crowd of one-thousand-odd school children burst into song. They sang a specially-composed anthem to Christine in Mandarin. This show of affection for our daughter stunned us. A huge silk sheet hung as a backdrop to the stage. On its center was a massive copy of the drawing Christine had made in front of Chen Chin-hsing during that night of terror. A heart encompassed a cross on which was written "I ♥ God." Christine's name was emblazoned across the top of the sheet, and the children in the school had signed their names on it.

Formally welcoming us, the principal related the story of our hostage-taking to the audience of children, and we were then presented by the foundation with gloriously-wrapped parcels containing our Chinese national dress. While the children resumed singing, we were led backstage where we quickly changed into the new costumes.

Resplendent now in our distinctive attire, we re-emerged on stage to thunderous applause from the audience of elated school children: Christine in a smart, emerald-green, two-piece suit; Anne in a crimson tunic decorated with a silver-and white-orchid pattern, and a black skirt with crimson beading; myself with a plain, purple Mandarin tunic.

Speaking from my heart, I told the school that we would never forget the warmth and support we had received from the people of Taiwan during and after our ordeal as hostages. Seizing the opportunity to give public thanks to our many benefactors, I explained that despite the terror of our frightening, nightmare experience, words would never be able to convey our appreciation for all the letters, cards, gifts, faxes, e-mails, and phone calls—often from strangers; all supporting and encouraging us.

I told them that of all the happy memories we would take home to South Africa, the most lasting would be the warmth, friendliness, and hospitality of the people of Taiwan. I was grateful this time to see many newspaper reporters and TV camera crews, as they ensured that my message was spread throughout the island.

Christine then addressed the children and shared with them how to react in a crisis and how to remain calm. I was surprised to see the normally self-confident Christine hesitate. She seemed almost intimidated. It was another sign of the toll the publicity and media pressure was taking on her. She expressed herself well, though.

Christine sat on the floor of the hall with children all around her and reporters interviewing her. Anne and I were also surrounded by media on the stage. They asked us endless questions, mostly about how we felt about Taiwan, how we felt about leaving, and about future relations between South Africa and Taiwan. I called on whatever diplomatic skills I might have developed to speak a lot and yet say nothing. All the time we were being interrupted by squealing children, excitedly asking for our autographs. We must have signed hundreds of books, cards, and little bits of paper thrust into our hands.

Then Christine was presented with an honorary student certificate. We were all given more gifts, and then the fifth-grade children circled us and sang a joyful Christian hymn in English. Obviously they had spent many hours practicing it during the weeks before this event, and it brought tears to our eyes. Christine was given a tape recording of the school singing "Christine's Song" and a bag full of farewell cards.

We waved goodbye as we left, and children pressed all around us in the school yard and teachers thrust more gifts into our hands. Patient Jimmy waited in our car. What a memorable experience.

And it was not the only one. One Sunday we appeared at the Ling Leung Tang, the largest church in the city. Situated in downtown Taipei in a seven-story building, with a congregation of several thousand, it is compelled to hold services throughout the day on Sundays in order to accommodate all the worshippers. In a country where only two percent of the population claim to be Christians, the Ling Leung Church plays a significant role.

We addressed the Sunday School children on one floor of the church, which has several auditoriums. Speaking through an interpreter, Christine then shared her experience with the excited kids and their parents.

Later we attended a special Christmas Eve service there. Through an interpreter, Anne and I testified about our experience before a packed audience.

Church members were only admitted to the service if they brought a visitor. This is standard practice for the Sunday night services, and they always have a full house. It was a memorable opportunity to tell people about the power and the love of God and the reality of Jesus Christ.

There were secular invitations as well. I gave a talk to a

Rotary International dinner crowd representing Rotary Clubs from all over Taiwan. Anne, Christine and I had our photo taken posing with literally dozens of Rotarians, as we moved from table to table.

Then came official farewell dinners and visits to the Chiefs of Staff and Commanders-in-Chief of the various branches of the military, with more speeches and exchanging of gifts. I received exquisite, highly-valuable items and beautifully-inscribed plaques. I presented our hosts with hand-painted statuettes of South African soldiers, sailors, and airmen.

However, the greatest honor which I as a soldier could receive came when the President of the Republic of China conferred on me the Order of the Resplendent Banner with Cravat.[1] A most embarrassing self-induced escapade preceded the investiture ceremony, though.

For many months I had eyed the beautiful mountain bikes produced in Taiwan. I set my heart on a particular model, with marvellous shock-reducing front and rear suspension, thumb-shift gears and a lightweight aluminum frame. Making up my mind to take one of these bikes back to South Africa with me, I went with my wife and daughter down to the local Giant Bicycle Shop in Tien Mu to make the exciting purchase.

By then, I was recovering well from the shooting injury. I could walk without the aid of a stick, and although I still retained a limp, I had again started driving the car. At the shop, I looked over the chosen bicycle, wanting to be quite sure I had selected the right one.

"Why don't you try it out?" Anne said.

No further prompting was needed, so I mounted the machine, jammed my feet into the stirrups and pedalled along the open sidewalk for about 100 metres. It felt wonderful. Thrilled with my choice, I slowed down to turn back. I was almost at a stop and as I turned I felt the bike tip over slightly to the left. It would normally be a simple enough matter to withdraw the left foot from the stirrup and place it on the ground to restore one's balance. But now my injured leg would not respond with the necessary alacrity and over I went, my foot still firmly in the stirrup. The side of my shot knee received the full force of my impact with the pavement and I felt a searing pain lance through it. Christine was at my side before I could extricate myself from under the bicycle and, leaning on her and a sales assistant I hobbled back to the shop, unable to place my weight on my left leg. In spite of the excruciating pain, I bought the bike. Anne drove us home.

I had to slide up the stairs to the bedroom on my bottom. After a night with very little sleep I rose the next day aware that I was in no condition to attend the investiture ceremony I had been anticipating with such enthusiasm. It was scheduled for that afternoon. Jimmy fetched me and he took me straight to the Veterans' General Hospital. An X-ray confirmed a broken bone at the top of the fibula.

Through tears of rage at my own stupidity, I watched Dr. Huang fashion the cast around my leg. He was philosophical about my anger, pointing out that it would not change the reality of my condition. I had to agree. Glumly I collected my crutches.

During the formal ceremony at the Ministry of National Defence, attended by Ambassador Scholtz, my fellow military attachés, generals and admirals with whom I had worked, and my proud and loyal wife and daughter, the splendid decoration was hung around my neck by Admiral Lee Chie.

Then, propped on my crutches and trying hard not to appear undignified on such a solemn occasion, I gave a farewell speech. Though it was a moving occasion, it was tinged with sadness and a little embarrassment, as there was no replacement military attaché for me to present as my successor.

The various farewell dinners were more relaxed. Christine, still very much the little heroine in the eyes of Taiwan, was invited to all these dinners. Our hosts admiringly conversed with and complimented Christine and sang her praises to Anne and me. She was a centre of attraction and was even asked to make a speech at the formal dinner for the Ministry of National Defence. For the most part, she relished the attention, but occasionally the strain began to tell. One evening, after we got home, Christine turned to us tearfully.

"Why does everyone say we are the perfect family?" she demanded.

I winced. We had been placed on a pedestal by a society which was probably aching for sound, stable family relationships and which desperately needed to look up to an infallible model. Alas, we could not be that model, and neither could any other family. They needed to turn to a far more profound and reliable example

"People like to think we're perfect, my sweetheart," I tried to explain, "because it makes them feel better to believe that it is possible to achieve perfection. But you know that we've never pretended to be perfect. We know that we're full of flaws and shortcomings.

"Only Jesus is perfect, and His sacrifice on the cross was made in order for us to become perfect in God's sight. No one can be perfect of their own accord or through their own ability. Perfection is a gift of God, given by grace to them that repent of their sins and accept Christ as their personal and only Saviour. Haven't we always taught you that?"

"Yes, but we're not perfect," Christine replied, unconvinced and with heartache in her voice.

"Not now, we're not," I returned. "Because we're living in a broken, sinful world and we're surrounded by the effects of this world. Our earthly bodies are still the products of all this sin, but one day in glory with our Lord Jesus we will really be perfect. Until then, we live according to His Word, trying every day to be more perfect through His grace but at peace because we're assured of our future in eternity.

"All these people who are longing for perfection need to accept Jesus in their lives, then they would not need to look to still-imperfect people like ourselves."

Christine sighed and went off to bed, perhaps not quite fully persuaded by my late night theology lecture.

Anne and I sat down in the midst of the packing and chaos of our house, and in sheer exhaustion and heartache, just cried and cried.

22

‣Back To South Africa◂

WE MUST HAVE LOOKED haggard and worn, as the constant round of farewell dinners and parties continued right up to the end. One night when we arrived back at the hotel where we were spending our last few days in Taiwan, we were close to exhaustion. We found a card from Christine on our bed.

> *Dear Mom, Dad,*
> *I know everything is getting rough, but we're the*
> *"Alexanders." We can live through hostage-taking,*
> *we can live through this!!*
> *I ♥ U*
> *Love, Christine*

We tiptoed into Christine's room and both gave our sleeping daughter a kiss, thanking God for giving her to us, and for sparing her.

On our last day, 31 December 1997, we rose long before dawn to prepare to leave for the airport.[1] It was still dark as Jimmy drove along the familiar highway.

He knew that once we got to the airport the tempo would again increase and this short journey would be the last time he would have alone with us. So as he drove he presented us each with a farewell gift: a pen for me, a handbag for Anne, a necklace and a wind chime for Christine. We were deeply touched. Jimmy had driven me so many thousands of kilometres along the highways and byways of Taiwan over the past two years; he had fetched Anne to take her to official functions on so many occasions; and now it was all over.

Television crews met us at the airport. We had become accustomed to them by now; but we hurried through check-in procedures to get away from cameras and questions. We bade the faithful Jimmy farewell. Struggling along on crutches, I had to leave most of the hand-luggage to Anne and Christine. In the VIP lounge, we at last appeared to be safe from the ravenous media.

We had no sooner settled onto the comfortable seats, than we had a very pleasant surprise. In walked Lieutenant General Huang Yun-dea, the Deputy Chief of the General Staff for Intelligence, accompanied by three other military officers. We profoundly appreciated this meaningful gesture. Not every military attaché is seen off by a lieutenant general, and I was acutely conscious of the significance of this generous action.

For about half an hour we chatted. Then suddenly a camera appeared. Somehow the media had obtained permission to enter the passengers-only section, and now they swarmed all over us, ending our pleasant conversation. We found ourselves again being interviewed and posing for photos. General Huang and his officers accompanied us all the way to the boarding gate, and so did the cameras. After a very public goodbye we entered the tunnel to the aircraft. The camera people filmed us until we disappeared.

On board, the Chinese stewardesses recognized us and gave us extra-special treatment; but less than two hours later, we landed in Hong Kong, where a pretty young stewardess was waiting for me with a wheel chair. Embarrassed, I thanked her but politely declined. I really was quite capable of managing without help. Anne found my embarrassment hugely amusing.

Even in Hong Kong, where we spent the day shopping, people recognized us and stopped us in the streets, although it had been six weeks since they had seen us on television and in their newspapers. People were friendly and excited to see us, telling us how glad they were that it had turned out well.

That night we boarded the South African Airways flight for Johannesburg. The overnight journey brought us to our own country as the sun was rising over the African *veld* on New Year's Day 1998.

Retrieving our motor car, we drove to Pretoria, where Shona was spending the weekend with a friend. Although we were thrilled to see her and her fiancé William again, we sensed a definite reserve. Our relationship would take a lot of rebuilding.

Next, we spent three days of rest on a peaceful farm in the company of friends. What a wonderful tonic. For the first time since our ordeal, we had an opportunity to reflect on events. Conversation with my friend James, a former comrade-in-arms, inevitably turned to the days when we, as fellow para-troopers, had spent long months on active service, while our wives kept the home fires burning. Anne and I began to real-ize how great a role our lives as a military family had played in equipping us for the hostage ordeal we had experienced. Yet no amount of preparation could have been sufficient. In the final analysis, it was the hand of God that delivered us.

Soon we were off to start our new life in Pietersburg. I commenced my new job as the Senior Staff Officer of Oper-ations at Far North Command and began to reacquaint myself with the situation on our country's northern borders.

On Saturday 30 January 1998, Shona and William were married and happily, Melanie was back from America to attend. Christine was bridesmaid. We saw William and Shona frequently during the next year and a half, and gradually our relationship with our daughter was repaired, and she became her friendly self with her sharp wit and mischievous smile.

On our arrival in Pietersburg, the Officer Commanding

the Far North Medical Command, Colonel Grobler, asked in passing what psychological counselling the family had undergone after the hostage-taking. He was mortified to hear that we had had none, and he immediately arranged counselling sessions for all of us.

The psychologist, after tallying up the points normally allocated for traumatic experiences to indicate degrees of stress experienced, shook his head in disbelief: loss of a parent, loss of a child, being held hostage, moving house, changing jobs, marriage of a child, new school, writing exams, closing down an office, etc. This would be a heavy load to bear spread over a year, but our family had experienced all this in less than three months.

He dispensed with further counselling for me after two sessions, and Melanie had only a few sessions before she returned to America. Anne and Christine continued to attend sessions for several weeks. The psychologist was amazed at how well we had all come through the experiences of those past months. Unamazed ourselves, we gave thanks to God for giving us the strength and fortitude needed. We know that the strength was His; it certainly hadn't come from us.

In South Africa we continued to be asked to testify at churches of the power of God as we had experienced it during the hostage drama. Several magazines interviewed us, and Anne was asked to write articles on her experience.

Six months after our return, Anne began to feel depressed and for the first time she started questioning herself as to whether she had done all she could for the rest of us during the hostage-taking. She had been the one who was not tied up; couldn't she have prevented Melanie and myself from being shot? It was the onset of post-traumatic stress and she was quickly referred to a psychiatrist. He prescribed medication and she was soon a lot better. The medication had to continue for many months, though, and there were times when she lapsed into despondency. But a year later the doctor expressed his wonder at her recovery and that, given what she had been through, her symptoms were so mild.

"It really is a miracle," he told Anne. "It could only have been the spiritual reserves which you were able to draw on that carried you through that period."

After Melanie had completed her exams, she had interviewed with social welfare agencies in South Africa and submitted endless written applications, but with no success. The job market in our country was not encouraging. Affirmative-action policies were attempting to right the wrongs of the past; and Melanie had little chance of employment as a white woman. Disillusioned by six months of vain effort, during her visit to the United States she discovered a great demand for people with her qualifications. So she decided to return to America.

In Boston she had immediate success, with very tempting offers; but first she had to go through the time-consuming and frustrating procedure of obtaining a "green card."

In June 1998 we received a phone call from Michael Letts. He asked me for Melanie's hand in marriage. This didn't surprise us. But Anne found the prospect of her daughter bringing up a family in such a distant land daunting.

After a wonderful trip to America for Melanie's wedding, we returned to our mundane life in Pietersburg. Yet even in this distant little town, the spectre of the hostage-taking continued to haunt us. When the representative of the Taipei Liaison Office in South Africa, Mr. Ling Du (the ROC's "unofficial ambassador" in South Africa) invited our family to a dinner at his luxurious residence in Pretoria in August 1998, we were grateful for the opportunity to again enjoy the lavish, traditional Chinese hospitality.

However, also present at the dinner was a gentleman from Taiwan's China News Agency, a Mr. Chang. We chatted very affably about our stay in Taiwan. He assured me he was "off duty" and that he was not out to get a story on our family. Two months later, the agency distributed a report on a "recent interview" with the family in which we were reported as saying we missed Taiwan and that we had felt much safer there than we do in our own country.

Sadly, the sentiments reported were accurate, even in the country town of Pietersburg, where we had been burgled barely two weeks after we'd moved into our home there.

23

▸The Miracle Bullet◂

Despite the high crime rate in South Africa, the demands of a new job, and the emotional stress of daughters getting married, our lives became quieter and more settled. Gone were the never-ending cocktail circuits and social engagements. Gone were the media hounds and the whirl of interviews and the glare of publicity.

In the small town of Pietersburg, we got involved in church activities and made new Christian friends in the mainly-black congregation of the local Assembly of God. As we shared our experiences with them and talked in a calm and restful environment, certain issues became clear to us.

Up until then, we had seen the evacuation of Melanie and myself from the house after our shooting as the turning point in the whole saga. But with deeper reflection, we began to recognize the miracle God had manifested. In the terror of the crisis, we had fervently asked God to send us a miracle. The miracle He sent had amazingly come in the form of a bullet.

How could we regard an instrument of destruction, which had cut down my daughter and myself, as a miracle of mercy? It was quite simple, once we contemplated the horrible possibilities had we *not* been shot.

**Bullet holes riddled the windows of the
lounge where Chen held the Alexanders
hostage in their Taipei home.**
(Photo: Fan Lee, *The Journalist*)

On that ghastly night, Chen Chin-hsing had seen me as a
threat right from the start. As the only adult male among his
captives, he had neutralized me first and most effectively,
using his only pair of handcuffs. He had diligently kept a safe
distance from me even after I'd been tied up and only exchanged Melanie for me as a human shield with reluctance.

His suspicions were justified. My feelings of frustration
and helplessness had reached virtual breaking point. I am
normally a self-controlled person, able to keep a bridle on my
emotions in public. However, on the occasions when I do
become angry, I sometimes do things which I later regret. At
the time we were taken hostage, I came very close to giving
vent to my anger. I had been exercising patience through a
deliberate act of will, but my patience nearly snapped.

What might I have done then? One can only surmise. In a
fit of rage, I might have butted Chen with my head; or tried to
kick him, or trip him, or bump him down the stairs. Such

tactics almost certainly would not have worked and most definitely would have provoked a violent response from Chen. His past actions indicate that he would probably have had no compunction about shooting me dead on the spot.

The effect on my family would have been devastating and it would have put Chen into an even more desperate frame of mind. I believe now that God knew I had become a danger to the peaceful resolution of the crisis and He needed to extract me from that situation in order to bring about calm. The bullet through my knee was His way of achieving this.

The surgeon Dr. Huang himself called it a miracle. He said given the point of entry and the point of exit of the bullet in my leg, nothing else could account for the fact that it caused no severe damage to bone, nerves, or vascular tissue.

As for Melanie, it was equally important for her to be removed from the situation. Chen was guilty of raping many young women and his attention had been focused on our eldest daughter from the time that he had first set eyes on her. Melanie is a very attractive woman, and this had most certainly not escaped his notice. Mercifully, he did not have opportunity to give free rein to his sexual impulses, largely because of his single-minded purposefulness in accomplishing his self-imposed mission.

Yet the man's record as it subsequently came to light would infer that, once a lull in the siege had taken place he would in all likelihood have exploited it to satisfy his cravings. I believe God sent the bullet to come between Melanie and the man's debased desire. Even after she was wounded, he tried to prevent Chief Hou You-yi from removing her. Thank God the policeman remained resolute and insisted on carrying her out in the face of Chen's protest.

Again, the doctors confirmed the miracle. The surgeons who operated on Melanie expressed unanimous wonder at her miraculous condition. One of the surgeons, who was a Christian, told Anne that the path of the bullet could only be ascribed to the hand of God. It passed through her wrist without touching any bone, missed her spine by a few millimetres, travelled almost twenty centimetres without touching any vital or reproductive organs, and came to rest in her pelvic area, right between two main arteries. But it didn't sever any of the arteries. A centimetre to the left or right, and Melanie would have bled to death in minutes from a massive internal hemorrhage. The doctors shook their heads in disbelief, exclaiming that her limited injury was a physical impossibility.

The shock of the bullet entering her body did cause some damage to the nerves leading down her left leg. The resulting numbness and dull pain in that leg has continued to trouble Melanie. However, she was not permanently impaired in any way, and her recovery was quite remarkable. The doctors ascribed her rapid recovery to her youth and good health and mine to my physical fitness. However, it was to be over a year before I could return to my favorite physical exercise of jogging. (I substituted cycling and walking in the interim.)

We remain totally convinced that the limited bodily damage and our recovery were nothing short of miraculous.

But the miracle did not end there. The bullet quite clearly also had an effect on Chen. Inexplicably, he seemed to be gripped by a feeling of remorse when he realized that he had inadvertently shot us. It was the nearest he came to panic throughout the entire hostage-taking episode. Otherwise, the hardened criminal who had previously been untouched by the suffering he caused to others, would scarcely have called for the police (who had just tried to kill him) to send up medical assistance for his wounded victims.

After our evacuation, Chen showed a marked softening in his attitude toward Anne and Christine. The level of tension subsided, and he displayed an almost apologetic tone in his further dealings with them, particularly when using Christine as a shield. Any designs he might have had on my wife and youngest daughter were almost certainly dispelled by the shock of what he'd done to Melanie and me.

Chen was not the only person to be shocked into exercising restraint by the miracle of that one bullet among the many fired that night. The over-zealous police appeared to have been abruptly sobered by this blood-letting of innocents. The high drama of our evacuation seemed to suddenly bring home to them that the whole world was watching their antics, because it was only from this point that they took stock and began to approach the problem professionally. Until then, the police were probably as great a danger to our safety as was the gunman. This would not necessarily have changed, if not for that miracle bullet.

However, this was not the most miraculous aspect. As Christians, we saw the greatest miracle as being the manner in which the people of Taiwan showed such a sudden interest in hearing of the love of Christ. This love and faith seemed to be what everyone wanted us to share with them.

During those hectic days in hospital, in the mountains of mail we received was a letter from Catherine Lin (Lin Yih-ling) chief editor of the *Christian Tribune,* a Chinese-language weekly intent on spreading the Christian gospel to the people of Taiwan. Catherine told us the story of the Ladies' Fellowship in Hsinchu who had initiated Chen's spiritual encounter by praying for him and placing the advertisement showing the praying hands with an appeal to him and Kao Tien-min. Catherine had been instrumental in getting the ad placed in the *United Daily News* the day before we were taken hostage.

In her letter, she traced the thread of Chen's encounter with God's love — from the ad, through Christine's drawing, and finally to Anne's display of Christian love. She wrote to request an interview so that she could publish an article to continue the encounter for Chen and to touch others as they read the full story. We willingly granted her the interview, done with an interpreter. The *Tribune* eventually published an in-depth article, with photos, which was later produced as a full-color, large-size gospel tract in Chinese. Catherine's desire was granted as it touched the hearts of many hundreds of

Chinese in Taiwan.

Besides all the television and newspaper interviews in which we were openly able to witness about the role of Jesus in our lives, we were told by missionaries and other Christians of how doors were suddenly and unexpectedly opened to the gospel. One missionary couple told us how they had struggled for many years without success to share the gospel with people in the area where they lived. Now, after the hostage-taking, those same people were eager to hear what they had to say.

We heard of school children asking their teachers whether they, too, could ask Jesus to help them when they found themselves in danger. We heard of Christians being accosted at work and in the streets by people anxious to hear more about the love and forgiveness of Christ. At the official receptions which Anne and I attended, Taiwanese people and foreign representatives would take us aside and tell us that they were Christians who had "hidden their lights under a bushel," but that now they were proud to come out into the open and share their faith with others. All this, to us, was a mighty miracle indeed.

And yet, even this was still not the end of the miracle. There was more to come, and we were to be truly awed at the changes wrought by God in the life of our ruthless captor, Chen Chin-hsing.

24

▸The Miracle Conversion◂

THE CENTRAL FIGURE in the siege of Cherry Hill unquestionably
was Chen Chin-hsing. In fact, he was the central figure for
many people in the whole bizarre story stretching back to the
kidnap and murder of seventeen-year-old Pai Hsiao-yen.
After a life of social deprivation and crime and prison, charac-
terized throughout by violence, Chen had embarked on his
seven-month terror spree with his two cronies, culminating in
a hostage-taking and shoot-out, and was the only one to
emerge unscathed. He was a survivor.

His stony, poker face had come to represent many contra-
dictory things to many people: cruelty and suffering; oppres-
sion and resistance; selfishness and selflessness; strength and
weakness; and many other conflicting characteristics and
emotions. Some people identified with him; some felt they
understood his motives, given his circumstances. Others
hated and despised him. He had embarrassed the authorities
and shown up some of their weaknesses and failings. Doubtless this played no small part in the begrudging respect he
seemed to gain for a time among the common folk of Taiwan.

Ordinary people often feel helpless in the face of a mighty

government bureaucracy which they can do nothing to influence. Here was someone who had succeeded in forcing just such a monolithic bureaucracy to pay individual attention to him. Was this not every frustrated and bitter citizen's ideal? That he had resorted to violent and illegal means was what made the respect begrudging. No "ordinary person" could possibly condone the means used by Chen Chin-hsing, and I am sure the people of Taiwan at no time did so.

Chen predictably denied that it was he who had done the actual killing. After his surrender, he was interrogated for several successive days. He steadfastly maintained that in the murder of the plastic surgeon and his wife and nurse, it was Kao Tien-min who had pulled the trigger.

However, within days of Chen's surrender, reports were circulating that DNA tests indicated that he may have raped more than fifteen women. It was thought likely by Criminal Investigation Bureau sources that Chen was the notorious "Wolf of Chungshan," a serial rapist the police had been trying to find for several months. Initially, police discounted the possibility that Chen was responsible for these crimes. But Chen now admitted that he and the other two rogues had hidden in Taipei City for most of the seven months that they had been on the run. Chen had ample opportunity to commit the rapes.

Fourteen of these rape cases took place in Taipei and one in Taipei County's Yungho, when he had attacked the young vocational high school student. Despite Chen's denial, it was reported, the test results also identified him as having raped the nurse Cheng Wen-yu before she was murdered.

Between January and November 1997, the Chungshan district had reported twenty-three rape cases, eleven of which had yielded no identity of the perpetrator during investigation. Chen confessed to nine of those rapes, and this was confirmed by DNA testing, according to police. Police were reported as saying that he said he had raped so many women that he forgot the actual number.

Despite the string of indictments against Chen, the trial progressed speedily. There was a blaze of publicity as the evidence was systematically laid before the court. On Thursday 22 January 1998, just over two months after he'd been apprehended, the notorious criminal was found guilty. The attractive young judge Tuan Ching-jung passed sentence.

Chen received five death sentences: one for abducting and killing Pai Hsiao-yen; one for the ten rapes for which he was found guilty; one for the killing of the plastic surgeon Fang Pao-feng, his wife and the nurse; and two for the separate kidnapping and extortion of Taipei County Councillor Tsai Min-tang and businessman Chen Chao-yang.

For our hostage-taking he was sentenced to life imprisonment; and he received another life sentence for attempted murder in an arson case. He was also sentenced to a total of fifty-nine-and-one-half years in jail for various other crimes. Judge Tuan proclaimed that her harsh sentences were intended to ensure that no one was persuaded by the criminal's bid to portray himself as a hero.

Chen's wife, Chang Su-chen, in her retrial, was absolved of guilt in the kidnap and murder of Pai Hsiao-yen, but she received a sentence of nine months for harbouring her husband during his efforts to evade the police. As she had served this period in detention already, she was released from prison and it seemed that Chen had achieved what he'd set out to do when he took us hostage. Chang Su-chen's brother Chang Chih-hui was acquitted, but ten others received sentences ranging from five to eighteen months in prison for complicity in the Pai case.

Chen appears to have received the verdict stoically. It was not yet over, though. In Taiwan there is an automatic appeal to the High Court for all death sentences, so the appeal trial would still have to take place. In the meantime the public had been appeased, though Pai Ping-ping and others were incensed by the release of Chang Su-chen and her brother.

Chen Chin-hsing began his wait in the cell on death row,

with a guard mounted over him twenty-four hours a day. He was regarded as an extremely dangerous and desperate criminal, and the authorities were taking no chances.

▶▶▶▶▶▶▶◀◀◀◀◀◀◀

Shortly after the hostage crisis, Anne had received a letter from Jennifer Sun, associate editor of *Campus Magazine*, a Christian publication in Taiwan. Jennifer wrote: "As Christine walked out of the hostage situation, our tears of prayer burst into tears of joy. People were amazed how each member of this family from South Africa could have acted so nobly, courageously and lovingly towards this most notorious criminal suspect, Mr. Chen."

Jennifer asked Anne to write an article for the magazine which they would translate into Chinese. Anne wrote it while the movers packed boxes and crates around her. She barely had time to e-mail the article to Jennifer before the computer was packed up for shipment to South Africa.

That magazine, with Anne's article in it, later found its way into Chen Chin-hsing's prison cell. Back in Pietersburg, South Africa, we got news from Jennifer.

Chen Chin-hsing, Jennifer said, had "amazingly converted into a new person, a born-again Christian brother in our Lord. In his correspondence to me, he asked me to send his best regards to you. Since the letter he wrote to me is pretty much his personal testimony, I've decided to translate it into English so that you may be able to read it yourself."

We were over-awed. Shortly before this we had received a letter from Carol, my former secretary, who had told us very excitedly that Chen was reading every day from the Bible we had given him. This encouraged us, but now we were just stunned by the greatness of God's grace.

We felt embarrassed before God by our own lack of faith. Ever since the night Chen Chin-hsing took us hostage, we had prayed for his salvation, that he would repent of his sins and accept Jesus into his heart. Now it had happened, and we could hardly believe it!

Why do we bother to pray at all unless we believe that the prayer can be answered? Then why do we express surprise when it *is* answered? We were certainly learning a lesson in faith.

Reportedly, on a visit to Chen Chin-hsing in his cell, Pastor Huang had counselled him to the point where he fell to his knees, weeping and confessing to God his transgressions and sins. He repented, asked for God's forgiveness, and obtained it by accepting Jesus Christ as his Saviour.

Chen wrote the following to Jennifer Sun:

> *Sister Jennifer in the Lord:*
>
> *How are you? Thanks for the letter and the Campus Magazine. If you write to the South Africa Military Attaché family, would you please write a few extra lines to their family, including my appreciation and apology.*
>
> *Pastor Huang and Brother Sun* (note: they belong to the Renewal Fellowship and they spend quite a lot of effort to spread the gospel to the prison inmates) *have already led me to Jesus Christ before the Chinese New Year. Since the time I've walked out of the past, I read the Bible daily, and books about God's gospel. I have a wonderful feeling in reading these. May He not abandon me for the last days I have on the earth, not desert me, but teach me and lead me. I also try to pray daily, talking to God with my heart opened, just like the letters I write to some Church brothers and sisters. I declared: My belief, sincerely without lying, is not for the "benefit" of everlasting life. I confess before God and before the judgement of the court, but I do not seek for forgiveness (from human or from heaven). My conversion is not for the sake of escape away from the crimes I committed. I write in words, in front of God. Church brothers and sisters, along with Pastor Huang, can all witness for me, I am willing to be punished with hellfire, whether I am indeed repent or not, for there is no need for anyone's approval. God alone knows.*
>
> *Today, I believe in Jesus without any regret. The reason I believe is that God really exists, and has plans for*

everything on the earth. As I look up, oh, we human
beings, how small and unworthy compared to God. The
impact of the event in Attaché house has affected me till
this day.

It has made my whole body immerse in God's loving
grace. The memory of Attaché family, their whole hearted
devotion to Jesus (although I did not understand their
prayer) indeed has made me tremble in the deepest of the
heart. When I saw Christine's picture of the HEART with
a Cross, it shivered me for no apparent reason. Oh, how
can one describe the feeling with words in this world? I
think there is definitely a purpose why God has allowed
me to live to this day. Now, my only wish is that he will
take away all the thoughts I have in this world, cast all
my worries and burdens for my families to him.

Then will I truly be "born again," a "new" man. May
God's kingdom come to you and Attaché family. May
God bless and protect yours and Attaché family forever,
and have peace.

Thanks to the Lord Jesus Christ, Amen.
Chen Chin-hsing
11 February 1998

A note from Ina van der Schyff confirmed Chen's conversion. She sent us an extract from a Baptist magazine which reported how Chen had listened intently when Pastor Huang and "Uncle" Sun visited him and how he clearly prayed to receive Christ.

Ina mentioned that "so many people were praying for him."

Both Anne and Christine felt the need to write to Chen about his conversion. His execution was scheduled for June, and they both felt they wanted to encourage him in his newfound faith. They e-mailed letters to Jennifer Sun, who translated them and had them delivered to Chen in prison. He immediately wrote back, and again Jennifer had to be the post office and interpreter. However, so impressed was she by the high standard of Chen's calligraphy that she sent his original letters to Anne to keep.

Jennifer's translated text of Chen's letters revealed to us afresh just how great the miracle was that God had performed in the life of this formerly callous and brutal criminal.

We read Chen's words with lumps in our throats and tears in our eyes:

> *Dear Mrs. Alexander,*
>
> *How are you? Whenever I think of what happened on that day, I feel deeply that I need to apologize to your family. These days, I keep on thinking: God has arranged everything! Indeed, I am positively sure of it without any doubt. Sometimes I struggle for being influenced by human thoughts, but the work and power of the Lord are even greater and amazing. Again and again, the Lord has cleared my confusion and has corrected me not to walk astray again. To skip one or even three meals a day is not a problem to me, but now I cannot live one day without reading His words in the Bible. I also practice how to pray and talk to God. In the earlier days, I felt shy and so awkward to open my mouth. I talked nonsense, but now I am gradually improving so that I may express myself a little bit better. I am indebted all this to the grace of the Lord. I see some changes of me and it makes me feel happy.*
>
> *Thanks for Melanie's concern for me. I really thank God for His protection over her. I feel relieved to know that she is doing well, but I still owe her an apology. May God bless her with peace and joy. How is Mr. Alexander doing? I feel so shamed that I have frightened all of you, and harmed both Mr. Alexander and Melanie. This is one of those many evil deeds that I have committed. These crimes are still lingering in my heart, and I find it very difficult to forgive myself. May God also bless Mr. Alexander with peace and joy.*
>
> *I like to thank all your prayers for my family and me, they (including my mother-in-law, my wife and my son) have accepted the Lord too. My wife and my son visit me a lot, and they also write to me. Because of the Lord's grace, I can see that my wife has changed also. Though she may still feel sad and melancholy, she becomes brighter after she knows the Lord. She also believes that*

God has destined all this. I think this has helped her somehow. I tell her many times, that since the Lord would not give up on a sinner like me, He will certainly not forsake her either. However, my wife used to worship false god idols, the understanding of God and the emotional transition may be slower for her than for me. I believe that she will gradually grow up to know that the true religion is depending and looking up to our Lord solely. I pray to the Lord to help her and guide her.

I especially like to thank your whole family for praying and blessing. I believe that is why the Lord saves me now. I am a new man now. It is different from what I was before. I can tell that this is a true feeling inside me, and that I can not pretend it. I think it is the mighty power of Jesus that has changed me. I like to thank all brothers and sisters in South African Church, for their prayers and support. I will do my best not to disappoint all of you. I thank you, and your family one more time, and thank all the brothers and sisters in the Church. May the Lord Jesus be with all of you forever, Amen.

Chen Chin-hsing,
26 March 1998

▶▶▶▶▶▶▶◀◀◀◀◀◀◀

Dear Christine,

How are you? My life here is kind of peaceful and quiet. I am really sorry that I frightened your family on that day. The loud and sincere praying of your family is why the Lord saves me. After I came out, I sincerely confess my sins before God and before the law at court. I know the old me is dead already, I am a brand new man now. My feeling is so real, I am bold and fearless with peace to come before God. Although I still can not carry out some things that I desire to do, yet I know the Lord Jesus will change me gradually. Less and less evil thoughts, day by day I sentenced them to death. In the meantime, I gain joy by looking up and trust on Him. I owe all this to our Lord's gracious work through your family.

Do you remember the Cross in the loving heart that

you drew? The painting has shivered my soul incomprehensibly. Later, afterwards, when I spoke to you or to your Mom, or pointing my guns, I felt that it was not necessary for me to do so. I felt that you are so close to your Mom, and trusted her, though I was still pointing my guns without surrender, but deep inside my heart, there was a voice telling me: "I am doing this for police outside, it is to them not to you." I was holding the guns because I knew they may break in, they were downstairs and some were upstairs. And I knew I would shoot myself once they came in. Moreover, I remembered that both your Dad and your Mom said in English "NO!" to me, I could not describe their tones and eyes, it seemed that there were sadness, sympathy and sincerity. That was the first time I was touched. But I forgot it all for so many other things happened later.

In the last days of my life, my soul was saved and I had the chance to know God through your family. He is almighty and He knows everything. He has showed me the right way. My life and my thought have been changed greatly through reading the words in the Bible. I gradually feel relieved. It is hard to describe my feeling. The only thing that I can do now is to thank Him, and you all. I love every one of you greatly too.

South Africa is beautiful. That was what I said to you when you showed your family photos from South Africa. I believe everyone loves his own hometown and think it is the best place in the whole world. But your hometown is indeed beautiful. You are still young, please do your best when you have the opportunity to go to school, OK? May the Lord bless you with peace and joy, forever be with you. I thank our Lord!

Thank you for praying for me.
Chen Chin-hsing
26 March 1998

Perhaps the most thrilling part of these letters was, for us, the news that the family of Chen Chin-hsing had, like him, accepted Christ as personal Saviour. Anne especially experienced this as deeply rewarding and rejoiced as she shared it

with everyone she knew. In an article which she wrote for
Joy!, a South African Christian family magazine, she quoted
Chen's letters in full and she read them out to churches where
she was asked to testify. When she would share their contents
at women's prayer groups and Bible studies, the ladies
listened, misty-eyed.

But as the year passed, there seemed to be strange things
happening in Taiwan and our joy was to receive a jarring
blow. The new-found faith of Chen Chin-hsing and Chang
Su-chen was to be severely tested and the whole testimony of
the hostage-taking was to come under a direct assault from
Satan.

May, June, and July passed and Chen Chin-hsing's appeal
trial dragged on. It was complicated by the trials of the other
accused. After the revision of Chang Su-chen's sentence to
only nine months, her prosecutor immediately appealed.
There was also an outcry from certain sectors of the public
who demanded a heavier sentence. However, at the hearing
which took place in May 1998, her lawyer expressed his confidence to Ingomar Lochschmidt that the sentence would not
be increased. Ingomar, himself a doctor of law, attended the
hearing and wrote to tell us this.

He also told how Chang Su-chen had been supported by
members of her new church who had been there. He had
spoken to her and described her as "a lovely person," who
had asked that her best regards be conveyed to all of our
family. Chen himself had expressed in a letter to Ingomar that
he felt really bad during his appeal trial when the defense was
trying to get his death sentences reduced from five to four.

On Saturday 5 September 1998 the Taiwan High Court
handed down its verdict: Judge Li Hsing-chu completely
reversed the Panchiao District Court's acquittal of Chen's
brother-in-law, Chang Chih-hui, by sentencing him to life
imprisonment for being an accomplice in the kidnapping and
murder of Pai Hsiao-yen. Chen's wife, Chang Su-chen, had
her sentence (for knowingly concealing her husband after he

committed the kidnap-murder of Pai Hsiao-yen) increased
from nine months to fifteen years in prison. The High Court
cited new circumstantial evidence to justify these harsh
increases in the sentencing. It upheld all five death sentences
passed on Chen Chin-hsing by the Panchiao District Court, as
well as his life sentence for taking us hostage.

That Monday, 7 September, the prison authorities at the
Tucheng Detention Center on the outskirts of Taipei where
Chen was being held, arranged an interview with Chen by the
print and broadcast media, allowing him to voice his reaction
to the revised sentences. I thought it strange for a convicted
murderer and rapist to be afforded such a privilege.

Chen, showman and a manipulator of the media *par
excellence*, exploited this opportunity to the utmost. During the
interview in a special visitors room in front of all the media
persons, he whipped out a small blade that he had been concealing and dramatically slashed his neck twice. As he did so,
he called out that he no longer believed in God.

Prison guards dashed forward to intervene, confiscated
the blade and stanched the bleeding. As he was dragged away
to the prison health clinic he shouted at reporters that he
would refuse to cooperate with authorities in further investigations because of what he considered to be unfair sentences
passed on his wife and brother-in-law.

It was later reported that the blade which Chen had used
was a small art knife which he had concealed inside a tooth-
brush that he kept in his jacket pocket. Chen, it seems, sustained only minor neck injuries from superficial cuts. The
deputy director of the detention centre told reporters that
Chen was in a stable condition after receiving medical treatment. He added that he had ordered an investigation into
how Chen had acquired the blade.

Despite telling the media that Chen was both emotionally
and physically stable and was receiving the same treatment as
other inmates, the prison had placed Chen under a twenty-
four-hour watch in a cell for mentally ill prisoners and he had

been forbidden to meet visitors.

This episode in Chen's story came as a considerable shock to our family. We had been rejoicing in the man's conversion to Christ, and sharing the news of this miracle with everyone with whom we came into contact. On Sunday 6 September 1998, the day after the revised sentences on Chang Su-chen and Chang Chih-hui were handed down and the day before Chen's attempted suicide, Anne and Christine testified of our hostage experience to the Liberty Community Church in Johannesburg. I had been deployed on active service, commanding a military task group in the violence-wracked Richmond area of the KwaZulu-Natal Province, so I was unable to be with them.

Blissfully unaware of developments in faraway Taiwan, Anne enthusiastically told the large congregation how Chen had turned from his evil ways and accepted Christ as his Saviour on death row. Now, the day after his suicide attempt, she received e-mail from friends in Taiwan telling the awful news of his public rejection of God. Anne was devastated.

She contacted me by cell phone as I drove through the muddy, rutted streets of Richmond checking on the patrols of my soldiers. Immersed as I was in the tensions of the armed conflict between warring factions, I received the news as a blow to my own faith. The miracle of Chen's conversion had been the hinge on which our experience hung. Now it seemed a lie. Had our family been through everything in vain?

I could hear the hurt, disappointment, and confusion in Anne's voice. I didn't know what to say. I knew our faith was again being sorely tried. Once again, we could only pray.

And once again, Anne found herself under pressure, this time without me. Jennifer Sun and ORTV, themselves embarrassed and hurt by Chen's angry retraction, decided to release to the media the letters that Anne and Christine had written to Chen. They were immediately published in the Taiwan newspapers with the explanation that we were unaware of Chen's suicide bid. Taiwan Television Enterprise then phoned Anne in South Africa and conducted a telephone interview with her and Christine which they broadcast live. Anne told them that she could understand how Chen felt, particularly his sadness and disappointment at the outcome of the trial. Christine confirmed our family's concern over his recent actions and told them that we were all praying for him.

There were other phone calls from the media in Taiwan and once again Anne, under treatment for depression at the time, began to feel hounded. But through prayer and a strong reliance on her faith, she was again able to cope. She sat down and wrote a letter of encouragement to Chen, e-mailing it to Jennifer Sun for translation by her husband Daniel.

Even before the letter got to Chen we received fresh news. Chen had made a statement that his rejection of Christ had been an emotional act in the heat of the moment. He regretted having said what he had and wanted to reaffirm his commitment to Christ. I was skeptical. The man was beginning to sound like a politician.

But then we heard that Pastor Huang had been seeing a great deal of him and had been counselling him daily. Much later we received a letter from Pastor Huang in which he told us the details of what took place in the condemned man's life inside the prison. Huang described Chen's condition at the time of the sentencing of his wife and brother-in-law by the High Court as "the lowest point of his life."

In the wake of Chen's suicide attempt, Huang said, Chen was locked up in a separate part of the prison with only one other inmate. Stripped of all visitation privileges, he faced a lonely incarceration. Yet, miraculously, the prison authorities allowed Pastor Huang in to see him and to counsel him.

When Jennifer Sun passed Anne's letter to Huang, he read it to Chen. As he was reading, Chen broke down and wept. During another visit a few days later, the hardened criminal again dissolved into tears of repentance. Gradually he was released from the hatred he felt towards the authorities and his faith in the Lord Jesus was restored. According to Pastor

Huang, he then experienced remarkable spiritual growth, fully accepting God's will in his life.

25

‣A Mind-Boggling Request◂

AFTER CHEN RECEIVED Anne's translated letter, he wrote a
reply to her and we found it difficult not to be convinced by
what he said and the way that he said it. Yet that letter
introduced further turmoil into our unsettled lives.

> Madam Anne: Peace!
>   I received your letter on the 12th October. Thanks for
> the loving concern and encouragement from your family.
> I am a man with great transgressions, but it also made me
> more appreciative of the Lord Jesus' teaching. How can a
> man comprehend God's will? Through me, human weak-
> nesses and indecision can be seen. I'm a fool, and even
> though I know I am not worthy, I still ask for the Lord's
> mercy and forgiveness. It's all because of the prayers of
> church's brothers and sisters hold me, and make me able
> to stand up again quickly.
>   The cost for my wrongdoing was not worthwhile in
> the first place, and I should not have done it, but if there
> were no Lord's watching and judgement, then I would
> have surely died in my transgressions.
>   Now I am happy of the real peace I enjoy after all
> these things. After all these things, I carry less worry and
> feel much relaxed in this world. At this moment, there is

nothing that can prevent my love toward the Lord. Whether the outcome is blessing or misfortune, God knows everything. No matter how long I may still live on this earth, I am satisfied while the Lord is with me. Yes, if my sins can be forgiven, then I will know everything when I meet the Lord face to face. Although I do not understand at this moment, I firmly believe that the Lord's will is definitely good, because His will and His ways are higher than man. I am sorry, because my weakness and my fall makes you recall the previous unpleasant memory. Your family was calm in that chaotic situation, and I have a very strong impression of your steadfast dependence on the Lord. Especially your husband, Mr. Alexander. I still recall the way he looked at me, and it can only be described with the word "compassion". God was with your family during the hostage crisis, and my crime and spirit can testify it.

Madame Anne, I am also of great hope that we will meet in the home of our heavenly Father, the better homeland. Would you and your husband please not worry about the situation here? Even though God is God of Israel, isn't he also God of the Gentiles? I am completely obedient, and I trust Him with peace, because I truly understand that I am a Christian, no matter if I am alive or not. Doesn't God purify the gold in His furnace? I am willing to do anything, and I am no longer pondering with any doubts. May God place me in the place that will satisfy Him. Every moment I have on this world, I am looking up to Him. Our God and His name should be praised.

Your homeland is beautiful indeed. I remember that your daughter, Christine, showed me a picture of South Africa. It moved me deeply, and made me want to go there, but all I can do now is to keep it in my memory. I read local newspaper and I have learned of the rioting in South Africa. Your husband is amidst the riot, and God must be with him. I believe the riot will be settled soon. I will also pray for your family, for God to abide with you and give you all peace. How is Christine doing? Could you please give my regards to her? Melanie and the little baby were mentioned in the last letter, which was written by you and Christine. I wrote a return letter to you. How are they doing? May God bless that Melanie will have a wonderful marriage. How are you doing?

I have a very discourteous question for you. It is that I will give away my second son (he is three years old). Would you like to have a boy for yourself? Otherwise, do you have a friend willing to adopt him? The adopter must be a Christian family. Would you please look around for me? It will be really great if you are willing. I am looking forward to hear from you. I would like to thank you again for you and your husband's loving concern and encouragement.

May God bless your family with peace and joy.
Your brother in the Lord,
Chen Chin-hsing, 12 October 1998
(translated by Daniel Sun)

Anne and I discussed this new development over the telephone. Were we being manipulated by this master of the practice? We decided to pray about it while Anne tried to find out more about Chen's children. She began to e-mail Christians in Taiwan while I mulled over the idea of us becoming parents again in our fifties.

Her enquiries revealed to Anne a heart-rending story of two little boys in the care of their impoverished grandmother while their parents languished in prison. Enrolled in a pre-school, the eldest son found himself rejected and victimized when people learned who his father was. A group of the children pushed the lad into a fish pond, hurling taunts and jeers after him. Some parents withdrew their children from the school.

Unable to care for both boys, the grandmother appealed to the imprisoned parents to agree to an alternative. They decided to allow the youngest boy to be placed in foster care. A Christian pastor and his wife from the Taichung area offered to take the three-year-old into the temporary shelter which they ran near the city, known as the House of Faith and Hope. It offered a temporary home to drug addicts and orphans.

Realizing the hopeless future that their boys faced in a hostile Taiwan, Chen Chin-hsing and Chang Su-chen at this stage decided that the younger boy should be offered for permanent adoption to Christian parents abroad.

The pastor and his wife asked Chang Su-chen to let them have both boys, saying they would care for them until such time as adoptive parents could be found for them in some other country. It was a magnanimous gesture, as once parents were found it was estimated that the adoption process would take between a year and two years to be finalized. Should no adoptive parents be found for them, the House of Faith and Hope would raise them in Taiwan.

Anne and I considered taking both boys. We simply could not separate them. Anne contacted Jennifer Sun to find out if Chang Su-chen would agree to this. She would. Jennifer also told us that Chang wanted her sons to forget the shadow of their past and to start a new life with a new surname.

Anne and I were torn emotionally. On the one hand we saw an opportunity to give these two children who had been thrust into our lives a chance to escape from the dark shadow of their father's evil deeds. But on the other hand, did we want to have two teenage boys when we were in our late sixties? We considered the implications and thought and prayed.

My tour of duty in Richmond ended and I returned home. Anne and I made up our minds to take the two boys and we were quite excited at the prospect. Right from the start, Christine had been very enthusiastic about adopting them. The idea of having two little brothers appealed to her. Shona thought it a great idea. Melanie, however, viewed the matter less superficially than the rest of us.

As a trained social worker, she looked at many aspects that the rest of us had not fully considered. But there were also personal issues at stake concerning which Anne and I had not shown proper sensitivity. We had not been aware of how lastingly the hostage experience had affected Melanie. She had been a human shield for the best part of an hour, in the midst of near-continuous gun battle. She had been subjected to an extreme form of terror and had been shot in the process.

Gently, Melanie reminded us that every time she would see those boys she would again feel their father roughly dragging her, bound and frightened, back and forth as he fired at the police. She would feel the empty cartridge cases striking her cheek, smell the cordite and hear the terrifying echo of the gunshots right next to her ear. We would be condemning her to live with this horror for the rest of her life.

This, together with the reality of social, financial, and age considerations led us to make the difficult decision that we could not adopt the two boys. Anne wrote a letter to Chen Chin-hsing informing him of our decision and assuring him that besides praying for his sons, we would do all that we could to find adoptive Christian parents for them.

Would our decision have a detrimental effect on Chen's apparently shaky spiritual state? We were underestimating God. Despite that outburst when his wife's sentence had been reversed, Chen was a lot more steadfast in his Christian conviction than we realized. The miracle God had performed in his life was a lasting one.

ORTV e-mailed pictures to us of Chen in prison, shackled and always under guard, being baptized and leading a Bible study with other inmates. We later learned that Chen had led three of his prison mates to an acceptance of Christ as their Saviour. His face in the pictures reflected peace and his smile spoke of an inner joy and happiness.

We thought back to the cruel, steely-eyed determination and unhappy turmoil we had seen in that face a year ago. Truly, this man's conversion was a mighty miracle of God.

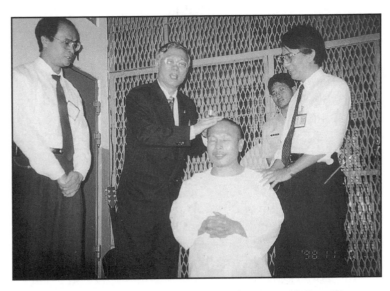

Chen Chin-hsing baptized in prison by Pastor Ming Huang.

Spiritually re-born Chen, with other converted inmates and prison ministers.

26

▸Execution◂

On Christmas Eve 1998 the Taiwan Supreme Court upheld
three death sentences and two life terms for Chen Chin-hsing,
thus removing the last legal obstacle to his execution. But the
Supreme Court threw out the death sentence for his role in the
killing of Pai Hsiao-yen. Similarly, the life sentence for our
hostage-taking was overturned for lack of conclusive evidence. We wondered whether this had been due to a poorly
prepared case by the police and prosecution, or whether it
was because we had refused to testify in court.

The Supreme Court then ordered a retrial of Chen on
certain charges and a reopening of investigations into whether
his brother-in-law Chang Chih-hui had helped detain the
kidnap victim and whether his wife Chang Su-chen had helped Chen to elude arrest. Though Chang and Chen's friend, Lin
Chih-neng, were aware of some of Chen's criminal acts, the
Supreme Court ruled, there was no evidence that they had
aided him in carrying out these crimes. Chang's fifteen-year
sentence and Lin's eight-year sentence were therefore overturned. The Supreme Court, however, upheld the eight-year
sentence passed on the fourth defendant, Hsu Chia-hui.

During his long wait on death row, Chen was ministered to on a regular basis by Pastor Huang and other dedicated Christians of the Prison Fellowship of Taiwan. Huang testified that Chen read his Bible and prayed to God every day. He greatly loved the book of Romans in the New Testament, saying that it listed all his own transgressions, but it also stressed the importance of faith in God. The description of the unrighteous found in Romans certainly fit the Chen Chin-hsing who had taken us hostage:

> They have become filled with every kind of wicked-ness, evil, greed and depravity. They are full of envy, murder, strife, deceit and malice. They are gossips, slanderers, God-haters, insolent, arrogant and boastful; they invent ways of doing evil; they disobey their parents; they are senseless, faithless, heartless, ruthless. (Romans 1:29-31)

But the new Chen Chin-hsing had now received

> This righteousness from God, (that) comes through faith in Jesus Christ to all who believe. There is no difference; for all have sinned and fall short of the glory of God, and are justified freely by his grace through the redemption that came by Christ Jesus. (Romans 3:22-24)

It was clear to us that this book of the Bible had come to mean so much to Chen because he had experienced the truth of Romans 6:23:

> For the wages of sin is death, but the gift of God is eternal life in Christ Jesus our Lord.

Two months after his suicide attempt, Chen was baptized. Pastor Huang, who performed the baptism, said that he and other Christians involved in ministering to Chen, had pro-longed the sacrament until they were fully convinced that he really had repented. At the same time the prison inmate who had been sharing Chen's cell was also baptized. Chen Chin-hsing had led him to an acceptance of Jesus Christ as his Lord and Saviour! But for his suicide attempt, Chen would never have found himself in a position to tell this man of the grace of Jesus Christ. For Anne, there was now an understanding of why the Lord had allowed that trying event to take place.

Chen's wife Chang Su-chen, his mother-in-law Lin Shih, and his two young sons were also baptized a short time later. Chen's own conversion was showing a multiplication effect. Three other prisoners and four members of his family had accepted the Lord. Eight souls were saved as a result of our terrifying hostage experience! We now saw answers to Christine's question that night: "Daddy, why is this happening to us?"

At this time, Chen began writing down the story of his life. When he had finished, he handed his Christian friends the 50,000-character "confession." The Christians were anxious to have it published, as it contained the details of his deprived childhood, his early start on a life of crime, his wayward and wicked adulthood, and finally the testimony of his conversion in prison. They believed that it would be a strong witness for the spreading of the gospel of Jesus Christ.

The Ministry of Justice, however, felt differently about what Chen had written and showed considerable alarm at the plan to have the "confessions" published. Their strong reaction prompted the Christians under Pastor Huang to postpone publication until Chen's sentence had been carried out. Even then, Police Chief Hou You-yi was quite vehemently opposed to any such publication, no doubt feeling that it would again raise the wrongdoer to a place of unwarranted prominence.

On Monday 21 September 1999 Taiwan was struck by a calamitous earthquake which caused widespread death and destruction, particularly in the central parts of the island. Within a few days the toll had been reckoned as over 2,000 dead, more than 4,000 seriously injured and about 2,700 unaccounted for, presumed trapped under the rubble. Whole towns were destroyed and damage to property was estimated at around US$3.2 billion. Some five million homes were left without any electrical power and over 100,000 people lost their homes. It was one of Taiwan's worst recorded disasters and certainly the biggest earthquake experienced on the island during the twentieth century.

Concerned for all our friends in Taiwan, we sent off frantic e-mail messages, but were soon reassured by those we knew living in Taipei: they had escaped the worst of the effects. We also enquired after Chen Chin-hsing, wondering whether the terrible quake had caused damage to the prison. We were told that the prison was unaffected, but what we did not know was that on Wednesday 23 September, in the midst of all the carnage that Taiwan was experiencing, the high court had reaffirmed Chen's death sentence for Pai Hsiao-yen's kidnap and murder.

In the aftermath of the dreadful national tragedy caused by the earthquake, we received an e-mail from Daniel and Jennifer Sun, bringing us the latest news on Chen's case. After retrial, Chang Su-chen's final sentence was nine months in prison. In effect, this made her a free woman as she had already served far longer than that. Her brother, Chang Chih-hui, was given a life sentence. There was no longer any legal reason to prolong Chen Chin-hsing's execution and it was rumored in the media in Taiwan that it would be carried out within the next three days.

On Taiwanese television Chen was reported as saying: "God is righteous. I am prepared to die for the crimes I have committed. I will donate my organs so that others can have the chance to live, and I will trust the Lord for the unfinished work he has brought about in me."

The news report also made mention of the lifting of an embargo on visits to Chen by family members and on receiving letters. Sometime earlier, Anne had written a letter to Chen and sent it, with some family photos, to Daniel and Jennifer. Jennifer now told us that, after translating the letter, she had forwarded it to Chen as soon as she had heard that the embargo had been lifted.

Anne and I waited a few days and heard nothing. I had to go for a week to the beautiful Wild Coast of the Transkei area of South Africa. The Joint Military Task Force of which I was the Chief of Staff was holding discussions with chiefs and headmen of warring tribal factions in the remote Majola district.

In Taiwan, Chen's last chance for a stay of execution, it seemed, lay in an extraordinary appeal. Prosecutors however, concluded on Tuesday 5 October that no grounds existed for such an appeal. Prosecutor Chang Hwei-chiung, having reviewed Chen's case, submitted the execution order to her superiors. All it required for the execution to be carried out was the signature of Minister of Justice Yeh Chin-feng.

▶▶▶▶▶▶▶◀◀◀◀◀◀◀

Anne received an unexpected phone call on the afternoon of Wednesday 6 October from a TV station in Taiwan. We could only guess where they had obtained our home phone number in Port Elizabeth, location of our latest posting. The interviewer informed Anne that Chen Chin-hsing was scheduled to be executed by shooting at 9:00 P.M. that night, Taiwan time. That was 3:00 P.M. South African time, only a few minutes away.

Anne told Christine the sad news, and the two of them sat together as three o'clock drew near. They held hands and prayed for the condemned man, now a brother in Christ, and for his family. They asked for strength for Chen as he faced his final ordeal before going to be with the Lord.

Execution in Taiwan is by shooting. The condemned man has his head shaved, is made to lie face down on the ground, and is then shot in the back of the head. Not a pretty image to contemplate while praying!

About forty minutes later the phone rang. It was the TV reporter in Taiwan. The execution had been delayed by just over half an hour, but she confirmed that Chen had been shot to death at 9:33 P.M. Taiwan time.

How did Anne feel about the execution? The reporter
wanted to know. They would broadcast her answer live.

"Of course I feel sad that he had to die," Anne said, "and I
accept that the law had to take its course. But I am happy
because we know where he has gone. He accepted Jesus
Christ as his Saviour before he died, so he at least had peace
for his soul."

"But how could you and your family forgive the man after
what he did to you?" persisted the reporter.

"We can never condone what he has done, neither to us
nor to others in Taiwan," replied Anne. "But Christ died for
our sins and has forgiven us; he has also forgiven Chen; so
who are we to withhold our forgiveness? Jesus hates the sin,
but loves the sinner."

The woman seemed satisfied with what she had heard,
though we thought she may have been hoping for a ghoulish,
vengeful outburst.

The next day Anne received several e-mail messages from
Taiwan. There were also phone calls from other Taiwanese TV
stations. The conversations followed more or less the same
line as the previous day, but with a fresh angle: how did Anne
feel about the death penalty? What was her stand on capital
punishment? This was the latest and probably final controversy surrounding Chen Chin-hsing.

Always straightforward, Anne did not hesitate to tell them
that she supported capital punishment for murder, rape, and
other violent crimes.

"I believe it is consistent with the laws of Scripture and
after experiencing the vast increase in violent crime in South
Africa since the abolition of the death penalty here, I am quite
convinced that it is a deterrent."

This was no intellectual debate—Anne merely said what
she believed and the reporter had to accept it. Perhaps it
sounded incongruous to the reporter, particularly in the light
of an article which had appeared on the back page of the

China Post that day quoting Pastor Huang as saying that a hug from the South African military attaché's wife marked the turning point in the killer's life. When Anne hugged Chen and told him, "God loves you," at the time when he surrendered to the police, Huang explained, the hug became a symbolic act of love to Chen, although he was initially unable to comprehend the merciful act.

To Anne, as to all our family, acceptance of Christ as personal Saviour did not absolve one of responsibility for acts committed in this life. Chen had been forgiven by God, but not by the government of his country. Retribution had to still be exacted by the worldly authorities. Though acceptance of Jesus' sacrifice meant that the sinner was granted eternal life in the hereafter, the earthly laws which had been broken would have to be answered for in this life.

We believe the Scriptures clearly teach that governments are instituted by God to bring order into society and that they are to be obeyed by Christians (See Romans 13:1-7). The difference for Chen, as a Christian, was that he went to his death with the sure knowledge that life eternal with Jesus Christ was awaiting him; whereas an unsaved criminal could expect only eternal damnation.

In Taiwan, the media continued to sensationalize Chen Chin-hsing's execution. Newspapers carried gruesome pictures of his body being rushed to the Chang Gung Memorial Hospital in Linkou for the removal of his organs for transplantation. Even this last wish of the condemned man was immediately the subject of further controversy. A potential recipient of one of his organs was reported as refusing outright to have the transplant done, saying that he would rather die than accept the body part of such a vicious criminal.

Chen's final moments were described in the media, where it was said that he was interviewed by a psychiatrist shortly before his execution, when he is said to have admitted his guilt and to have asked for forgiveness.

"Why did Chen suddenly decide to repent as he was

facing death?" Police Chief Hou You-Yi asked in an interview reported by the media. "It seems that he was only using religion to lower the impact of his sins and that is actually a very selfish action. Is that real repentance? He even lied to God when he said he repented."

I am sure the police chief's professional experience with the very worst of Taiwan's criminals had produced a deep cynicism regarding their words and actions. Anne and I had no doubt in our minds that Chen's repentance and conversion were genuine, but of course the psychologists would in all likelihood put that down to our wanting it to be genuine. And probably Hou would agree with them.

Chen's letters spoke to us very clearly of a remarkable and real conversion and we are fully convinced that an experienced prison pastor like Huang Ming would not have been mistaken about the sincerity of the man's decision.

Naturally, Hou You-yi is entitled to his opinion. The seasoned policeman went on to say that Chen had attempted to portray himself as a tragic victim by his donation of his organs for medical transplants. Many ordinary people and other criminals had made similar offers, but no publicity was accorded to them.

"For Chen to be made out to be a tragic figure and a victim is in fact unfair to the families of his victims. Chen is being elevated far too much, at the cost of the real victims," Hou pointed out.

Hou indicated that Chen appeared to have a split personality. When committing his crimes he was bloodthirsty and violent, but while being interrogated he appeared calm and serene. Hou saw this Jekyll-and-Hyde phenomenon as a cunning ploy by the criminal to present a defensive measure during interrogation.

"To a certain extent," Hou admitted "it worked, and the police were often led astray. But he never changed as he would have had people believe he did."

Whether this was in fact so, or whether the police were

merely expressing their frustration at not having been able to solve the cases which they ascribed to him, the ones he said he did not commit, we have no way of knowing. There were times though, when Anne and I discussed this and came to the conclusion that some of what was said just might border on sour grapes.

Chen was said to have been clothed in a white garment for his execution. White, in Chinese custom, is the color of mourning. Ironically, in Christian tradition white represents purity and innocence, qualities imparted on Chen by the grace of Jesus Christ when he had repented of his sin and accepted Christ as his Saviour.

During the execution, numerous Taiwanese television teams had maintained a vigil on the rooftop of a building overlooking the detention center, hoping to record some gory details of the event. They were disappointed, as no gunshots were heard outside the walls of the institution. However, prison workers believed to have been the execution team were seen emerging from the main prison building a few minutes after the execution had taken place, and had, in a Taoist tradition, burnt "ghost money" and incense to appease the dead man's departed spirit.

Pai Ping-ping, interviewed hours before the execution, remained adamant in her refusal to forgive the criminal for what he had done to her daughter.

"I still cannot forgive him," a tearful Pai said, "whether he regrets what he has done or not. The harm has been done and I can never be compensated for it." She then told the media that she would no longer speak of her daughter's murderer, as "he is not worth human speech." It hurt her every time she heard Chen's case being discussed, she claimed.

Chen, on the other hand, expressed three desires to Pastor Huang:

> 1. that his family be accepted by society,
>   although he realized that it would probably

be only at church that they would be
accepted;

2. that his book would help dissuade juveniles
from turning to a life of crime;

3. that he would be able to testify to the world
of the love of Christ.

27

▸Dead To Sin;
But Alive To God◂

"I DIE TO SIN, but I live to God," Chen told Pastor Huang, before he was taken to die. The condemned man was paraphrasing chapter six of his beloved book of Romans.

Pastor Huang of Prison Fellowship later described Chen as having been very sensitive to spiritual matters during the eighteen months that he ministered to him. He wrote that Chen was "just like a dry sponge in his hunger to draw in God's living water." During the time that Huang spent alone with him the day before his execution, he thanked the pastor for all he had done to help him finally learn the lesson of total commitment. He also told him that if it had not been for so many Christians praying for him, he would have perished long ago.

Of course, Chen was speaking of spiritual life and death, and to back this up he quoted from James 5:16 to Huang:

"The prayer of a righteous man is powerful and effective."

Pastor Huang saw this as pointing to the prayers of many people:

> ▶ the group of women who placed the newspaper ad appealing to Chen even before he had taken us hostage;

> ▶ our family's prayers during the hostage-taking;

> ▶ the prayers of the thousands of Christians in Taiwan and around the world during the crisis;

> ▶ and the Christians, especially from Chang Su-chen's church and from Prison Fellowship Taiwan who had prayed for Chen through his long months of incarceration.

During the final hour before Chen's execution, as he had waited for 9:00 P.M. to come, the condemned man had read from the small Bible which Anne had handed him nearly two years before. Awaiting his death, he marked the date and time, 6 October 1999 (evening), in a margin beside Psalm 27.

> The LORD is my light and my salvation
> — whom shall I fear?
> The LORD is the stronghold of my life;
> of whom shall I be afraid?

Chen's Bible was given to Pastor Huang by the prison authorities after the execution, and he has kept it, in the hopes of one day giving it to Chen's sons when they are bigger.

About ten minutes after the execution, Chen's body was removed from the Tucheng Detention Center in an ambulance and rushed through to the hospital so that his organs could be saved. Medical personnel were on hand, keeping his organs functioning by means of pumps and other apparatus.

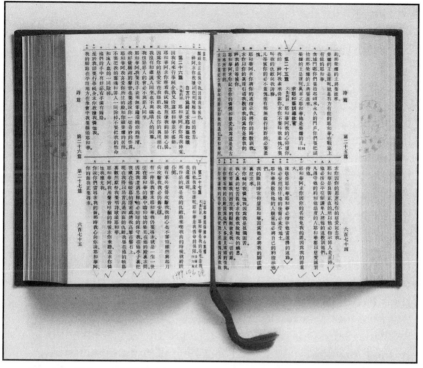

Chen's Chinese Bible, open to Psalm 27, which he was reading before the execution on 6 Oct. 1999.

The now-widowed Chang Su-chen appears to have been waiting at the hospital for the arrival of the body. Front page photos in the newspapers showed the distraught woman beside the stretcher containing Chen's body, its head gruesomely wrapped in a blood-soaked bandage.

Chen had donated his heart, kidneys, lungs and corneas, but his liver could not be used because he had contracted hepatitis sometime in his past. A twenty-eight- year-old male patient received Chen's heart at the Taipei Veterans' General Hospital after an eleven-hour marathon transplant operation. The patient and his family were informed beforehand who the donor was, and after considering the situation they decided to go ahead with the transplant.

However, a patient awaiting a lung transplant at Taipei's National Taiwan University Hospital, when offered Chen's organ, was not so ready to go through with the operation. After long and careful consideration with her husband, she decided to forego the opportunity. To many people in Taiwan, the transplant of an organ from a criminal was seen as something which would negatively affect their personalities.

But the kidneys of the executed man were transplanted into two male patients, a forty-one- and a fifty-three-year-old. At the Chung Gang Memorial Hospital the operations were declared a success.

Earlier on his final day, Chen had been allowed a last visit by his wife. Reporters questioned her afterwards. She said her husband had not been emotional about his imminent death. But she deeply regretted that he was refused permission to see their two sons one last time. She lamented that "society did not give him (her husband) a chance."

This claim was mercilessly rejected by some. An editorial in the *China Post* maintained that he had countless chances to rectify his behavior, but that he had persisted in living the life of a criminal. He was said to have rejected the advice of his mother, his stepfather, police officers, and prison counselors. He had lived badly and he had died badly, alone and with nothing to show for it, said the editorial.

But Christians believed he had much to show:

▶ his personal conversion to Christ was a miracle in itself;

▶ he had led three of his fellow prisoners to the Lord;

▶ he had donated his organs so that others could live;

▶ and he may have died alone and hated, but

> he was now in heaven with the hosts of other
> departed saints of God.

Yet in a sense, Chen Chin-hsing did not die alone. Seven other convicted criminals, all sentenced under the same controversial "bandit law," were also executed at approximately the same time in prisons across the island of Taiwan. Three were shot in Taipei, three in Taichung and one in Kaohsiung. The crimes for which they had been convicted were robbery, rape, and manslaughter, for all of which the death sentence was mandatory under the "bandit law."

Human rights groups and some legal experts argued that the so-called "bandit law" under which Chen and the other seven were tried and sentenced was a violation of basic human rights and was in any case no longer valid. The law had been passed by the military government of Chiang Kai-shek in 1944, when the government was still located on the mainland and World War II was still raging. Large parts of China were occupied by Japanese troops and internal strife was prevalent in those parts under Chinese control. The law, intended to cover a wide range of vaguely-defined offenses, was needed to curb banditry in mountainous parts of the country during a time of virtual anarchy and extreme emergency. Modern Taiwan presents a very different situation.

Another case involving three other convicted men known as the Hsichih Trio was believed by human rights groups to be seriously flawed. The prisoners claimed that their convictions had been based on forced confessions, extracted under torture by the police. In the wake of the executions of the eight, a wave of media and human rights protests swept over Taiwan. The freeing of the Hsichih Trio was now seen by human rights activists as the one way in which Taiwan could redeem itself and take its rightful place beside other "civilized nations."

I found this *naïveté* astounding. Anyone with only an inkling of international affairs and the complexity of the

Taiwan issue must surely understand that human rights play a pathetically insignificant part in international recognition. One has only to look across the Taiwan Straits to see that.

The debate in the media moved away from the "bandit law" and centered squarely on the issue of the death penalty. The Taiwan Association for Human Rights was a vociferous participant in this war of words. When I saw that public support for the death penalty had been assessed at 70 percent in Taiwan in 1994, it made me think rather cynically of my own country.

When the crime rate in South Africa had soared after the abolition of the death penalty, many supported its re-introduction. Pressured to hold a referendum on the issue, the government had refused. The reason given was that the death penalty is morally wrong, regardless of whether the majority of the population are in favor of it. Democracy, it seems, is fine, as long as you don't disagree with the ruling party. Equally, censorship is despicable, but not if it is applied by those same self-appointed intellectual superiors.

Of course, many Christians are not in favor of the death penalty. They regard it as totally irreconcilable with their Christian beliefs. In fact, one of the first people to contact us after Chen's execution was our good friend Ingomar Lochschmidt. He is a vehement critic of anyone taking the life of another person, even if the act of execution is carried out by the government authorities. His bitter e-mail referred to the execution as "murder." Although Ingomar acknowledged that Chen appeared to have been fully prepared to meet the Lord, he decried the fact that this brother in Christ had been condemned and executed under the unconstitutional (as Ingomar saw it) "bandit law." He claimed that in any case Chen had never confessed to committing the murders for which he had been executed. "He and his children were denied the right to see each other again," wrote the outraged Ingomar.

Adele Booysen, a Christian South African working for ORTV in Taiwan, e-mailed Anne and sent her a list of ques-

tions from Catherine Lin of the *Christian Tribune*. These were
to obtain Anne's feelings as a Christian at the time of Chen
Chin-hsing's execution.

Out in the wilds of Pondoland where I was involved in
dialogue with the chiefs of the feuding tribal factions, a group
of media people were covering the tribal discussions. From
one of them I learned of Chen's execution. One reporter
immediately asked for my response. I told the reporters that it
was always sad when a life was lost, but that I rejoiced in the
sure knowledge that Chen had gone to be with Jesus.

After returning home I was contacted by Jason Blatt, the
one-time reporter from the *China Post* in Taiwan, who was
now working for TVBS. He heard that I was writing a book on
the hostage drama and he interviewed me by phone on my
approach to writing the story. Not long after this I was also
contacted by the *Christian Tribune* in Taiwan with many
questions about my proposed book. It was apparent that for
the public of Taiwan, the saga of Chen Chin-hsing remains
powerfully relevant.

The tempestuous and controversial earthly life of the
arch-criminal of Taiwan may have been terminated; but the
issues raised by his life and death are likely to haunt Taiwanese society for many years to come.

▶▶▶▶▶▶▶◀◀◀◀◀◀◀

About a month after Chen's execution, Anne received an
e-mail from Jennifer Sun. She related that Chen's two sons
had been told that their father was to be executed and that
they had prayed for him at the time. Jennifer did not know
whether Chen had received Anne's last letter to him before he
died. She did, however, receive a letter from the condemned
man, written just one month prior to his execution, in which
he had referred to Anne, Christine and myself and the role
that our actions had played in leading him to Christ, as well
as how his own prayer had been answered. Jennifer sent us
her translation of the letter. Anne and I read it with a feeling

of wonder that God could so powerfully use a Christian's simple gestures of love:

> *Dear Sister Jennifer,*
>
> *May Lord be with your family! I would like to thank you for writing to me! It strengthens my faith and increases my joy, thank Lord, He listens to my prayer! The beauty and the goodness of His Holy children are treasures to me. I haven't contacted you and your husband for a long time, not because I had forgotten you, but because my special situation. How are you all doing these days?*
>
> *Do you believe: it is through prayer that Mrs. Ann sent her letter asking you about me. Just like a little boy asking candies from parents, I am asking our Lord in my secret prayer for Mrs. Ann to write to me. The reply came rapidly. It sounds like I am making a story, but it is true indeed. Please rejoice with me. Our Lord Jesus is Omni-presence God. He builds me up and leads me day by day. Though I am an unworthy man, yet the new heart and the new Spirit given to me by our Lord are growing daily like cedars of Lebanon. My soul thirsts for Lord, I long for his filling me up with His love, so that I may decrease, and He may increase.*
>
> *The Lord's grace unto me is indeed abundant, He has taught me through all kinds of ways, people, letters and Bible teaching to testify that He is with me. But, just like a little boy who starts to learn how to walk by himself, the boy is happy to walk alone, but he fears sometimes that he may get lost or stumble, he keeps watching if his parents are around. That's how I feel these days. Praise our Lord, Hallelujah! Your letter indeed is the evidence that our Lord answers my prayer, He proves His love to me once more. May His love fill up the whole universe forever and ever! Amen!*
>
> *It is been a long time, isn't it? I am afraid to write to friends because of my criminal condition, so I tell our Lord instead of writing letters. I will pray only, and ask for reply mails as evidence that Lord hears my prayer. I know I can't be justified in doing so, my pastor warned me not to tempt the Lord. Our Lord knows that I am just*

like a naughty boy. He knows my weakness and anxiety.
He has mercy for me, your letter came in time! I thank
Lord and thank you too.

Thank you for sending me the information concerning the family of Alexander letting me know that they
are remembering me in their prayers. Let me tell you, the
joy fills my heart, I felt that I can fly up. I am so glad that
Mr. Alexander is promoted to Brigadier General, I feel so
honoured. Our Lord is taking well care of Mr. Alexander's family, everything is under His control. I am so
pleased to hear that they are all doing well, and Christine
has grown up. Oh, how wonderful is their love toward
me! My glory and praise be unto our Lord. All my family
(especially I), would like to thank them for they lead us to
our Lord, and let us have a chance to know our Lord that
I can be saved by Lord's grace.

The ways and the works of our Lord are incompre-
hensible. It has been almost two years from then. Your
letter came in as a miracle to me. Please tell the Alexander
family that they are the most blessed, the most holy people
I ever know, who trust our Lord's love. Would you please
tell Mr. Alexander that I always remember the way he
looked at me in his house. To be frank with you, I don't
look back to my notorious life in the past, but the eye of
Mr. Alexander is such a vivid image in my mind, it is
dearer than my loving families, for it is full of love, mercy
and understanding, all focusing on that look. Please tell
Mr. Alexander that the way he looked at me somehow
opened my heart, it is a seeing with faith. Tell him that on
that special night, Jesus descended through Mr. Alexander, and the bullet is on Him too, this is indeed true,
Amen!

I share with my pastor my feeling, which I described
above, the love of our Lord came upon me in such way,
and my life is changed ever since that moment. I shall
bow down and thank Him. I am thinking a lot of things
these days. What is man that He is mindful of him? I am
such an unworthy, but our Lord does not abandon me, He
has showed me the full extent of His love. I have learned
to trust and to obey through His love, His love comforts
my weary body, and His love helps me and leads me every

day. I am so content at this moment. Please rejoice with me, ask your family and the Alexander family to rejoice with me. All because their prayers, and the loving heart with cross which Christine drew, and Mrs. Alexander's "God loves you!", all these have made God's promises come true. He has proved His omnipresence and His eternal being to me. How limited is our human life, we met and we parted, yet the perfection is hiding in the imperfection, because His love is hiding inside.

I pray that our faith will all be strengthened and we will all be glorified in beauty. May all the glory be unto our Lord, our God.

Thank you again, and send my best regards to your husband. God Bless You All with Peace.

Emmanuel.
Your brother in Christ,
Chen Chin-hsing, 6 September 1999

▶▶▶▶▶▶▶▶◀◀◀◀◀◀◀◀

Chen may have had a profound affect on society in Taiwan, but he also had a very deep affect on our lives as a Christian family. His conversion taught us a lasting lesson about the power of one's behavior. Never again should we underestimate the importance of actions to back up words when sharing the love of Christ with others.

▸Epilogue◂

Time has passed since our family's hostage ordeal and life has continued. Our own circumstances have altered so drastically since the event, that sometimes it all seems like a distant dream. The emotional scars will probably always be there to remind us of what took place on that fateful night in a far-off land. Anne displays an agitation and an occasional depression which she cannot explain, but which she never experienced before we were taken hostage. Melanie still has difficulty dealing with what happened to us. Shona finds it hard to relate to our experience, given her unfortunate exclusion by those who could have kept her informed and encouraged. Christine sometimes manifests behavior which indicates that the sudden massive publicity to which she was subjected and its equally sudden termination has not made her teenage years any easier. Although my training and long experience as an active paratrooper probably contributed to my being better equipped to handle the psychological after-effects than some of my family, I too have been through times of deep regret that my dear family were subjected to such indescribable terror. Zachary, perhaps and very thankfully, was the only one to come through it all truly unscathed.

Yet, somehow we will never cease to be grateful for what happened. We're grateful and humble that God saw fit to use us in a situation which profoundly influenced the lives of so many people and which allowed the gospel of Jesus Christ to reach untold numbers of those who would otherwise perhaps never have heard it.

> Who shall separate us from the love of Christ?
> Shall trouble or hardship or persecution or famine
> or nakedness or danger or sword?
> As it is written:

> 'For your sake we face death all day long;
> we are considered as sheep to be slaughtered.'

> No, in all these things we are more than conquerors
> through him who loved us.
> For I am convinced that neither death nor life,
> neither angels nor demons,
> neither the present nor the future, nor any powers,
> neither height nor depth, nor anything else in all creation,
> will be able to separate us from the love of God
> that is in Christ Jesus our Lord.

> ~Romans 8:35-39

Notes

Chapter 2

1. Though I was disappointed in the outdated content of the course, our composition as a group was extremely interesting. The new South African National Defence Force had been constituted by combining seven different armed forces, some of them erstwhile foes. The bulk of officers came from the old South African Defence Force, but there were also members of two liberation groups' armed wings: the ANC's *Umkonto weSizwe* (MK) or Spear of the Nation, and the Pan Africanist Congress's African People's Liberation Army (APLA). Then there were the defense forces of the four "republics" created by the *apartheid* government, but recognized by no one but South Africa: Transkei, Ciskei, Bophuthatswana, and Venda.

Four of these seven former armed forces provided members of the Joint Staff Course which I attended. This diversity, together with the mix of army, air force, navy, and even some civilians made for stimulating discussions.

Chapter 4

1. It is customary, in the East, for the surname—always a single syllable—to come first, followed by the name—usually two syllables. Many Chinese people who have regular dealings with Westerners

adopt a Western first name. In such a case the Western name is given first, followed by the surname in the conventional Western manner. The Chinese two-syllable name then falls away. In this account both practices are used, depending on the preference of the individual. The Chinese do not have the variety of surnames that Westerners do. This can lead to confusion in a narrative of this nature. So many key figures have the same surname (for example, Chen and Chang, Yeh and Yang, Lee and Huang are all surnames which occur frequently.) that it is usually essential to give the full name, even though this could appear as overly repetitive.

Chapter 5

1. Throughout the events of the evening, Chen Chin-hsing displayed two very marked characteristics: first, a single-minded purposefulness — he knew exactly what he wanted and he was working towards achieving it at all costs; second, a strange but definite professionalism in the defensive measures he took in the house. Besides ensuring that he always had at least one fully-loaded pistol in his hand, regardless of how much shooting he had done, he also showed many other signs of having received specialist military training in defending an occupied building.

His selection of the inside balcony which we used as a TV room for his defensive position was ingenious. He could fire through the front door and large windows downstairs without coming near them, so he never made himself a target. In addition, he could cover both the stairs leading up to the balcony and those leading down from the bedrooms without having to be near to them. Anyone approaching along either stairs would be seen by him long before they would be able to spot him. This gave him a decided advantage. Furthermore, he had cleverly barricaded both sets of stairs with chairs and tables, making a successful assault by the police extremely difficult, if not impossible.

He kept the whole house dark, except a low-wattage light shining in from my study, which provided sufficient light for him to see what he was doing. But the area where he held us could not be seen from outside.

Besides these measures, he evidenced a criminal cunning, in all likelihood born out of a lifetime of living on his wits and desperately avoiding capture by the law. This we saw in his shrewd assessment of the police and his accurate anticipation of their actions. It was clear to me that he knew he would need to first win a gun battle with the police before they would be prepared to allow him to negotiate. Hence his careful defensive measures and his phenomenal supply of ammunition. Later we saw he had not two, but three 9mm pistols to ensure that he could maintain a constant and high rate of fire when the police assault came.

His trump card, of course, was the holding of foreign hostages. The bonus he had not planned on was that they were diplomats. This elevated his escapade to the level of an international incident, with South Africa's imminent break in diplomatic relations providing a further boost to the profile of that incident.

The impression I gained was that Chen had no illusions regarding the certainty of a police assault. He also knew that the assault would not be a rescue attempt, but that it would be aimed at killing him. He therefore thought he had to use one hostage as a shield. That hostage would probably be sacrificed in the assault, but if it helped to repulse the police it would probably also bring them to their senses and force them to resort to negotiations.

Chapter 7

1. Later we learned one reason for the absence of the special task force, who had become accustomed to interminable false alarms about Chen's whereabouts. Earlier that day, the police had received reports that Chen was in the vicinity of Keelung Road, in a completely different part of the city. The specially-trained SWAT team had rushed to that area to follow up the report. So they were delayed in responding to our situation. Most likely the police considered our report to be just another false alarm, anyway.

My personal opinion is that the police only took the matter seriously when Chen fired his first shot, and that must have been about 8:20 P.M., more than an hour after he had taken us hostage.

2. The language difficulty exacerbated the problem. Not one diplomat at the South African embassy in Taipei could communicate reasonably in Mandarin. On the other hand, the average police officer in Taiwan had no working knowledge of English.

Chapter 17

1. Many people contributed immeasurably to easing our burden, but the greater significance of the missionaries lay in the fact that they could speak Mandarin. Most other expatriates living in Taiwan had to get by with a superficial course of "Survival Chinese." We would have experienced extreme difficulty in handling the situation in the days and weeks after the event if it had not been for the linguistic expertise of the missionaries and for their willingness to sacrifice time and effort for our benefit. We salute these unsung heroes, dedicated to uplifting their fellow man and to spreading the Gospel of Jesus Christ.

Chapter 18

1. Americans comprised the biggest Western group in the country. Christine attended an American school, we fellowshipped at an American church, and we had long been members of an American Club. The people of Taiwan were greatly enamoured with the American culture, many of them actively promoting celebrations such as Thanksgiving.

A group of couples we met at United Marriage Encounter prepared a traditional Thanksgiving dinner and brought it to us in the hospital. We arranged for tables and chairs to be brought into the ward's small lounge, and we all gathered there on the Wednesday evening 26 November. With Christian friends we joyously tucked into roast turkey, mashed potatoes, corn-on-the-cob and cranberry pie.

The next day was the actual Thanksgiving Day holiday, and a long time back we had accepted an invitation from Mitch and Sally Mitchell, unofficial American military attaché, to attend a Thanksgiving celebration at their home on Yang Ming Mountain. Dr. Huang let me out of the hospital for a few hours and Jimmy drove us up to the Mitchell's house. What a wonderful evening, with Bernard and Annie Malavieille from France, Rafi and Hana Bouhnik of Israel, Roger and Christie Dong, and the new Korean couple.

We had many reasons to celebrate and give thanks: our lives had been spared; our injuries were not serious; our family was still intact; our friends had stood by us; we had been shown love by people whom we had never even met; so many people were showering us with kindness; and the gospel of Jesus Christ was being proclaimed.

2. Rachel de Beer was a 19th Century South African *Boer* heroine. A refugee fleeing across the harsh African *veld*, the young girl removed her own garments to cover her small brother during a snowfall at night, and died of exposure as a result.

3. "Bravo Zulu", from the military phonetic alphabet, is the naval code used to denote "well done!" It is normally transmitted to seaborne elements on the successful execution of a mission.

Chapter 19

1. Some weeks before our hostage-taking ordeal, I had been contacted by John Chandler, a retired British army officer holding the CBE and now chairman of ICI Taiwan Ltd. He was a member of the Kinkaseki Prisoner of War Memorial Committee, and he invited me to attend the dedication of a memorial obelisk on Sunday 23 November 1997 at the site of the former Kinkaseki Prisoner of War Camp. I felt honoured to be invited and accepted with pleasure.

During the Second World War Taiwan had been a Japanese possession. Ceded to Japan by China after the latter's defeat in the Sino-Japanese War of 1895, Taiwan was for the next fifty years governed as a part of Japan. The Japanese developed the backward island's infrastructure and built up an efficient economy and educational system. But they ruled the island with an iron fist. In 1942 a prisoner of war camp, known as Kinkaseki, was established on Taiwan at the village of Chinguashi, near the port of Keelung.

Commonwealth prisoners mainly from Britain, Australia, and Canada, captured during the Japanese campaigns against Hong Kong, Malaya, Singapore and other parts of the old British Empire in the East, were sent to Kinkaseki. More than a thousand Commonwealth and other Allied prisoners at this camp performed forced labour at a nearby copper mine for the two-and-a-half years that the camp existed between November 1942 and May 1945, when U.S. forces rescued the survivors and took them off the island.

Subjected to a harsh regime of malnutrition, physical abuse and privation, more than 365 prisoners died at Kinkaseki. Whenever the Americans bombed Taiwan, prisoners would be tortured in retaliation. My father had fought with the South African forces in the

Second World War and the father of a close friend of mine had been a prisoner of war under the Nazis. Attending this memorial service was very meaningful to me personally, as I identified strongly with the Allied cause. But I was also the only Commonwealth military attaché in Taiwan, and I would be the only representative of the former Allies entitled to be there in uniform. I knew that this also meant a lot to the organizers and I did not want to let them down.

However, I was in hospital with my leg heavily bandaged, being kept carefully isolated from the media vultures. It was only four days since I had been shot, and the ROC authorities were still very sensitive about the welfare of my family and myself. I decided to discuss the matter with Dr. Huang. He smiled as I explained the situation to him. He wasn't inclined to engage in an argument with me about the matter.

"Of course you can go, Colonel," he offered good-naturedly. "Just be very careful, don't get yourself into a stressful situation, and make sure that you come straight back."

Excitedly, I called my driver Jimmy and made arrangements. Mericia and Christine collected my uniform from the house and brought it to the hospital. Sunday morning I dressed in all my military finery, managing to get my bandaged leg through my trouser leg and pull a brown military sock over the foot to hide that portion of the bandage. Then, taking my ash cane I climbed into a wheelchair. I wrapped myself in a blanket to cover the uniform. Donning a baseball cap, I pulled the peak low over my face and tucked my chin deep into the folds of the blanket so that no one would see my conspicuously un-Chinese thick, grey beard.

A nurse wheeled me out of the ward and into the elevator, then across the spacious entrance foyer of the hospital to where Jimmy was waiting with my official car. I quickly slipped into the back seat and the nurse took the blanket and wheelchair back to the ward. If there were any media reporters there, they most certainly had not spotted me!

Jimmy drove me out to Keelung and then up the winding road into the hills where the village of Chinguashi was situated. We soon found the site where the memorial had been erected and joined the 150 or so people gathered for the dedication ceremony. John Chandler and the other committee members were very pleased to see that I'd come, and I was particularly privileged to meet three of the camp survivors: Jack Edwards from Hong Kong, George Williams from

Britain, and eighty-four-year-old Les Davis from Canada.

Inevitably, reporters were present to cover the ceremony. They converged on me as soon as they saw me, but I quickly dismissed them by informing them that I would under no circumstances grant them an interview on such an occasion.

"We are here to honor the real heroes," I told them sternly. To their credit, they never bothered me again during the proceedings.

Also present were representatives of other Commonwealth offices in Taiwan (including Nikki Scholtz, our ambassador), the members of the Kinkaseki Memorial Committee, and a number of the local residents, including older persons who had lived there when the camp had existed and who could recall the horrors of the Japanese occupation. I sat alongside the patron of the memorial committee, Admiral Soong, a retired former ROC Chief of the General Staff.

The memorial itself was a simple grey plinth with an inscription in English and Chinese. In his address, Committee spokesperson Michael Boydon described the memorial's symbolic significance: "It faces west, towards the setting sun, which for the men of Kinkaseki meant the end of another day of work and a day closer to freedom. It also faces away from their place of imprisonment and towards their homes far across the sea." He portrayed its dedication as "a celebration of courage and fortitude."

I went forward to lay a wreath, as did many others, while a piper played a lament. During the emotional ceremony I was heartened to see my old friend there from Calvary Church, Dawson Kwauk, himself a veteran of the Second World War. Afterwards I quickly left, receiving lots of help back up the short slope to where Jimmy was waiting with the car on the road. He drove me back to the hospital in Taipei where I was again met by Ina and a nurse with my wheelchair and "disguise" at the casualty entrance.

Chapter 21

1. In view of the pending termination of official diplomatic relations between South Africa and Taiwan this was an unexpected honor indeed. It is not unusual for military attachés to be decorated by their host countries if they have performed outstanding work during their tour of duty. However, as South Africa was not decorating attachés from Taiwan over this period, I expected reciprocal

action from the ROC authorities. Great was my surprise and pleasure to be informed that I would be decorated before my departure. Whether or not the hostage-taking influenced the decision of the authorities in Taiwan in any way I do not know, but I did wonder whether the impact of that event didn't ultimately transcend the niceties of diplomatic protocol.

Chapter 23

1. Before we left our rooms we heard a knock at the door and there was Dawson Kwauk and his son, who is a medical doctor in the USA. Dawson was a good friend from Calvary International Baptist Church who had long assured us that he would bid us farewell on our last day in Taiwan. They helped us load our luggage into the embassy minibus which Jimmy had brought to the hotel. After final goodbyes, we were on our way.

Acknowledgments and Sources

MOST OF WHAT IS WRITTEN here is based on my own experiences and those of my wife and daughters, as we have been able to recall the events. However, I have used many other sources in an effort to achieve as much accuracy as possible and in order to check and correlate the facts as we remember them. We are reasonably certain of the facts as I have recorded them. Nevertheless, there was much confusion at the time, and any mistakes, inaccuracies and omissions are not intentional.

In attempting to piece together all that happened during the hostage drama, I was almost overwhelmed by the complexity of the story. I have tried to focus on the personal aspects of the drama, as experienced by my family. Nevertheless, so many ramifications and implications necessitate further explanation that at times I despaired of ever unravelling all the threads. I cannot claim to have been successful, particularly as our return to South Africa made it impossible to follow the detailed subsequent unfolding of events during the trial of Chen Chin-hsing.

This is a human story. Feelings and emotions are an inseparable part of it. I make no excuses for expressing opinions in what I have recounted. Where these are the opinions of

307

others, they are ascribed to sources. For the rest, the opinions are my own and do not in any way reflect the viewpoints of the South African Government, the South African National Defence Force, the South African Ministry of Defence, the South African Department of Foreign Affairs, or any other body or individual, private or official, in South Africa, Taiwan, or anywhere else.

The story I have described undoubtedly places some individuals in a poor light. This should not be seen to reflect the standard of the organisations they represent.

Shortly after the events described in this book, I drew up a detailed report for the Republic of China (Taiwan) National Police Administration, the Panchiao Public Prosecutor, the South African Department of Foreign Affairs and the Directorate of Foreign Relations of the South African National Defence Force. This was not a classified report, but I do not consider it prudent to make public certain of the observations and recommendations contained in it. These were done in my professional capacity as a soldier and a diplomat. But, because it was written when the events were still fresh in my mind, I have drawn substantially on this document to try to ensure the correct sequence of events and to recapture some of the emotions which I felt at the time.

As an accredited diplomat I very deliberately refrained from making any comment at the time on issues which could have been seen to have a political connotation in my host country. However, as I am no longer a diplomat, and three years have passed since the events described in this book, I have been more open in my comment. The story could not be fully told without including political issues. I am a soldier, not a politician; I do not espouse any political ideology. However, as a thinking human being, I do have opinions.

Clearly my family played a major role in reconstructing the events. My wife Anne's recollections have been particularly valuable, even to the extent of correcting my own. She was, of course, the victim who was held hostage the longest, being with Chen Chin-hsing for about twenty-five hours.

She also was able to observe and recall what happened when Chief Hou You-yi entered the house and rescued my daughter Melanie and me, at a time when I was barely conscious from the pain and blood-loss of my wound.

A major difficulty in commencing with the writing of this story six months after the events described is the fact that we have moved back to South Africa and do not have access to many of the people who were involved, nor to other sources located in Taiwan. Accordingly, I have made a great deal of use of contemporary newspaper reports. Many of the newspaper articles did not indicate the author. Author's names are included whenever possible. Articles and news items which were published in Chinese characters had to be translated by friends in Taiwan, and they often only provided us with some of the contents of the article and not always the heading. In many cases, we have only the newspaper name and date of issue.

I gleaned what information I could from Chinese-language newspapers. Translations by my wonderful former Mandarin teacher, Margaret Ren were particularly useful. Her warm Christian love was a great encouragement. Terry Li, the official translator at the South African Embassy in Taipei, also translated several articles from newspapers for me.

Many people from our church in Taipei, the Calvary International Baptist Church, added information, as did other friends from the diplomatic and quasi-diplomatic community, the Taipei American School, the American Club in China, the ROC Ministry of National Defence, the Taipei International Church, the United Marriage Encounter couples in Taiwan, and even the carpet salesman, Saif Sindhu and his nephew.

Photographs were obtained from newspapers, periodicals, and well-wishers, but because of the confusion of those few days it has been impossible to recall all of the exact sources. I have tried, as far as is humanly possible, to give acknowledgement where I could.

Besides the press, both radio and TV supplied further sources. Tapes of an interview conducted with our family by Jeffrey Mindich of International Community Radio Taipei (ICRT) and of telephone interviews broadcast on the South African radio station *Cape Talk* served to remind me of certain details. Anne's sister-in-law, Carol Leech, made audio and video taped recordings of some of the news reports which were broadcast in Cape Town during the crisis. One of Taiwan's major television stations, TVBS, very kindly presented us with a video tape of most of the footage they took during the crisis, as well as a magazine news story they aired after the event. ORTV, the Taiwan Christian TV company, gave us a video tape copy of the talk show on which Anne appeared, as well as of the documentary program on the crisis, which they broadcast on national TV on Christmas Day, 1997. All these helped recall the reality of what happened to us and enabled me to add details and accuracy to the story.

Particularly useful in verifying facts and obtaining personal experiences was a visit to the USA in December 1998 and January 1999 to attend our daughter Melanie's wedding. Many of our American friends from Taiwan who were involved in the crisis had returned home to the USA by then, and were able to go over the events with us. From Kevin and Rosie Garske, adoptive parents of our foster child Zachary, we learned something of the terror they experienced in the far off USA on hearing of their infant son's being taken hostage in Taiwan.

For the typing, retyping and correcting of the original manuscript I am indebted to Val Ferns. She it was who had to decipher my scrawl, sometimes written by lamplight in a tent, sometimes written while perched in the cab of a military truck, sometimes written while sitting in an uncomfortable aeroplane seat, often written during breaks in a hectic study program or between arranging military assistance to our own Independent Electoral Commission during voter registration. Always, Val was patient, long-suffering and understanding and her typing was fast and accurate. With the constant changes and alterations I had to make as more information became available to me, I am sure she blessed the advent of computers!

I must also acknowledge the role my family played in boosting and encouraging me during the crisis, during the months afterwards, and during the writing of this book. Not one of these periods has been easy, and I will always be grateful for the support of my family. Our daughter Shona especially, who had to endure the crisis from a distance of 10,000 kilometres, showed herself to be our real hero.

The part played by the hundreds, thousands, perhaps millions of Christians (very few of whom actually knew us) who were praying for us during and after the crisis can never be overestimated. I hope that this story does some justice to their prayers. We can never reward them, but God will.

We have not been able to reply to every message of support and encouragement we received. Many letters were written in Chinese from people we do not know and who did not include a return address. We hope that they will understand that we deeply appreciate their love and their care.

Finally, I cannot but acknowledge that God alone gave me and my family the strength and fortitude to bear this experience. We are eternally grateful to Him, that because of his grace the reality and love of Jesus Christ shone through like a beacon of light in a sea of darkness.

Chinese Newspaper Sources
(In Chronological Order)

CHINA NEWS, 10 October – December 1997.
"The Republic of China in Brief."
Robert Ruwitch, "Kao Identified in Clinic Murders."
"Chen Chin-hsing Contacted Relatives."
Jane Rickards and John Ruwitch, "The Final Act."
"Ministry of Foreign Affairs."
Anthony Lawrance, Mahlon Meyer, Jane Rickards and John
    Ruwitch, "Chen Surrenders."
Anthony Lawrance and Idelette von Papendorp, "The Inside Story:
    How It All Went Down."
—"Inside the House: How It All Happened."
Ian Lamont, "Media at Center of Hostage Drama."
Jane Rickards, "Neighbor Comes Home to Police Command Post."
Carl Davies, "Expat Community Relieved, but Sounds Wary Note
    Over Crime."
Editorial, "Let the Man Speak."
"Drama, Media Circus Unfolds."
"Chronology of Events."
Jane Rickards, "Prosecutors on Defensive."
Idelette van Papendorp, "'We Draw Our Strength From the Lord'."
Cadalina Lin, "TTV Criticised After Interview With Chen."
Andrea Chen, "Role of Media Comes Under Scrutiny."
"Hsieh Receives Accolades."
"Ho Applauded for Heroic Deeds in Bringing Peaceful End to

Standoff."

"Criminal Investigation Bureau Chief Submits His Resignation."

Idelette van Papendorp, "Drama All Too Real for Friends of
    Hostage Family."

Mahlon Meyer, "Lots of Sympathy for Chen."

Editorial, "Showing Their Colors."

"DNA points to Chen Raping More Than 15 Women."

Jane Rickards, "Justice Minister Defends Actions."

MahlonMeyer, "TAIP Officials Apologise for KMT."

—, "Authorities Incensed at Sympathy for Chen."

"Pai Fears Sympathy for Chen May Affect Sentencing."

Editorial, "A Textbook Trial."

Mahlon Meyer, "'Barbaric' Legal System Blamed for Hostage
    Crimes."

Douglas Habecker, "After Tina."

Kang Shen-ping, "Rough Justice."

John Trenhaile, "They're Coming to Get You."

Anthony Lawrance, "A Model of Irresponsible Journalism."

Richard Vuylsteke, "Taiwan's Media in Perspective."

"Police Chief Has 'Regrets'."

"Lu Calls for Hostage Crisis Protocol."

Cadalina Liu, "Hsieh's Defence Offer for Chen Criticised."

Editorial, "Good While It Lasted."

Eric Mader-lin, "Chen is Nothing but an Evil Monster."

Steven Schaufele, "Criminals Can Be Heroes Too."

"Kidnapping Was No Random Act."

Jane Rickards, "Senior Cop Admits Flaws in Pai Case."

"Chen Hints at Extortion Case."

Phelim Kyne, "Taiwan's Allied POWs Take Rightful Place in
    History."

Editorial, "Finding The Right Cure."

"Claims mounting against Chen."

"Watchdog Won't Probe Torture Claim."

"Prosecutor Slams Media."

Jane Rickards, "Parents of Victim Wish to Give Money to 'The
    Needy'."

—, "Confusion Reigns in Chen Investigations."

"NT$20Million Reward Given Out."

"Jewelry Store Heists May Have Provided Funds for Chen."

Jane Rickards, "Three-Month Amnesty for Handguns Begins
    Today."
Andrea Chen, "Chen's Rape Victims Receive Support."
Mahlon Meyer, "Journalists' Association Calls for More Self-
    Discipline."
Dave Smith, "Pai Lights Way."
Jane Rickards, "Hsieh Reveals Secret Tape."
Editorial, "The Truth Will Come Out."
Idelette van Papendorp, "Love the Sinner, Hate the Sin: Alexander
    Family."
Jane Rickards, "A New Breed of Cop."
"Security for Taipei Expats Stepped Up."
John Ruwitch, "Prosecutor Launches Chen Case."
Douglas Habecker, "Police Bungle Kidnapping Rescue Bid."
"Alexander Visits Top Cop."
"Outlaw's Death Sentence Upheld," December 98

CHINA POST, 24 October – 30 December 1997
"Plastic Surgeon, Two Nurses Found Brutally Slain."
"Plastic Surgeon Slayings Linked to Pai Murder: NPA."
"Anonymous Letter Sent to Police, Witness Account in Clinic
    Slayings Claimed."
"'Shoot to Kill' Order for Pai Suspects."
"Kidnapped Boy's Body Discovered by Roadside."
"Leads in Clinic Murder Case Growing."
Yueh Fei and Brian K.Y Hsu, "Pai Suspects in Police Shootout."
Pingling Hsu, "Police Under Fire Over Kao Shootout."
Flor Wang, "Criminal Investigation Police Force to See Hike."
Pingling Hsu, "Fugitive Eludes Police Again."
Editorial, "Elusion of Pai Murder Suspect Puts KMT in Crisis."
Pingling Hsu, "Pai Suspect Escape a 'Humiliation': Soong."
—, "Two Reports of Pai Suspect False Alarms."
—, "Letter From Chen Surfaces in Media."
Editorial, "Fugitives Can't Get Special Treatment."
Pingling Hsu, "Police Refuse Dialogue with Wanted Suspects."
"Pai Suspects Hunted in Yungho."
Pingling Hsu, "Fugitive Search Continues Following Futile Patrols."
—, "Another Letter from Pai Case Suspect Chen Revealed."
—, "Taipei Police Promotion Snubbed."

—, "Kao Behind Clinic Murders: Police."
—,"Two Women Released After Being Held Captive."
Editorial, "Public Support Essential in Fighting Crime."
Robert Taylor, "Pai Suspect Takes Hostages."
"Remorseful Chen Says He's Guilty, Ready to Kill Himself."
Yueh Fei, "One Minute with Taiwan's Most Wanted."
Pingling Hsu, "Chen Surenders to Police."
Simon King, "Chen Chin-hsing Profile."
"Chronology of Events Related to the Pai Hsiao-yen Case."
"Pai Ping-ping Condemns Crime."
Stephanie Low, "Government Vows Protection of Foreigners."
"South Africa Thanks ROC."
H.C. Chia, "Well Done China Post Over Hostage Drama."
Jeffrey Parker, "Hostage Case a Media Free-for-All."
Maubo Chang, "Police Lead to Gun Used in Clinic Slaying."
"Hunt Starts for New Pai Accomplice."
R.L.Chen, "Chen Hostage Crisis Shames the Nation."
Richard Dobson and Lloyd Roberts, "Foreign Community Reacts to
    Hostage Drama."
Editorial, "Let's All Take a Hard, Long Look at This Issue."
Pingling Hsu, "Chen Admits Pai Murder During Interrogations."
—, "Police Officer in Hostage Drama Offers to Quit Anew."
Sofia Wu, "Foreign Minister Visits South African Diplomat."
Laurie Underwood, "Mayor to Taipei: Breathe Easy, Crime is
    Down."
Eddie Y.T. Song, "Defence Set for Chen's Wife."
"Diplomat's Wife Discusses Ordeal."
Debbie Kuo, "Youngest Hostage Set for New Home in U.S."
Editorial, "Irresponsible Journalism."
"Negotiator Under Fire in Hostage Drama."
Lillian Wu, "Police Official Pays Visit to Alexander Family."
Debbie Kuo, "'Irrelevant' People to be Barred from Hostage Talks."
"Hostage-Taker Linked to Rapes."
Eddie Y.T. Song, "Frank Hsieh: Taiwan's Human Rights Lawyer."
Martie Olson, "Chen Chin-hsing is No 'Folk-Hero'."
Pingling Hsu, "Chen Admits to Other Crimes."
"Deputy Denies Rumour of Chen Kidnapping."
Sofia Wu, "Citizens Rewarded as Pai Case Nears End."
"Taipei Deputy Admits He Was Robbed by Pai Suspects."

Jason Blatt, "Alexanders Air Feelings."
Editorial, "Stricter Law on Gun Use Laudable."
"Hostage Negotiator Vows to Clear His Name With Chen Tape."
Sofia Wu, "Taipei, Pretoria to Meet Again on Ties."
"Captive Chen Tells of Hsiao-yen Death."
Daniel J. Bauer, "After Hostage Crisis, Color Gray Gives Way to
    Hope."
"Nurse Shot by Criminals Given Grand Funeral."
"Hu Concerned Over SA Envoy Attack."
Akie Ang, "Goodbye to the Alexanders."
Lillian Wu, "S. African diplomat Given Warm Farewell."
"Murder Suspect Chen Appears in Court."
Sofia Wu, "S. African Diplomat Visits Police Official."

Hsieh Kuo-lien, "Former Post Intern to Wed Hostage Figure," 17
    June 98.
"Ex-Hostages Send E-mail to Chen Chin-hsing," 10 September 98.
"Chen Chin-hsing Put on 24-Hour Suicide Watch," 11 September 98.
"Notorious Killer Chen Executed," 7 October 99.
Francesca J. Lee, "Chen Turned to God Near End of Life," 7 October
    99.
Editorial, "Chen Chin-hsing Had Many Chances," 7 October 99.
Andrew Lai, "Killer Chen Gives Life After Death," 8 October 99.
Chris Lang, "Executions Spark Row Over 1944 'Bandit Law'," 8
    October 99.
"Chen Never Truly Repented,' Says Policeman," 8 October 99.
Yueh Fei, "Former South African Attaché to Put Hostage Experience
    in Memoirs," 20 October 99.

SOUTH CHINA MORNING POST, 19-22 November 1997
"Top Fugitive Shoots Two."
Stella Lee, "Siege Gunman Surrenders."
—, "Families Offer to Adopt Fugitive's Children."
Glenn Schloss, "Attack Note Aimed at Pretoria, Says Minister."
"Long Reign of Terror."
Vivien Pik-kwan Chan, "Task Force Hopes to Track Triad
    Supporters."
"Media's Star Role in Race for Stories."
Stella Lee, "Messages of Support for Christine, 12."